Using a Microcomputer in the Classroom

Gary G. Bitter
Ruth A. Camuse
Arizona State University

A Reston Computer Group Book
Reston Publishing Company, Inc.
A Prentice-Hall Company
Reston, Virginia

Library of Congress Cataloging in Publication Data
Bitter, Gary G.
  Using a microcomputer in the classroom.

  "A Reston computer group book."
  Includes bibliographies and index.
  1. Computer-assisted instruction.   2. Microcomputers.
I. Camuse, Ruth A.   II. Title.
LB1028.5.B47   1984   371.3′9445   83-16043
ISBN 0-8359-8144-4 (pbk.)

Photographs by Dennis Camuse

AIM is a registered trademark of Data Processing Consulting, Inc.
Apple, Apple II Plus, and Apple IIe are registered trademarks
    of Apple Computer, Inc.
ATARI is a registered trademark of Atari, Inc.
BIG TRAK is a registered trademark of Milton Bradley Co.
Commodore and PET are trademarks of Commodore Business
    Machines.
Honeywell's DPS 88/81 is a trademark of Honeywell
    Information Systems, Inc.
IBM and IBM 3038 are registered trademarks of International
    Business Machines, Inc.
PFS is a registered trademark of Software Publishing
    Corporation.
TI 99/4A is a registered trademark of Texas Instruments.
TRS-80 is a registered trademark of Tandy Corporation.
VisiCalc is a registered trademark of VisiCorp.

© 1984 by Reston Publishing Company, Inc.
        A Prentice-Hall Company
        Reston, Virginia

10   9   8   7   6   5   4   3   2   1

Printed in the United States of America

Contents

Preface

Using a Microcomputer in the Classroom was written to help classroom teachers, laypersons, and school personnel understand the role of microcomputers in education. Based upon our experiences with children, adults, and school districts, we attempt to clearly explain the most important information about microcomputers and their possible applications in the educational environment. We have avoided technical computer jargon as much as possible. No assumption of previous knowledge or experience has been made. Feeling that many options have been overlooked in the past, we discuss alternatives to be considered when planning the use of microcomputers in education. So read the book from cover to cover for a total perspective, or pick out the topics of interest to you.

Because many people, particularly teachers, may have access to a microcomputer but have no previous knowledge of computers, Chapter 1 presents information needed when you are "Getting to Know Your Microcomputer." Brand name is not an issue; we have carefully planned the development to apply to most microcomputer systems. This discussion includes the general terminology of computers and their components. Much of this information would also be meaningful to students as they experience computers for the first time.

Computer literacy is the emphasis of Chapter 2. The discussion includes a general look at the topics important in a computer literacy curriculum (totally outlined in Chapter 8). This is followed by an overview of microcomputer applications in society as a whole, and the microcomputer's potential contributions to the school and home. Because no chapter on computer literacy is complete without an outline of how we got to where we are today, we include a brief historical discussion of the early calculating devices up to and including the four generations, and speculations on the fifth generation.

Computer-assisted Instruction (CAI) is carefully outlined in Chapter 3. All curriculum areas are included in the discussion. The unique feature of this chapter is a case study discussion of each application area, including drill and practice, tutorials, simulations, computer-managed instruction, and problem-solving software. The chapter ends with a look at the way CAI can be integrated into the curriculum and presents information pertaining to the area of special education.

Chapter 4 details the use of the computer as a tool for instructional and administrative tasks, including examples of existing applications and offering ideas that should appeal to the imagination. Testing, grade keeping, word processing, music, art, work load generation, and other applications have been described. Our goal is to encourage you to explore many possibilities and then to decide how the microcomputer can best aid you and your students.

Chapter 5 offers a brief overview of the most common computer languages. Programming a computer is a must if you plan to tell the computer what to do. The discussion of languages gives you some basis for deciding which one to use for young children, average students, sophisticated programmers, and so forth. Appendixes K and L accom-

pany this chapter, providing steps for programming in BASIC which can be used by individuals, or in a workshop setting.

Chapter 6 provides information that can help in the continuing search for good software. Checklist forms are included. These can be used to train educators in the art of software evaluation and can also be used to conduct a thorough evaluation procedure for specific kinds of software. Four different checklists have been provided: drill and practice, tutorial, simulation, and word processing. We have found that one form won't work for all. Selection and review criteria are carefully discussed. Additional written and short checklist forms have also been provided, since they will be preferable formats for many software evaluation tasks.

If you haven't selected a microcomputer, then Chapter 7, "Choosing the Right Hardware for Your Classroom," is required reading. A form is supplied and details provided to help you set up a plan to select the hardware best fitting your needs. The criteria are all discussed so that you will understand the terminology. The chapter also includes a "real" hardware proposal request, prepared by the Glendale Elementary School District No. 40 in Glendale, Arizona.

A model scope and sequence computer literacy curriculum for kindergarten through twelfth grade is also provided in Chapter 8. The curriculum includes topics, objectives, and activities for each grade level. Awareness and programming topics have been listed separately. This should help you to decide what needs to be taught and learned at specific times and can give you guidance in developing your own computer literacy curriculum.

Organizing your classroom or center for computer use is the emphasis of Chapter 9. Actual examples are presented. The chapter also

includes ideas for scheduling students as well as pointers for proper care of equipment. Good organization assures that students will be able to get involved with computers, and that the computer can become an extra helping hand in your teaching.

Every book needs a chapter on the future. Chapter 10 highlights a few of the expected developments which will affect education, and it gives some idea of what impact technology will have on our lives. This topic requires that you read current news and articles in order to stay abreast of new developments. Obviously, many exciting innovations exist for the future.

Finally, the appendixes include enough information to get you started and moving, including lists of relevant magazines, books, hardware vendors, computer literacy materials, and so on. We strongly recommend subscribing to several magazines, for this will contribute to your knowledge base and help you keep up with the latest events. Often magazine articles will provide the information you've been seeking for a specific area of interest.

We hope that your microcomputer becomes part of your teaching in a meaningful, helpful way to your students, as well as to yourself.

Acknowledgments

We would like to express our appreciation to the persons and organizations who have contributed in some way to this publication. We thank Dennis Camuse for his photographs and for the hours of time spent in taking them.

Several school districts made possible the inclusion of photographs in the book. We wish to thank the following persons:

- O. Benning Fast and Barbara Evans of Glendale Elementary School District No. 40

- Merrill Harlan, Pamela Miller, Pat Sagersten, Karen Trop, and Jerry Byrn at Bicentennial Elementary School

- Shirley Frye of Scottsdale Public Schools

- Nancy Watson at Kiva Middle School

- Dr. Al Kwiatkowski, Doris Iacobelli, Amy Chick, and Maureen Sculza at Pueblo Elementary School

- Sarah Baker and Nancy Martin at Chaparrel High School

- Lee Gerwitz at Carson Junior High School

- Sheila Walrath at Marcos de Niza High School

We also appreciate the help given to us by the following persons and organizations.

- Apple Computer, Inc., Cupertino, California

- Pam Anderson, Syntauri Corporation, Los Altos, California

- Atari, Inc., Sunnyvale, California

- Robert H. Brown, The Databug Corporation, Tempe, Arizona

- James Burke, Department of Chemistry, Arizona State University, Tempe, Arizona

- Commodore Business Machines, King of Prussia, Pennsylvania

- Data Concepts, Tempe, Arizona

- Lloyd C. Ferguson, Evans Newton Inc., Scottsdale, Arizona

- Hewlett-Packard Inc., Palo Alto, California

- Richard M. Hirsch, Businessland Computer Stores, Tempe and Phoenix, Arizona

- Fred Jipson, Gompers Rehabilitation Center, Phoenix, Arizona
- Gary Kwok, Software Connections, Santa Clara, California
- Suzi May and Marlene Zappia who created the Logo designs
- Don McCracken, International Business Machines (IBM), Phoenix, Arizona
- New York Public Library, New York, New York
- Radio Shack Computers, Tandy Corp., Fort Worth, Texas
- Texas Instruments Corp., Dallas, Texas
- Barbara Van Fleet, Honeywell Information Systems, Inc., Phoenix, Arizona
- Mike Walker and Pete Johnson, Walker Johnson and Company, and Terak, Inc.

As you read this book, concepts involving software will be illustrated by screen displays of actual programs. The companies involved in creating and/or marketing these programs are listed here:

- Bank Street Writer, Scholastic Software, Englewood Cliffs, New Jersey
- Bumble Plot, The Learning Company, Portola Valley, California
- Cyberlogo, Cybertronics International, Inc., Morristown, New Jersey
- Dragon's Keep, Sunnyside Soft, Fresno, California
- Facemaker, Spinnaker Software, Cambridge, Massachusetts
- The Factory, Sunburst Communications, Pleasantville, New York
- Gertrude's Secrets, The Learning Company, Portola Valley, California
- Hot Dog Stand, Sunburst Communications, Pleasantville, New York
- The Math Machine, SouthWest EdPsych Services, Phoenix, Arizona
- MasterType, Lightning Software, Palo Alto, California
- MECC Elementary Volume 7, Minnesota Educational Computing Consortium, St. Paul, Minnesota
- Meteor Multiplication, Developmental Learning Materials, Allen, Texas
- PAINT, created by the Capitol Children's Museum and distributed by Reston Software, Reston, Virginia
- President Elect, Strategic Simulations, Mountain View, California

Getting to Know Your Microcomputer

WHAT IS A COMPUTER?

To some people, computers are intimidating, omniscient, omnipotent humanoids in the process of taking over the world. These people suffer from frightening images of an impersonal, inhuman future presented in such literary works as *1984* and *Future Shock*. They fear that computers will violate their right to privacy, irreconcilably complicate their lives, and result in a society of human beings no longer capable of thinking for themselves.

Such fears are the result of a fundamental misunderstanding of what computers actually are and how they function. Simply put, a computer is a machine that processes information electronically. It accepts input, manipulates data, and produces output in some form for display. The key concept to remember is that computers follow the instructions they are given. They are the obedient servants of those who program them.

Although computers are powerful tools, there are many things that they cannot do. Computers cannot turn themselves on or off. They must depend on humans to do this. Computers cannot maintain and repair themselves; when they malfunction, a specialist called a computer technician must be called in to remedy problems. Computers cannot make moral judgments; therefore, they can be used by unscrupulous humans to commit unlawful or immoral acts. Again, the human operating the computer is responsible for the computer's performance. The computer cannot act on its own without a set of written instructions and a human to control its mechanical operation.

Given a cooperative working relationship between the computer and the humans who use it, the computer is an invaluable tool because of the many things it *can* do. Computers can save a vast amount of time, a precious commodity in today's hurried society. The homeowner who saves time by using a microcomputer to balance a household budget or to prepare income tax forms may use the extra time gained to enjoy leisure activities. For the businessperson, computerizing procedures that are usually performed by humans is one important way of cutting operating costs. To an emergency room physician using a computer to diagnose medical problems and prescribe treatment, the time saved may mean a life saved.

Computers are also extremely accurate under normal operating conditions. Human errors can be almost entirely eliminated from many business procedures, again saving time and money. Not only are computers fast and accurate, but they can work at high speeds for extended periods of time without becoming fatigued. This also helps to reduce errors that human workers make when they are tired or must work under a great deal of pressure.

The computer never becomes bored with repetitive tasks as humans often do. It can perform the same task almost infinitely without complaining or requiring a break. Also, the computer is used to perform tasks that endanger human lives. For example, radioactive materials in a nuclear power plant may be controlled by a computer which is not sensitive to radioactivity as are human workers.

Analog computers represent numbers internally by measuring quantities and then converting electrical energy into impulses that run mechanical devices. They perform work that is tiring, boring, or dangerous for human workers. A gasoline pump utilizes an analog computer.

In contrast *digital computers* (Figure 1-1) convert information in the form of numbers, letters, and special characters into digital form. The digital system is binary; that is, it depends on the system of numeration that includes only 0 and 1. Information is converted into electrical impulses during which a switch is either off (0) or on (1). The digital computer accepts input, converts input into electrical impulses, processes and manipulates data and information, and produces output.

Figure 1-1
Large Digital Computer, Honeywell's DPS 88/81
(Courtesy of Honeywell)

Whether analog or digital, computers depend on the humans who design, build, program, operate, and maintain them. Used properly, the computer is a tool that can help humans accomplish the work necessary to preserve an increasingly complex society.

With this definition in mind, computers are no longer to be feared, an attitude that reflects outdated ideas which are counterproductive figments of some science fiction writers' imaginations. Computers function now in our daily lives, and rapidly advancing computer technology promises to increase the number of computer applications in the near future.

Almost daily newspapers and news broadcasters report some new advance in computer technology. It is vital that people become familiar with computers and their capabilities because, in all likelihood, computer systems will be standard in new homes, and will play an integral part in many businesses and industrial occupations. Used widely, computers can and do enhance the quality of our lives.

There are a number of terms that are basic to an understanding of computer operations. One such term is *software*. *Software* refers to written instructions composed by computer programmers who are responsible for instructing computers to perform the tasks they are given to do. Another term for software is *computer programs*.

Basically, there are two types of software. *Systems software* instructs the computer to carry out its basic operations. Language interpreters, which allow one to program in various computer languages, are examples of systems software. The second type, *applications software,* instructs the computer to carry out specific tasks, such as writing payroll checks.

Software may originate from one of several sources. Large computer installations usually hire computer programmers on a full-time basis to write software to meet the installation's particular needs. Smaller computer users may purchase prepackaged programs from commercial software developers. Many personal computer users learn computer languages that enable them to write software for use on their own systems, allowing them to tailor software to their own individual needs.

In contrast to software, computer *hardware* is the physical machinery that makes up the computer system. Hardware is the equipment that you see when you visit a computer room or computer retail store. Computer hardware is sophisticated electronic equipment that must be handled and used appropriately and safely, and maintained properly in order for the computer system to operate with optimal efficiency.

The heart of the computer system is the *central processing unit* (*CPU*) (Figure 1-2). The *CPU* controls all the computer's functions since it is made up of circuitry that interprets and carries out instruc-

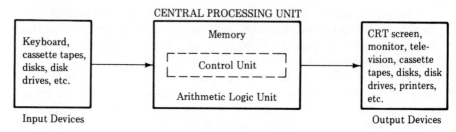

Figure 1-2
CPU Diagram

tions written into software. The CPU also retrieves software instructions before decoding and executing them. The components of the CPU are the *arithmetic/logic unit (ALU)*, the *memory,* and the *control unit.*

The *ALU* is that part of the CPU capable of performing mathematical calculations required for many data processing applications. The ALU performs these calculations with greater speed and accuracy than humans do. Imagine, for example, how the mathematical capabilities of the computer's ALU have revolutionized the work of the Internal Revenue Service.

The *memory* of the CPU is made up of integrated circuitry where information can be stored. Software instructions are retained in memory that is directly accessible to the CPU. When the computer requires these instructions for operations, the CPU retrieves them from memory, decodes them, and then carries them out.

The *control unit* of the CPU controls the flow of the computer's operations including data transfer, acceptance of input, functioning of the ALU, and other related functions. Clearly, the control unit is a vital part of the operation of the computer system as a whole.

PRIMARY COMPONENTS OF A MICROCOMPUTER

Electronics technology has resulted in computers that are both more powerful and physically smaller than computer systems used in the early 1960s. As computer technology advances with increasing rapidity, computer systems are becoming more affordable and, hence, more accessible to the average person. Gone are the days when only very large corporations could afford the advantages of computer capabilities. According to computer scientists, the increased sales and usage of microcomputer systems witnessed during the past several years is merely the tip of the iceberg. Eventually, they say, microcomputers will be standard appliances in our homes, our workplaces, and our lives.

Microcomputers are big business primarily because they put computer power in the hands of individual users. They are now being used

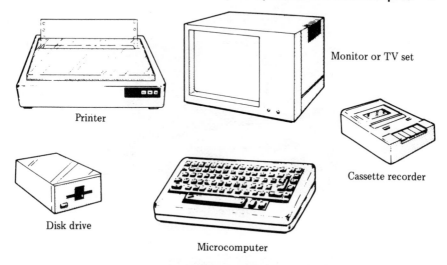

Printer

Monitor or TV set

Cassette recorder

Disk drive

Microcomputer

Figure 1-3
Microcomputer

to maintain household budgets and accounts; provide hours of challenging, entertaining, and often educational games; supplement traditional methods of classroom teaching; edit textual material; and expedite the business procedures of small business owners. The list of microcomputer applications seems limitless, indeed.

What is this powerful "little giant" that promises to make daily life simpler and more enjoyable in the future? The microcomputer system is made up of several hardware devices that function similarly to very large computer systems.

The Keyboard/CPU

The brain of the microcomputer system resides in the keyboard/CPU (Figure 1-3). Through the keyboard, instructions and data are entered into the computer system. The microcomputer keyboard is similar to a standard typewriter keyboard. It is made up of keys that represent letters of the alphabet and numbers, as well as special symbols such as @, $, %, and *. In addition to these familiar characters, the microcomputer keyboard usually includes special keys that instruct the computer to perform specific tasks. The microcomputer keyboard is simple and comfortable to use.

In many microcomputer systems, the keyboard is included in the same housing as the CPU. As in larger systems, the CPU is made up of the control unit, the ALU, and memory. The size of a microcomputer system's memory is vital to the speed and efficiency with which the system will operate.

Figure 1-4a
ATARI* Microcomputer

Figure 1-4b
Apple® Microcomputer†

Figure 1-4c
PET Microcomputer

---

*Indicates trademark of Atari, Inc.
†Apple is a registered trademark of Apple Computer, Inc.

Figure 1-4d
TRS-80 Microcomputer

Microcomputer Memory

The advent of the microcomputer age began with silicon chip technology. The technical properties of silicon chips will be discussed later, but it is important to note here that the silicon chip has brought about the miniaturization of electronic equipment. Consequently, a greater amount of memory capacity can be included in the CPU than was previously possible. This has significantly increased the power of microcomputer systems.

The typical microcomputer system includes *boards* onto which chips with memory capability have been fastened (Figure 1-5). At the time of purchase, a microcomputer will possess a certain amount of memory capacity; this amount can be increased according to the user's needs by inserting additional boards. Adding memory to a microcomputer is a simple process that most users can perform themselves.

To determine the memory size of a microcomputer system, it is necessary to understand several quantitative terms that apply to com-

Figure 1-5
Motherboard of an IBM Personal Computer

puter capability. Because the digital computer operates on a binary system, a *binary digit* is called a *bit*. A *bit* is the smallest unit of digital information. A *byte* is the number of bits necessary to store one character of text. A byte is usually, but not always, eight bits. These eight bits represent combinations of 0's and 1's, according to the binary system.

Computer memory capacity is generally measured in *kilobytes* (*K*). In the decimal system of numeration, the prefix *kilo* indicates 1,000. In the binary system, a kilo refers to 1,024, or two raised to the tenth power. The amount of memory capacity required to store 1,024 bytes of information is referred to as a *K*.

A major advantage of microcomputer systems is that extra memory space can be added simply and quickly as the needs of the user expand. Extra memory space allows the system to operate with greater speed and efficiency. More complex programs with lengthier instructions can be stored and run on a system to which extra memory space has been added.

There are two major types of semiconductor memory: *Random Access Memory* (*RAM*) and *Read Only Memory* (*ROM*). RAM is designed to store new data and programs. Data and program instructions are entered into the memory of the central processing unit and then accessed, or retrieved from memory, in random fashion. RAM is not permanent memory. For example, if the computer system loses power during operation, the information stored in RAM is lost forever. This requires that the lost information be reloaded into memory.

To maintain program instructions and data in the assigned RAM locations, the system must "refresh" its memory. The system does this by supplying small amounts of electricity to memory locations at the rapid speed of several hundreds or even thousands of times per second.

In contrast to RAM, ROM (Read Only Memory) is comprised of computer chips that have had program instructions manufactured into them permanently. Information stored on ROM chips cannot be lost in the event of a power failure. ROM chips contain programs that are used repeatedly for various applications; programs that control the video terminal and programs that control the mechanical operations of devices such as disk drives are two examples.

ROM can be built into computers at the time they are manufactured, or it can be purchased in modules to be inserted into special receptacles built into a computer. Some ROM chips contain programs that make the task of programming easier or more enjoyable. For instance, some ROM chips include a shape table—much like a dictionary—that holds a set of shapes already done so that the programmer can reuse these shapes numerous times without having to recreate them for each use.

The primary difference between RAM and ROM is that RAM is

programmed by the user and ROM is programmed by the manufacturer. There is one variation of ROM, however, that cuts across the distinctions between RAM and ROM. This variation is *Erasable Program-*
mable Memory (EPROM) or *Programmable Read Only Memory*
(PROM). EPROM chips come with program instructions stored on the
chips by the manufacturer. If the purchaser wishes to alter these program instructions, it is possible to erase them and then store new
instructions on the chips.

Memory Storage Devices

Another essential part of computer hardware is the storage device.
Storage devices retain data and instructions outside of the computer's
central processing unit. This allows the data and instructions stored to
be used repeatedly or kept for future reference. Several popular storage devices are available for use with microcomputer systems.

Perhaps the most popular storage device in use for computers in
general is the *magnetic disk drive*. The disk drive reads and records
information stored on *magnetic disks*. These *hard disks* (Figure 1-6a)
look very much like the plastic forty-five rpm disks used to record
music. Each disk has two recording surfaces—top and bottom. On the
recording surfaces are concentric circles moving outward from the center of the disk to its edge. Inside the disk drive are mounted several
read/write heads that record and retrieve information on magnetic
disks. Usually two or more disks are inserted into the disk drive at one
time.

Information stored on magnetic disks is relatively safe from loss.
Loss of stored material may result from writing too much information
onto a disk. Disks may also be erased by a computer-controlled device
called a *bulk eraser*. Accidental loss of information stored on magnetic
disks is unusual, though, and this factor adds to the popularity of
magnetic disk storage.

Figure 1-6a
Hard Disk

Although the *floppy disk* functions similarly to the hard disk, it is different because it is flexible rather than rigid. The floppy disk is eight inches in diameter. Usually only one surface is used for recording, although two-surface disks are becoming increasingly popular. The *diskette* (Figure 1-6b) is a smaller version of standard magnetic disks. It is five and one-quarter inches in diameter and is used with most personal computer systems.

Another popular storage device is *cassette tape* (Figure 1-6c). A major advantage of cassettes is that they are capable of storing large amounts of information. Cassette tapes used for information storage are quite similar to cassette tapes used to record and play music. The cassette is a reel of recording tape enclosed in a plastic cartridge. Cassettes are easily stored in a relatively small space.

Figure 1-6b
Floppy Diskette with Disk Drive
(Courtesy of Texas Instruments)

Figure 1-6c
Cassette Recorder

Cassette tapes are popular with microcomputer users because ordinary cassette players can be used as tape drives. The primary advantage of cassette tape storage is that it is considerably less expensive than other forms of external storage. However, there are two drawbacks to using cassette tapes. First, retrieving stored information is slow because information must be stored and, consequently, accessed in sequential order on tape; this can happen only at regular playing speed. Second, cassette tape performance is sometimes unpredictable.

As we have already seen, ROM chips are another way of retaining program instructions externally to the computer system. The instructions on ROM chips are manufactured into the chips and are, therefore, permanently stored on the chips. Hence, ROM chips are safe from loss of information.

Still another method of entering information is on special cards used with *optical card readers* or *scanners* (Figure 1-7). The *optical card reader* is a device that electronically "reads" information entered onto cards. The cards are relatively inexpensive, but because they are so bulky, they often cause a storage problem. Magnetic disks and cassette tapes are far more popular media for storage.

Display Devices

In order for the computer to work efficiently with the humans who use it, it must include some means of communicating. Display devices enable humans to see what instructions are being given to the computer; to respond to erroneous information; to enter data and verify data for correctness; and to see the output, or final product, of the computer's operation. Several hardware devices for display are available.

Figure 1-7
Optical Mark Scanner
(Courtesy of TRUE DATA)

Microcomputer systems rely on a variety of *video screens* for display purposes. Many computers can be adapted for use with ordinary television screens, the most common video screen in our society. Video games that plug into the family television set are one common and popular example. As computer graphics technology advances, the visual displays on video screens are becoming increasingly sophisticated.

Other terms for video screens are *monitors* or *cathode ray tubes (CRTs)*. CRTs rely on the same cathode ray tube technology that television is based on, but are designed strictly for use with computers. Simple CRTs display characters in green or white on a black background; more complex monitors can generate characters in a broader range of colors.

Printing Devices

Once the computer has completed its data-processing function, it is necessary to generate some human-readable, permanent copy of the resulting output. A record of computer transactions printed onto paper is referred to as a *hard copy*. Hard copies are often necessary for filing purposes or for reporting the results of data processing to many departments within an organization.

The printer is one device that cannot be used as an input device; it functions strictly as an output device. Data is read from the computer, processed according to instructions, and the results written out by the printer. Printers operate within a wide range of speeds from very slow to extremely fast—from ten characters per second to many thousands of characters per second.

Several factors determine the rate at which a printer operates. The type of printer is one factor. Some printers print material one character at a time, a relatively slow method of printing. A faster method is to set up a line of text at a time and then print the entire line. Another enhancement is to print in two directions—from left to right and then from right to left. This saves the time spent in returning to the left margin of the page to print each subsequent line.

One common method of printing is *thermal printing* which generates characters on heat-sensitive paper. These printers have the advantage of functioning very quietly, while other printers may cause a distracting level of noise in their immediate vicinity. However, thermal printing usually does not produce high-quality copies.

The other common method of printing is *impact printing*. In impact printing, characters are formed when the printing element, the part that includes the pattern or mold for characters, strikes or contacts the paper. This process is quite similar to the process of a typewriter key striking a ribbon against a sheet of typing paper to produce the image of a character.

A common type of impact printer is the *dot-matrix printer* (Figure 1-8a). The writing head of the dot-matrix printer is made up of wires that represent each letter, number, or symbol. Because each character is printed by a combination of separate wires, the resulting copy generally has a dotty appearance that may be unacceptable when high-quality copies are required. Dot-matrix printers that print a high density of dots per inch produce the best quality copies.

A higher quality impact printer is the *daisy wheel printer* (Figure 1-8b). These include print wheels that have letters, numbers, and other characters molded on them. The print wheel is rotated until the desired character is in the striking position on impact. Daisy wheel printers are usually more expensive and somewhat slower than dot-matrix printers, but they produce copies comparable to those produced by sophisticated typewriters.

Like all hardware technology, printer technology is advancing rapidly Many computer printers are available with graphics capabilities. These printers can generate reports with clear and illustrative graphs, charts, and maps. There are also special graphics plotters available that allow the user to keep the printer and the graphics printer separate. Newer models include color capabilities to make the output even more attractive.

USING YOUR MICROCOMPUTER

Now that you have a moderate vocabulary of computer terminology and can recognize the function of various kinds of computer hardware, you are probably eager to try your hand at working with the microcomputer. Microcomputers have an amazing amount of capability and using the system correctly will help to unleash its potential power.

Figure 1-8a
Dot-Matrix Printer
(Courtesy of Commodore Business Machines)

Figure 1-8b
Daisy-Wheel Printer
(Courtesy of Wang Laboratories, Inc.)

The microcomputer is user-oriented; that is, using a microcomputer system does not require an extensive background in computer science or an orientation toward electronics. Many owners of microcomputer systems begin slowly and find themselves learning more and more about their systems as they experiment with them.

There is, of course, a significant difference between *operating* a microcomputer and *programming* one. Operating the computer refers to the process of controlling the functions of the system, selecting software, and manipulating the equipment to cause it to perform given tasks. Programming, on the other hand, refers to the process of writing instructions that tell the computer how to perform its operations. Programming requires a more extensive knowledge of the computer and of computer languages than does merely operating the computer.

Often microcomputer users begin by learning to operate their systems using prepackaged software. Software is a fast growing field, and newer and better prepackaged software is available all the time. This software can perform a number of applications so that the microcomputer user need not know how to program the computer in order to use it.

Many prepackaged educational programs are available for use in homes and schools. More and more educational institutions are installing microcomputers in their classrooms for a number of reasons. Not only does the computer execute programs that cover topics that parents may not be familiar with, but it can also present those topics in interesting and colorful ways. In addition, the computer is a patient teacher offering feedback, reinforcement, repetition, flexibility, and remediation whenever appropriate.

Prepackaged educational software is available to teach mathematics, spelling, reading, grammar, and practically any other subject typically covered in traditional curricula. Whether students use such programs at home or in the classroom, they are learning several important lessons simultaneously. Not only are students tutored and drilled in academic subject areas, but they are also given an invaluable opportunity to become familiar and comfortable with microcomputer systems. This is especially important for today's children who will become tomorrow's adults in an increasingly computerized world.

Along with educational software, prepackaged programs that help the microcomputer user manage personal business are also popular. Some programs are written to keep track of household accounts and budgets. Others help the user to determine whether a hypothetical purchase is a wise investment or not. Still others store records of financial transactions for future reference. Computer scientists are now at work on software that will help the homeowner with physical tasks such as turning lights on or off, setting clocks accurately, and monitoring locked doors for security.

Software is available that maintains household inventories, computes income taxes, and even analyzes the stock exchange. Many microcomputer users find that computerizing their personal business makes such chores easier, faster to accomplish, and more accurate.

Perhaps the single most popular type of prepackaged software is software that entertains the user. These programs usually involve games of strategy, skill, or chance and are very popular with children. Some computer games can be played either with other people or with the computer itself as competitor. The computer keeps track of the score as well as recording each player's moves.

Many computer games can be adjusted for players at different levels of skills and may be enjoyed by players of all ages and abilities. Games that include graphics are exciting to play. Computer games are currently the fastest selling type of prepackaged software on the personal computer market.

The plethora of prepackaged software available for use on microcomputer systems makes operating a personal computer simple for the average, nontechnical person. Of course, the new microcomputer owner should follow instruction manuals and materials carefully in setting up the system properly. Most microcomputer retailers are happy to assist the novice in setting up and learning to operate a microcomputer system. Many personal computer owners find that once they have become familiar with the operations of their systems, they want to learn more about computers and about programming languages so that they can tailor software to their own individual needs.

PROGRAMMING YOUR MICROCOMPUTER

Occasionally, microcomputer users find that the prepackaged software they have located either does not meet their particular needs or has been written for use on a system other than theirs. In such cases, the user may wish to alter or rewrite program instructions to make them more suitable. At this point, the microcomputer user should begin to explore the process of programming a computer.

It is not always necessary for the user to have a thorough knowledge of a programming language such as BASIC, however. The novice can begin to learn about programming by using programs published in computer-oriented periodicals. Again, programs may be written specifically for use on a system other than the one the user owns, and changes may be necessary.

In the beginning, adapting such programs may be largely a trial-and-error endeavor. As in all new experiences, though, the user can learn as much from failures as from successes. The range of possibilities of writing and adapting microcomputer software is limited only by the user's imagination. Writing and altering programs also has the advantage of making the user's involvement with the microcomputer system more active and creative so that eventually the user becomes more computer literate.

Some microcomputer users will wish to study programming languages in a more structured way. There are a number of fine books available on the subject of computer programming. Also, as personal computers become more and more popular, numerous courses are offered by universities, community colleges, and technical schools. Any of these will provide an adequate background to the user who wishes to program. Also many communities now have clubs and organizations of personal computer hobbyists where the novice can interact with others having similar experiences and problems.

When users choose to study programming languages, they usually begin with a language called *Beginners All-Purpose Symbolic Instruction Code (BASIC)*. BASIC is a relatively simple, procedure-oriented programming language that is particularly useful to personal computer users. BASIC has the additional advantage of being used on most computers being manufactured today.

BASIC has still another strength as a starting point for the programming novice. Its editing capabilities make it highly useful for changing program instructions in existent software and for writing software that can be altered with relative ease in the future, if changes should become necessary. This gives the programmer the freedom to experiment with software.

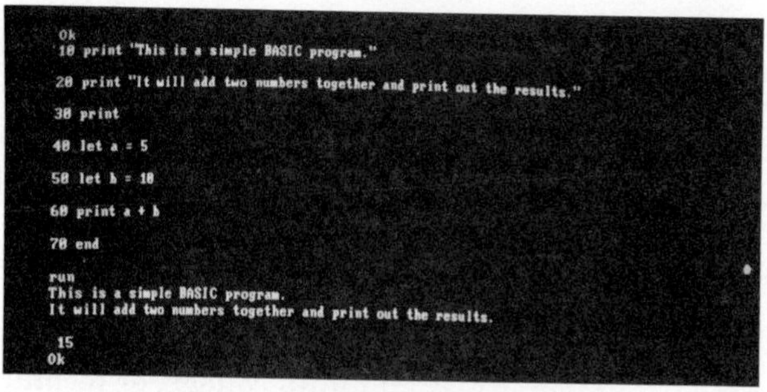

```
Ok
10 print "This is a simple BASIC program."

20 print "It will add two numbers together and print out the results."

30 print

40 let a = 5

50 let b = 10

60 print a + b

70 end

run
This is a simple BASIC program.
It will add two numbers together and print out the results.

 15
Ok
```

Figure 1-9
BASIC Listing on Video Screen

Figure 1-10
Hard-Copy Printout of a COBOL Program

Program instructions written in the same language will vary with different computer systems. For this reason, the user should own and consult the owner's manual that comes with the microcomputer system. Also, many books are available that tell the user precisely how to alter instructions for use on specific systems. (See "Suggested Readings" for books that teach the rudiments of programming in BASIC.)

BASIC is certainly not the only computer language in which software is written. Other languages exist which, although they may be more complex and consequently more difficult to learn, have been developed for various categories of applications. *Pascal* is a computer language often used to train computer scientists who will work with both large and small systems. <u>*Formula Translator*</u> (*FORTRAN*) is a higher-level programming language that is usually used for scientific, engineering, and mathematical applications. _Common Business-Oriented Language (COBOL)_ is another higher-level programming language that is widely used for business data-processing applications. Those wishing to work as computer professionals with corporations and businesses are well-advised to learn COBOL.

As with BASIC, the user can learn other computer languages from the many books available on various languages. It may be easier, however, to study more complex programming languages in a formal course offered by a university, community college, or technical school.

Microcomputer users who learn to write their own software will need to purchase hardware devices for storing and printing program instructions. As has already been explored, two popular media for information storage on the microcomputer system are magnetic diskettes and magnetic cassette tapes.

Besides needing to store the programs they write, microcomputer users will also want to generate hard copies of their software for their own use and so that they may share their software with other personal computer users. In order to do this, they must purchase a printing device. Computer retailers are trained to assess the user's needs and to recommend appropriate hardware.

SUMMARY

Computers are a vital part of our society today and promise to become even more pervasive in the years ahead. The personal computer industry is booming, indicating that a great number of people are discovering the benefits of home computing. This will require that microcomputer users acquire a greater degree of computer literacy.

Software refers to the written instructions that tell a computer how to operate. Hardware refers to the electronic equipment that carries out the software instructions. The central processing unit—the brains of the computer system—is made up of the arithmetic/logic unit, the control unit, and memory. Other hardware devices include storage devices such as magnetic disk drives and cassette tape drives, display devices such as the video screen, input devices such as keyboards, and output devices such as thermal printers and impact printers.

Microcomputers are said to be user-oriented because their operation does not require an extensive knowledge of computers. They are designed to be used by the average home computer owner. Many microcomputer users choose to learn more about computers and about programming languages such as BASIC. This enables them to tailor software to their own individual needs and to become more actively involved with their computer systems.

SUGGESTED READINGS

Alexander, Carole. *Feed Me, I'm Your PET Computer*. Manhasset, N.Y.: Cow Bay Computing, 1978.

Alexander, Carole. *Looking Good With Your Pet*. Manhasset, N.Y.: Cow Bay Computing, 1978.

Babcock, Eloise C. *Computer Readiness*. Phoenix: Think Ink Publications, 1981.

Carlson, Edward. *Kids and the Apple*. Chatsworth, Calif.: Datamost, 1982. (Atari, VIC, Commodore 64, Sinclair, TI99, and Panasonic versions also available.)

Dwyer, Thomas A., and Margot Gritchfield. *BASIC and the Personal Computer*. Menlo Park, Calif.: Addison-Wesley Publishing Co., 1978.

Dwyer, Thomas A., and Michael S. Kaufman. *A Guided Tour of Computer Programming in BASIC*. Boston: Houghton Mifflin Co., 1980.

Malone, Linda, and Jerry Johnson. *BASIC Discoveries: A Problem Solving Approach to Beginning Programming*. Palo Alto, Calif.: Creative Publications, 1981.

Stewart, George. *Getting Started with TRS-80 BASIC*. Fort Worth, Tex.: Tandy Corporation, 1980.

Zamora, Raymond et al. *Pet BASIC: Training Your Pet Computer*. Reston, Va.: Reston Publishing Co., 1981.

2 Computer Literacy: A First Look

INTRODUCTION

The idea that the children of today must be prepared for tomorrow's computerized society is commonplace. It is not only children, however, who need this preparation. The use of computers in our society is currently so widespread that adults who are unaware of, or uncomfortable with, computers are at a distinct disadvantage.

We encounter computers in banks, grocery stores, department stores, offices, libraries, and practically everywhere else in our society. We purchase and use appliances, toys, and automobiles designed with microprocesser technology. Simply put, we *live* with computers. It is obvious that we need to acquire some fundamental level of understanding of these electronic wonders which make our lives simpler and more enjoyable.

During the last decade especially, educators have debated the question of the schools' responsibility to instill in students this basic understanding of computers. Two terms often heard in this debate are *computer awareness* and *computer literacy. Computer awareness* refers to the development of a recognition of computers and their uses in society and a relative degree of comfort in working with computers. Computer awareness frees people from unfounded fears and prejudices about computers and causes them to become more willing to participate in computer-related activities. *Computer literacy,* on the other hand, begins with computer awareness, but involves a more fully developed understanding of and sensitivity to computers. Ankers (1980) recommends that computer literacy include knowledge of hardware and programming. Others recommend that computer literacy include exploration of applications of computers in the classroom, office, home, and other places where computers are in use (Bitter 1981, Bell 1979, Carpenter et al., 1980). Jay (1981) defines computer literacy as consisting of three realities or components: attitude, knowledge base, and ability or capacity to perform some functions or tasks with computers.

Although definitions of computer literacy vary, the term generally refers to a fundamental knowledge of computers, their uses and limitations, how they work, and their impact upon society. It does not refer to a sophisticated or professional level of computer capability, but rather a rudimentary knowledge of computers.

As microcomputer systems have become smaller, more powerful, and more affordable, they have become more feasible tools for use in the traditional classroom setting. Unfortunately, the attitudes of some traditional educators and administrators have not kept pace with this swift technological advancement. Some school systems appear reluctant to institute microcomputer systems in the classroom.

Some of this reluctance may be attributed to the erroneous belief that computer systems are too expensive to purchase and maintain, and acquiring and appropriating funds is an incessant concern of all school systems. However, especially during the past several years, the cost of microcomputer systems has decreased markedly, putting them well within the range of educational institutions.

The reluctance of educators to adopt computer literacy curricula may also derive in part from a lack of knowledge about computers. Teachers and administrators are certainly not immune to the attitude of resistance to computers that appears pervasive in our society. Setting up a microcomputer system in a classroom and introducing students to the system does require some level of computer literacy on the teacher's part. Some teachers may feel that this places additional pressure on them.

However, the alternative to teaching computer literacy—denying students the opportunity to acquire basic skills that they will need in an increasingly computerized society—is certainly more costly in the long run. After all, it is the responsibility of the schools to prepare children to become fully functioning, productive members of society. If a society relies on computers to accomplish much of its work, then members of that society must become computer literate in order to participate in that society.

No one would dispute that at present computer technology is revolutionizing practically every facet of our society. A brief survey of the myriad applications of computers in our society may serve to illustrate this point.

A BRIEF LOOK AT COMPUTER USAGE

In today's business world, computers have become standard equipment. The most familiar application of computers in business is data processing. Most businesses are faced with an overwhelming amount of accounting and bookkeeping procedures that must be performed routinely, quickly, and accurately. The computer's ability to perform mathematical calculations with lightning speed and virtual infallibility accounts for its immediate and widespread acceptance in the world of business.

Computers also have the ability to expedite the plethora of paperwork necessary to keep a business running. Computers perform inventory, record keeping, billing, payroll, and a seemingly infinite number of other functions routine to most businesses. Word-processing technology has changed the nature of secretarial work and freed many secretaries to perform other tasks that they were previously too busy to accomplish.

Yet another attractive feature of computers is that they can be programmed to make surprisingly accurate predictions that help managers make sound decisions. The computer can consider a wide variety of contingencies and predict what conditions will arise in the event of such contingencies (Figure 2-1a). Such predictions may save businesses vast amounts of money by anticipating adverse conditions and, in many cases, can increase businesses' profits by forecasting favorable conditions.

Not only is the computer an invaluable tool in the business office, but it is also becoming a vital part of industry. The use of robot technology in manufacturing is one example. Robots perform work that is boring, repetitious, difficult, or dangerous for human workers to do; indeed they can function around the clock without tiring or requiring breaks.

Figure 2-1a
VisiCalc Display on Video Screen

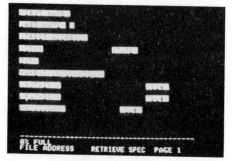

Figure 2-1b
PFS Filing System

Another application of robots is quality control. The robot is programmed with information about a product of acceptable quality. It can perform routine tests to determine if the items being manufactured meet acceptable standards. The robot is capable of checking minute details that may not be visible to the human eye.

Computers are also used widely in the field of engineering. *Computer-aided Design* (CAD) refers to the use of computers in designing and testing new products (Figure 2-2). The computer can speculate about various design ideas to determine which will work and which will not. It can simulate conditions for testing new products to determine their feasibility. In the past, design and research was an expensive and time-consuming process because engineers relied on actual physical models of designs to perform such tests. CAD helps eliminate costly mistakes in research and development.

The business world is not the only place where computers are found. Computer technology makes work faster and more efficient on the farm where computers help farmers evaluate climatic conditions, control inventory, feed and care for livestock, and keep up with many accounting and bookkeeping procedures. Although computers may seem out of place among chickens and silos, they are helping to make agriculture more productive and cost-effective.

Still another facet of society where computers have become an integral part is in the arts. In music, for example, electronic and digital sound synthesizers are producing a popular new sound. Computers are even being used experimentally in music composition, and they can also be useful in designing and choreographing marching band performances.

Another exciting development of computers in the arts has resulted from increasingly sophisticated computer graphics technology. Stunning visual displays can be created by computers with graphics capabilities. Animation created by human artists is time-consuming and astronomically expensive. Computers can create equally striking effects in a fraction of the time required for an artist to produce similar effects.

Computers expedite the complicated process of film making in other ways as well. They are useful in film editing, calculating the number of frames of film per scene, and controlling property inventory. The applications of computers to the entertainment industry are still quite new, but they promise to develop along with other computer technology.

Among the largest users of computers are federal, state, and local governments. Governmental agencies collect vast amounts of data that must be processed and stored in various ways. Consider, for example, the amount of data generated by a national census. Computers expedite the process of handling these data so that they can be used for

Figure 2-2
Terak CAD System
(Courtesy of Terak, Inc.)

research and allocation of funds and grants that improve the quality of the lives of many citizens.

The annual task of assessing and collecting taxes is one more job that has been simplified by the use of computers. Computers record vast amounts of information submitted by taxpayers and employers, calculate and verify tax returns, and generate refund checks. Without computers, tax collection would be an overwhelming task.

Governments also use computers for processes such as license renewal and vote tabulations. Using computers to tabulate election results has made for much faster and more accurate reports of election results. Computers are even used to predict election results while votes are still being tabulated.

Yet perhaps the fastest growing area of computer applications in our society is occurring in our own homes. Declining costs of owning and operating personal computer systems have put computer power in the hands of the average person. A popular use of personal computers is computer games, which are fun, challenging, entertaining, and often educational. They provide an enjoyable and nonthreatening means of interacting with the computer system. Advancements in computer graphics technology constantly improves the attractiveness of these games.

Personal computer users also perform accounting and record-keeping functions on their systems, much as large corporations do. Personal computers can also monitor checking accounts, maintain household inventory, generate budgets, store important records, and perform many other tasks that keep a household running smoothly.

Figure 2-3
Computer in Home
(Courtesy of Texas Instruments)

Still another application of the home computer is education. There is a great deal of educational software on the market that enables parents to supplement the education their children receive in a traditional classroom environment. The computer is a versatile tutor; it can help to teach reading skills to a small child or sophisticated, graduate-level university courses to a well-educated adult. It can be a useful tool in learning many subjects included in conventional academic curricula.

Personal computers keep their users aware and informed in an information-rich society. The personal computer user can gain access to nationwide data bases that provide the latest information about vocational and leisure interests. Many computer scientists suggest that in the near future, newspapers will be delivered not to our doors, but to our video screens. Electronic mail will expedite communication.

THE NEED FOR COMPUTER LITERACY

Obviously, computers are with us to stay. The number and range of computer applications in our society can only increase, and more than likely at an astonishing rate. It is only logical that people accept this fact and prepare themselves to take advantage of the many benefits offered by computer technology.

A strong argument in favor of computer literacy education is the increased job potential and earning power for people who become computer literate. The U.S. Bureau of Labor Statistics predicts that the demand for trained computer professionals will double in the next decade. And even those who work in fields not immediately connected with computers are likely to find themselves working with computers in some capacity. Computer literacy is fast becoming a vital job skill as basic as reading.

Unquestionably, the schools must begin to prepare students to function comfortably and knowledgeably with computers. But at what point is a child capable of working with computers? Is computer literacy appropriate at the high school level, or can it be introduced to elementary school children?

Computer scientist and educational technology researcher Seymour Papert has found that children as young as three years of age are capable of working with computers. Papert has designed Logo, a simple computer programming language that allows children to interact with computers without extensive instruction in computer languages.

In his landmark book *Mindstorms* (1980), Papert has pointed out that learning to work with a computer is analogous to learning a foreign language. Children seem to learn foreign languages with relative ease while adults find this task considerably more difficult. The earlier children are introduced to the world of computers, the more comfortably they will adjust to it.

Another advantage of introducing computers to very young students is that these children have not yet adopted the attitude of fear of the computer. Neither have they developed "mathphobia" and thus might be less likely to be intimidated by computers. Small children are open to a wide range of new experiences, and this openness can be a key factor in the success of any computer literacy program.

What skills are necessary to acquire before being introduced to the computer? In many systems designed for use in educational systems— Papert's Logo, for example—the student need only be able to recognize letters and numbers and possess very basic typing skills. Three-year-old children are able to recognize figures on a keyboard and manipulate the keyboard to enter data.

Although Papert might argue that BASIC is not a suitable first computer language, many teachers have found that children of elementary school age are capable of learning the rudiments of BASIC so that they can compose simple programs. By the time these children reach high school and have acquired several years of experience with computers and computer logic, they are able to begin to learn other languages such as COBOL and FORTRAN. Their early exposure to computers will make it easy for them to learn increasingly complex languages and skills.

Computer literacy, then, should be a concern of teachers of all grade levels and abilities. Computers have also been proven to be very effective in working with special education students because the computer allows children to function at their own pace. The key to effective computer literacy education is to begin with very fundamental concepts. The computer literate children of today will become the comput-er literate adults of tomorrow who function effectively and comfortably in a computerized society.

A BRIEF HISTORY OF COMPUTERS

A logical first step in becoming computer literate is to appreciate the origins of computers. Computers are the result of a long history of mathematical explorations and innovations. They have their earliest roots in primitive systems of counting that relied on fingers and toes or stones to enumerate objects.

Eventually, these primitive systems gave way to mechanical de-vices aimed at making complex calculations quickly and accurately. One of the earliest of such devices was Babbage's Analytic Engine. Charles Babbage was a nineteenth-century mathematician who de-signed the Difference Engine (Figure 2-4a). He saw a need for such a device because, in an era of increasing use of mathematics, people were making large numbers of errors in building logarithm tables. Babbage sought to eliminate the repetitive and time-consuming creation of these tables.

The Difference Engine was the first result of his efforts. It was a combination of rods, gears, and ratchets that jammed constantly and made the Difference Engine impractical to use. Undaunted, Babbage set to work on a more ambitious project: the Analytic Engine. A fore-runner of the computer, Babbage's device had an input section that read data from holes punched in cards. It also had provisions for print-ing results. More importantly, Babbage provided a control unit for operating the computer, a "mill" unit for performing calculations, and a "store" unit for holding up to 1,000 fifty-digit numbers.

The Analytic Engine was, in many ways, analogous to computers of today in that it could store, execute, and change instructions. The machine was doomed to failure, however, because it was a victim of its times. The state of technology in Babbage's day was such that the 50,000 parts necessary to manufacture a single Analytic Engine could not be produced.

The next influential invention was the census machine of Herman Hollerith. In the late nineteenth century, census taking had become a major task; tabulation of such a vast amount of data was slow and problematical. In an effort to find a faster way to compile raw statisti-cal data, the Census Bureau sponsored a contest. Herman Hollerith's device was chosen as the most effective and practical.

Hollerith had designed a device that read data from punched cards and kept track of the count (Figure 2-5b). The keypunch system of data processing was popular for many years, although recently it has suc-cumbed to faster and less cumbersome methods. Hollerith was so suc-

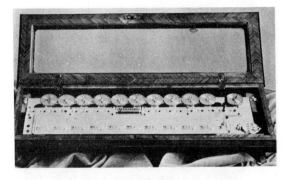

Figure 2-4a
Pascal's Mechanical Calculator

Figure 2-4b
Charles Babbage's Difference Engine

Figure 2-4c
Scheutz's Printing Calculating Machine
(Courtesy of New York Public Library)

Figure 2-5a
Historical Mechanical Keypunch Machine
(Courtesy of New York Public Library)

Figure 2-5b
Historical Card Tabulating Machine
(Courtesy of New York Public Library)

cessful, in fact, that he left the Census Bureau in 1896 to form International Business Machines Corporation—IBM, a recognized leader in the field of data-processing technology even today.

Then in 1939, the first digital-computing device was constructed by John V. Atanasoff. As the cost of producing electronic components decreased, a group of Harvard scientists headed by Howard Aiken and working in conjunction with IBM developed the Mark I. This computer is considered to be the forerunner of the first generation of computers.

The First Generation of Computers

Developed in 1944, the Mark I was primarily electromechanical; that is, it was made up of mechanical switches that are opened and closed by electrical current. It was 51 feet long, 8 feet high, and contained 1,000,000 components and over 500 miles of electric wire. It was capable of adding three 8-digit numbers per second. The Mark I was noisy, slow, and cumbersome compared to computers in use today.

The next major development in computer technology culminated in the Electronic Numerical Integrator and Computer (ENIAC) (Figure 2-6a). Designed by John W. Mauchly and J. Prespert Eckert, Jr., ENIAC was intended to be used by the military. It was programmed by means of switches and connections. ENIAC was more than one thousand times faster than the Mark I, performing 5,000 calculations per second. Weighing 60,000 pounds and containing nearly 2,000 vacuum tubes, ENIAC required tremendous amounts of electricity to power it and gave off large amounts of heat.

The most significant feature of ENIAC was that it introduced vacuum tube technology, and no longer were calculations and operations performed by moving mechanical parts (Figure 2-6b). This feature allowed for greatly increased speed of performance.

Figure 2-6a
The ENIAC

Figure 2-6b
Vacuum Tube Panel

The next computer was developed by Mauchly, Eckert, and others and was called the Electronic Discrete Variable Automatic Computer (EDVAC). It was smaller and more powerful than its predecessors. It also had two other important features: it used the binary numbering system, and it could internally store instructions in numeric form. Today all data and programs are stored in binary form. This method of storing instructions inside the computer is far more efficient than paper tape storage used with earlier devices.

Another member of the first generation of computers was the Electronic Delayed Storage Automatic Computer (EDSAC) built at Cambridge University in England. This computer introduced the concept of stored programs. Before this, computers often had to be rewired to be used for various applications. Their memories were incapable of storing more than one program at a time. EDSAC helped eliminate time-consuming and costly rewiring procedures.

At this point, computers were built primarily for scientific applications. In 1946, however, Mauchly and Eckert formed a corporation to build computers for commercial use; the UNIVAC (1951) was the first electronic computer used by large business firms. This launched the major growth of computers into the business field.

The first generation of computers, which thrived from 1951 until 1959, is characterized by vacuum tube technology. Although they were amazing devices in their time, they were large, took up valuable space, were expensive to operate, and required almost constant maintenance to function properly. The next generation of computers attempted to resolve some of these problems.

The Second Generation of Computers

The second generation of computers extended from 1959 until 1964 and was characterized by transistor technology. The transistor was developed in 1947 by John Bardeen at the Bell Laboratories in New Jersey. Bardeen studied substances that permitted a limited flow of electricity through them—*semiconductors*. Transistors that used semi-

Figure 2-7
Electronic Panel—Transistors

conductor material could perform the work of vacuum tubes, and took up much less space (Figure 2-7).

Because transistors were smaller, the distance between operating parts was reduced and speed of performance was increased significantly. Transistors were also much cooler than vacuum tubes, reducing the need for expensive air conditioning in areas where computers were housed.

Transistors did present several problems, though. They were relatively expensive because each transistor and its related parts had to be individually inserted into holes in a plastic board. Also, wires had to be fastened by floating boards in a pool of molten solder. The number of parts required for even the simplest transistors was staggering. Even though the distance between individual parts was reduced, it was still great enough to limit speed of computer operations. The next generation of computers helped to alleviate some of these problems.

The Third Generation of Computers

The development of integrated circuits in 1963 spawned the third generation of computers, lasting from 1964 until 1975. Integrated circuits developed from a need to mass produce transistors in a few simple production steps. The production process begins when tubes of silicon are sliced into wafer-thin disks that are chemically pure and cannot hold electrical charge. Then a preconceived design is etched onto the surface of the wafer with the use of light rays.

Once the entire surface of the wafer has been processed, the wafer is placed in an acid bath to eliminate all unexposed areas. To enable the wafer to carry an electrical impulse, slight traces of impurities must be added in a specified pattern. Finally, a fine diamond saw slices through the wafer and divides it into dozens of blocks, like postage stamps in a large sheet. Each tiny piece is now a chip. After discarding unusable chips, the manufacturer encases the wafer and connects it to the outside of the case with gold wires (Figure 2-8a). This is the integrated circuit—a sandwich of carefully treated silicon that now forms the transistor, a device that acts as an electrical switch.

The integrated circuit continued the trend toward miniaturization that has resulted in the popularity of the microcomputer and the personal computer system. Because the chips are tiny, the pathways through which electrical current must pass are short. Therefore, the number of calculations that can be performed each second is increased tremendously. Also, the chip is manufactured in such a way that its performance is virtually guaranteed for a practically unlimited life span.

Integrated circuit technology spawned a generation of computers that had greater storage capacity and terrifically increased speeds of

Figure 2-8a
Manufacturing Integrated Circuits
(Courtesy of Texas Instruments)

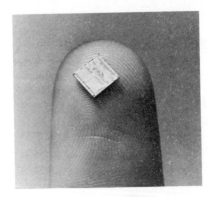

Figure 2-8b
Integrated Circuit
(Courtesy of Texas Instruments)

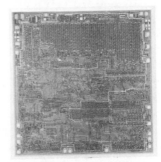

Figure 2-8c
Magnification of Integrated Circuit
(Courtesy of Hewlett Packard)

performance. Also during this period, many accessory devices were developed and marketed, such as magnetic tape drives and disk drives. Popular programming languages were developed and refined, many of which are still in use today. Time-sharing was introduced as a way of maximizing the efficiency of systems that performed calculations at incredible speeds.

Third-generation computers were not aimed at specific applications such as business or scientific use. Rather, they were designed as general-purpose computers. They represented a giant leap forward in the data-processing field. Not only were speed and reliability enhanced, but power consumption was decreased markedly. Computers became smaller and less expensive, putting computer power into the hands of a greater number of users than ever before. Computer technology began to snowball.

The Fourth Generation of Computers

Engineers were not satisfied with the degree of miniaturization that resulted from the integrated circuit. Also, the integrated circuits of the third generation were designed primarily with chips having only one function. For example, a chip might perform calculations or amplify weak currents in a television or radio. As engineers learned how to manufacture chips more easily, they conceived the idea of grouping an assortment of functions on a single chip, creating a microelectronic "system" capable of performing various tasks required for a single job. This technology became known as Large Scale Integration (LSI). Thus, the fourth generation of computers was born in the mid-1970s.

LSI had many applications other than large-scale computers. One such application is the pocket calculator so common today. This calculator had a single "block" that contained 6,000 transistors capable of adding, subtracting, dividing, and multiplying. Another device made possible by LSI technology is the digital watch. It contained 2,000 transistors on a single chip. Today's video games also rely on LSI technology.

Still another innovation of LSI technology is the computer-on-a-chip. Its manufacturers compressed nearly all the subsystems of a computer into $\frac{1}{20}$ square inch. Over 15,000 transistors combine to form a brain that stores, processes, and retrieves data with a capacity that rivals room-sized computers of a decade earlier.

LSI technology has also been responsible for the recent popularity of the microcomputer. These "little giants" fit easily on a desk top and put computer power in the hands of an increased number of people. Declining prices of powerful computer systems have also encouraged development of the electronics field in general. LSI turned computer technology into big business, and this trend will certainly continue in the foreseeable future.

Another benefit of LSI technology has been the production of computers that are easier to maintain and upgrade. The early computers required almost constant attention by highly trained computer technicians. Microcomputers, on the other hand, are relatively simple to own and maintain. This is one reason why so many people—adults and children alike—are being exposed to the many advantages of computers without needing to have a thorough knowledge of electronics.

Computer technology continues to advance at a tremendous rate. Today we are living with the fourth generation of computers, but already new developments are surfacing that give us some idea of what fifth-generation computers will be like.

The Fifth Generation of Computers

A hint of tomorrow's computer capability can be found in the IBM 3081, introduced in 1980. This computer is twice as powerful as its immediate predecessor. It was designed with Very Large-Scale Integrated (VLSI) circuitry, a concept that is essentially a refinement of LSI technology VLSI circuitry further increases the speed at which computers are able to function.

Multiprocessing—the simultaneous running of several programs by one computer—is likely to be developed further in the fifth generation of computers. Multiprocessing makes computerized data processing even more cost-effective. Another area that will receive attention is a new form of memory called *bubble memory*. Bubble memory eliminates the danger of data and instructions being lost when the system shuts down. In bubble memory, memory cells form a series of bubbles containing tremendous amounts of circuitry capable of storing data and programs in very small spaces. Available now for use with large computer systems, bubble memory will certainly become available for future microcomputers.

Certainly the trend of miniaturization witnessed throughout the past several generations of computers will also continue in the fifth generation, concentrating greater amounts of computer capacity in ever smaller spaces. Not only are computers becoming smaller, but

Decreasing Cost of Computer Operations

Generation	Technology	Cost per 100,000 Computations
First	Vacuum tube	$1.25
Second	Transistors	.25
Third	Integrated circuits	.10
Fourth	VLSI	less than .01

their prices are lower. Advanced manufacturing technology will lead to much more affordable computer systems within the near future.

As computers become more affordable, it is likely that many new applications will be found and explored. The average computer hobbyist, small business owner, school district, or other organization can now look to computers as a viable means of handling an ever-increasing flow of paperwork.

The message to educators is loud and clear. Tomorrow's society will rely heavily on computers and, consequently, on the people who work with computers. This indicates that the schools of today must adopt a computer literacy curriculum in order to meet those needs.

SUMMARY

Because computers are becoming more and more pervasive in our society, there is a great need for people—young and old—to develop some degree of computer awareness and computer literacy. Computer awareness refers to the ability to recognize computers and work comfortably with them. Computer literacy refers to a fundamental understanding of computer operations and terms, applications of computers in society, and uses and limitations of computers.

Even small children are capable of performing simple tasks with computers. Very likely, the earlier a child is introduced to computers, the better that child's attitude and experience with the computer will be. It is best to begin teaching computer literacy to children in elementary schools and then to present increasingly complex notions of computer science to the children as they mature and progress.

One reasonable place to begin with computer literacy is to gain an understanding of the history of the machines themselves. Although many primitive mathematical devices contributed to the development of computer technology, the first generation of computers is considered to have begun with the introduction of vacuum tube technology. The second generation of computers incorporated transistor technology in an attempt to resolve some of the problems presented by vacuum tubes. The third generation of computers was based on integrated circuit technology, which was enhanced in the Large Scale Integrated (LSI) circuits of the fourth generation of computers.

We can speculate about the fifth generation of computers based on the trends that are currently emerging. Very Large Scale Integration (VLSI) technology will certainly continue the trend toward miniaturization, making computer systems smaller and more affordable. As this occurs, computers will gain even more popularity than they presently have. The logical consequence of this trend will be an increased need for computer literacy for people of all ages and occupations.

REFERENCES

Bitter, Gary G. *Computers in Today's World*. New York: John Wiley and Sons, 1984.

Papert, Seymour. *Mindstorms: Children, Computers, and Powerful Ideas*. New York: Basic Books, 1980.

3 Computer-Assisted Instruction

INTRODUCTION

Computer-assisted instruction (CAI) is the most popular term used to describe the use of computers for instructional tasks. "Educational software," "courseware," CBI (computer-based instruction), and CMI (computer-managed instruction) are some other commonly used descriptive terms. CAI can be purchased in the form of *diskettes, cassette tapes,* or *cartridges.*

Several distinct types of CAI exist: drill and practice, tutorial, simulation, computer-managed instruction, and problem solving. These will be discussed in their purest forms. However, it should be recognized that any educational program may employ more than one of these techniques. A tutorial program, for example, typically includes drill and practice exercises after topics have been introduced.

No programming knowledge is necessary to use these "canned" software packages. The method for transferring the programs on disk, tape, or cartridge into the computer's memory varies for different brands of microcomputers, but is usually a simple procedure which can be learned in just a few minutes.

DRILL AND PRACTICE

As one explores the educational software available through software houses and educational publishing companies, it soon becomes apparent that much "drill and practice" type of software exists, and that a wide range of topics are represented. In general, drill and practice software allows learners to come in contact with facts, relationships, problems, and vocabulary until the material is committed to memory, or until a particular skill has been refined. The best drill and practice software possesses an interesting format which encourages reuse by students, thus ensuring mastery of the skill or establishment of the stimulus-response association required for memorization of certain facts.

Simple drill and practice programs can be designed and coded into computer language by students. Math fact drill, for instance, can be generated by several statements in a program which allow the computer to present randomly selected problems and then to test for the correctness of student responses. It is likely that these simple programs will not take full advantage of the microcomputer's capabilities be-

Figure 3-1a
Diskette and Disk Drive

Figure 3-1b
Cassette Recorder

Figure 3-1c
TI 99/4A Microcomputer with ROM Cartridge
(Courtesy of Texas Instruments)

cause extra programming knowledge is needed to add sound, music, color, graphics, or animation. Still, student-designed programs can be effectively used in the classroom for drill and practice purposes. The student can write and enjoy practicing with his or her own program, and can share the creation with classmates.

Any subject area can take advantage of drill and practice software. Because many microcomputers possess sound and music capability, software has been developed which increases ability to recognize notes, chords, rhythms, and so forth. As some music teachers have experienced, ear training in small or large group situations often leads to embarrassment for the students who most need the training. Use of ear-training software allows individual students to gain skill in a less threatening fashion, and with immediate feedback on accuracy. Other music theory topics that can be practiced through the use of computer software include aural intervals, enharmonics, key signatures, note types, visual intervals, music terms, whole and half-step intervals, scales, sevenths, and triads.

Drill and practice software can also be effective for learners in the area of vocabulary development. Computers can provide the proper

MECC Elementary Vol. 4

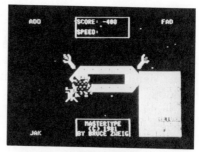

Mastertype

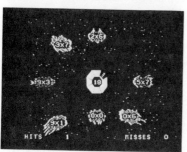

Meteor Multiplication

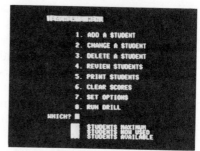

Math Machine

Figure 3-2
Drill and Practice Video Displays

amount of connections between words and their meanings, so that students can learn about words and their uses within our language. For example, the computer displays a definition. The student types in the appropriate word. This process can be repeated until the associations between words and their definitions are complete. The association method need not be so mundane as described above; gamelike formats, contextual clues, rhymes, riddles, and so on can help add much interest.

Similarly, students learning foreign languages, or those who are learning English as a second language (ESL) can use computer software to strengthen associations between corresponding words, expressions, and grammatical constructions. Many microcomputers allow sound and pictures to illustrate words, phrases, and sentences. Thus, the ESL student mainstreamed into a regular classroom can benefit from computerized, individualized instruction and may be able to communicate with his or her classmates in a shorter amount of time than would be possible otherwise.

Specific information on software is in Chapter 6 and Appendix A.

A Classroom Vignette

A group of children in Mrs. Evans's sixth grade class had been learning to add and subtract fractions. Diagnosis of error patterns in the children's work indicates that some children have poor mastery of multiplication facts. Others could not consistently determine the least common denominator (LCD) when adding fractions with unlike denominators. Further investigation convinced Mrs. Evans that the students did demonstrate understanding of the concepts involved, but needed further skill development. Therefore, she decided to employ two different drill and practice programs to supplement paper and pencil activities.

John, Jeff, and Margaret were sent to run a colorful math fact drill program which featured animated people and snippets of music for positive reinforcement purposes. The three children took turns sitting at the keyboard and recorded their scores at the end. As time passed, Mrs. Evans noticed that the children were adding in order to figure out some multiplication fact answers. Because the object of the lesson was math fact automaticity, Mrs. Evans accessed a "teacher-only" part of the program, and reduced the time limit for answering math fact problems, thus insuring that the children would need to recall facts from memory.

Mrs. Evans met with several other children to practice methods for finding the LCD. Later on during the day, these children ran a program allowing unlimited practice in finding LCD's and which increased their speed and accuracy. Because the program was written in

Figure 3-3
Child Using Drill and Practice Software

an interesting arcade game format, the children were encouraged to run the program over and over again.

TUTORIAL

As the name suggests, software of the tutorial type utilizes written explanations, descriptions, questions, problems, and graphic illustrations for concept development, much like a private "tutor." Often computerized or traditional written pretests are included with tutorial software to determine the most appropriate beginning lessons for a particular student or whether certain lessons should be skipped. After the tutorial portion of a lesson has been presented, usually drill and practice type exercises are offered. In some cases, the student has total control of the amount and type of exercises. Finally, a posttest for each objective or group of objectives will determine mastery of objectives. Student scores may be displayed as the lesson ends, as well as suggestions for further study and/or practice.

As you may have guessed, courseware of the tutorial type tends to require more complicated instructional design and programming techniques. The author of the tutorial must try to predict all possible correct responses and allow for insignificant mispelling and capitalization errors. The program must intelligently respond to incorrect answers and at best will predict the most common incorrect answers and offer specially tailored explanations and learning experiences according to which incorrect answer was chosen by the student. In addition, computerized tests must be as valid and reliable as their written counterparts, so that students are not subjected to already known material, and so that learning can be evaluated fairly and accurately.

Several different types of tutorial design exist. Tutorials which progress in a *linear* fashion will present a series of screen displays to all users, regardless of individual differences among the students.

However, incorrect responses to practice questions may serve to call in a reteaching sequence.

Branching tutorials, on the other hand, do not require all users to follow the same path, but will direct students to certain lessons or parts of a lesson according to results of computerized pretests and posttests, or to the student response to embedded questions within the tutorial. Figures 3-4a and 3-4b will illustrate tutorials of both types.

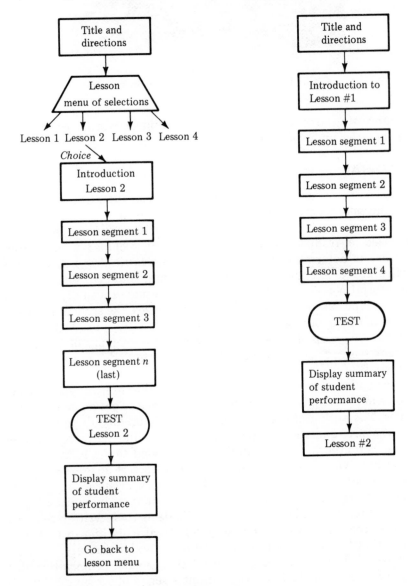

Figure 3-4a
Linear Tutorials

Well-written tutorials are the exception rather than the rule, so tutorials should be chosen very carefully.

- Are concepts developed in a sequential fashion which does not confuse the learner?
- Do you agree with the methodology employed?
- Do graphics and sound complement instruction?
- How valid are the pretests and posttests?
- Do they accurately measure student progress?
- Will the tutorial capture and hold the interest of its intended audience?
- Can the student control the pace of the presentation?

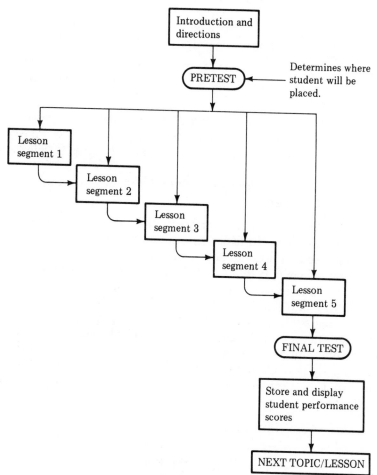

Figure 3-4b
Branching Tutorial Design

Figure 3-5
Microcomputer in Context of Classroom

- Is there some learner control over frame presentation so that previous material can be reviewed?

- And, ideally, does the program provide some way to automatically *record* student scores so that a teacher can easily access computer records and determine class and individual performance?

These and other questions should be answered before suggesting the purchase of specific tutorial software. See Chapter 6, "Choosing Appropriate Software," for more information regarding software selection.

Computer as Tutor: Unemployment Lines for Human Teachers?

Most of us have read articles or books that attempt to predict how children will be educated in the future. More often than not, children are depicted seated around their own bossy computers . . . at home! What about schools? If fine tutorials are developed for every subject area and for every topic, why are teachers needed at all?

A chilling outcome for teachers—and, it would seem, a plausible reason for resisting the placement of computers in schools.

But let's not accept the inevitability of robot teachers prematurely. Instead, contemplate the special abilities humans possess and the experiences only possible with the benefit of human understanding and leadership. Can a computer ever hope to replicate these abilities and activities?

> Dreaming . . .
> > Imagination . . .
> Holistic thinking
> Discovering Algorithms

Manipulation of concrete objects

Acting

Social Skills

Painting . . . Sculpture . . . Handicrafts

Experience with physical devices

Music . . . a chorus of human voices . . .

Gymnastics . . . Sports

Teacher as sociologist and psychologist

Fine distinctions

Field trips . . .

Smell . . . sound . . . touch . . . feel . . . see

Storytelling . . . Appreciation of good literature

Reading expressively . . .

Writing . . .

Sharing with friends

Computer no substitute

for curling up in a corner

reading

a good book . . . .

Advanced computer technology that is affordable to school systems has arrived, and is rapidly changing the nature of how we learn, what we learn, and how rapidly we can learn. Teachers can choose to resist all educational technology, thus ignoring the changes society is experiencing as a whole. Or they can meet the future by learning about innovations, using their creative abilities, and coming to conclusions about the true capabilities and limitations of computers. Only then can teachers play an important role in deciding how computers can *best* help in the educational process.

Two Classroom Vignettes

Mr. White's biology class will be learning about one-celled plants and animals this week. He has planned various laboratory activities which will allow his students to identify different plants and animals through the viewing of prepared slides for microscopes. In addition, students are assigned readings in various text sources, and they will be seeing several excellent movies and filmstrips.

At the end of the week, Mr. White prepares a quiz and administers it to his students. Results suggest certain areas of difficulty. Marie and John have failed the quiz miserably. Some students show little understanding of the process of cell division. Still others are unable to identify parts of a cell. To further complicate the issue, a new student has transferred into Mr. White's class.

Because the majority of the students passed the quiz with approximately 90 percent accuracy or higher, Mr. White feels that reteaching the entire class would be a waste of time for most students. Fortunately, the school's media center possesses several microcomputers and a software library which includes an excellent tutorial on one-celled animals and plants.

Mr. White asks the students who have not demonstrated mastery to go to the media center and sign up for a time to work on the one-celled animal and plant tutorial. As the tutorial begins with a pretest, those students who need more instruction about cell division but who otherwise understand the information and concepts included in the unit will be directed only to the lesson in the program dealing with cell division. John, Marie, and the transfer student will be presented with the lessons within the program to suit their individual needs.

The program keeps a record of student performance, so Mr. White can go to the media center to see who has used the tutorial, and what their performance was. Test No. 1 for the biology course will take place in a week, so at that time Mr. White will be able to determine if the tutorial has helped his students to master the appropriate objectives.

Percy School District is located in a rural location, over 200 miles away from a large city. The high school has an enrollment of about 500 students. Five students are very interested in learning more about economics. Though Ms. Jeffry is a capable social studies teacher, she feels that there is not enough time in her busy schedule to prepare for and teach an economics course for only five students.

But Ms. Jeffry has recently begun to explore microcomputer software and has located a tutorial for economics which is coordinated with other media, such as filmstrips and print materials. In addition, the microcomputer courseware is fully documented; student workbooks and a useful teacher's manual are provided.

Fortunately, Ms. Jeffry is able to locate and speak to Mr. Toliver, a teacher from another district who had used the economics courseware for a similar small group of students during the last year. Mr. Toliver was impressed with the individualized learning that took place, and offered Ms. Jeffry some advice on its use with students.

Armed with evidence of the courseware's successful performance, Ms. Jeffry is able to convince the principal to purchase the package, and to offer the economics course for use during the next quarter. It is planned that students work in pairs through the economics tutorials and meet one class period a week to discuss their findings and thoughts in a small group situation. Ms. Jeffry will be the first discussion leader, but by the second week, the five students will begin to take turns leading the sessions and planning discussion of relevant topics.

SIMULATION

Many of you have witnessed the space flights of the NASA program and have seen computer simulations of certain events which could not be shown through photography. Similarly, educational simulations allow students to experience situations which would be difficult or impossible to duplicate in a classroom setting.

Simulations allow students to make, and be affected by, their own decisions. Guided according to the data provided by the simulations, the student selects certain options or risks, and then witnesses the results of the decision.

"Lemonade Stand" is a famous simulation geared toward elementary school students. Each child who participates in this simulation must make certain business decisions every day.

1.   What price per glass of lemonade?

2.   How many advertising signs should be made?

3.   How many glasses of lemonade should be made?

Each child begins with a small amount of money and supplies (assets). If too much is charged for the lemonade, and too much lemonade is made in the morning, the lemonade stand owner will not sell enough lemonade that day to make a profit.

Also, certain factors are beyond control. The computer decides (by a math equation and a randomly selected number) whether the day will be clear, cloudy, or rainy. The weather, therefore, is a chance factor influencing the sale of lemonade. For instance, if a businesschild makes 100 glasses of lemonade and only one advertising sign, and charges $0.60 per glass, then a cloudy day may well mean a disastrous day for business and resulting loss to the bank account.

Of course, the object to this activity would be to gather the most profit possible over a certain number of business days.

Perhaps the most beneficial aspect of such a simulation is *involvement*. Though the lemonade stand is imaginary, the students do experience some of the feelings and problems associated with the owning of a business. They see the reasons for developing good business strategies and therefore begin to think in a more organized fashion. Business competition with other students lends an extra breath of reality to the simulation.

Social studies, science, business, and vocational type simulations can also be valuable learning devices, their use wisely integrated into the curriculum at appropriate times. Simulations do not serve as stand-alone units, but are most effective when used to illustrate and use skills, ideas, and experiences first explored by other means, such as lectures, questioning, textual material, discussion, and so on.

Simulations can also be used to train students in the operation of tools and different type of equipment. Such training would allow students to practice skills and procedures needed to safely and accurately operate the equipment—without danger to themselves or to the equipment.

In science labs, students can pour and mix dangerous chemicals via simulation. Mistakes do not blow up the classroom—or the computer! However, students can begin to make the fine discriminations needed for proper handling of chemicals. It is also possible to simulate experiments which have been too expensive, complicated, or time-consuming to replicate in school laboratories. Simulations provide a more involved experience than is possible through a reading assignment or lecture.

Social studies simulations can help students reenact historical events, learn about other societies, or experience governmental procedures, such as elections and lawmaking. When running simulation type software, students must first understand certain information and concepts in order to analyze situations and to make wise decisions; therefore, learning becomes more relevant and useful to them.

Though only a few areas of study have been mentioned, simulations can be created for any subject area where a simulated experience for a certain real life situation would contribute to increased learning.

A Classroom Vignette

Ms. Carson's junior high American history class has been studying early explorers and their voyages to the New World. When asked what

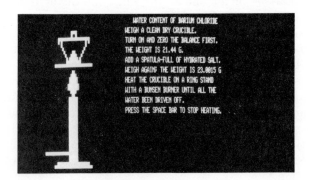

Figure 3-6a
A Chemistry Simulation Created by James Birk,
Arizona State University

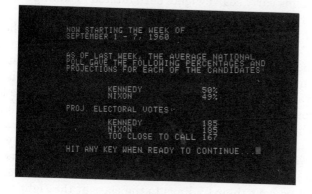

Figure 3-6b
President Elect Screen Displays
by Strategic Simulations

Figure 3-6c
Hot Dog Stand, an Economics Simulation
by Sunburst Communications

problems sea voyagers may have experienced, students mentioned the following:

1. Ran out of water or food
2. Ended up in China
3. Lost in a storm
4. Shipwrecked on a desert island, Tahiti, and so forth
5. Died from disease
6. Lost their way

The simulation "Geography Search"* will help to illustrate some of the problems early sea voyagers encountered in sailing west, hoping to locate "The City of Gold."

A teacher's manual and student workbooks accompany the simulation. Ms. Carson chooses to tell the story presented on the first few pages in the student workbook. Her expressive voice and gestures capture the interest of students. At appropriate moments, Ms. Carson refers to transparencies of ancient maps in order to illustrate locations and concepts. Some vocabulary words are new to students, but subsequent discussion and review questions ensure understanding.

At this point, Ms. Carson asks the students to suggest ways that ancient mariners may have used to ascertain their positions when at sea and on land. Some students volunteer to research topics more thoroughly and present their findings to the class at the right times.

Throughout the next few days, the concepts presented in the remainder of the workbook's chapters, along with excellent student reports, help the class understand the manner by which navigators were able to make sensible decisions. Diagrams, maps, games, and other learning materials and activities are utilized when appropriate. The teacher's guide suggests interesting projects and research topics.

Now the class is ready to set forth on an adventurous voyage from the imaginary land of Vesuvia, an island located at approximately the same position on the earth's surface as Spain. Thirty students are split into six crews, with one in each crew given the role of captain.

The queen of Vesuvia has commissioned these six ships to sail to the western continent and find its western side in order to locate a rumored "City of Gold," and then to bring back as much gold as possible to Vesuvia. There is a catch: the first ship will be rewarded more money per pound of gold than subsequently arriving ships.

First, the captains and their crews must decide whether to set sail, follow the coastline, or go ashore. According to the wind direction, a

---

*Thomas F. F. Snyder, computer simulation called "Geography Search," Computer Learning Connection (Webster Division, McGraw-Hill Book Company, 1982).

course must be chosen, and in addition, it must be decided how much of the day should be used for traveling.

Once the crews have established their plans, they begin to take turns at the microcomputer, inputting the necessary decision data. Then, according to these data, the ship will sail a certain distance, or if the "going ashore" option was chosen the crew will collect a computer-decided amount of supplies.

Finally, a display of information useful for navigational purposes will appear on the screen—but only for 15 seconds or so. Too much information must be recorded, so it is essential that each of the crew members be given specific jobs to do during those 15 seconds. One will record the data pertaining to longitude, another records latitude data, another the wind direction, and so on. Then the crew's turn is over, and the next crew goes to the computer.

Based upon clues such as the north star position, distance west from Vesuvia, the temperature, the terrain, and the ocean depth, the crew determines their navigational position, assesses their food and water supply, and chooses the best course to follow for the next day's sailing. Chance factors like the presence of pirates, however, may cause the captain to order that the ship sail off course until danger is past.

The simulation continues in a similar manner, until all the ships have returned to Vesuvia, or been lost at sea. And, by that time, the students have experienced difficulties, read navigational signs and clues, and have learned more about sailing in the time of the explorers than would have been possible in a more passive mode of learning.

The "Geography Search" has been so popular with the students that Ms. Carson plans to locate and use simulations for other topics in all her classes. An American presidential election simulation, she judges, will intimately acquaint her students with the procedures, strategies, and customs followed in planning campaigns.

COMPUTER-MANAGED INSTRUCTION

In its purest form, computer-managed instruction (CMI) does not offer instruction of any type, but rather *manages* instruction in a classroom or school through computer-assisted testing and record keeping which indicates students' mastery or nonmastery of specific objectives. Closely related to criterion-referenced testing, CMI programs can be powerful tools for a sensible individualized instruction plan. The computer does the tedious record-keeping work and provides reports that can guide the teacher in choosing the best student grouping arrangements for instruction leading to mastery of specific objectives.

CMI systems tend to be quite expensive—around the range of $500 to $3,000. However, many have the capability to manage instruction for a school's entire student population. Often, only one computer is required, though two disk drives and a mechanical device called an *optical card reader* may be essential peripheral equipment. If the CMI program requires a card reader to be connected to the microcomputer, students may take pretests or post-tests on computer cards. When the cards are inserted into the card reader, the test results are automatically stored for each student and mastery level for each objective tested is determined by the CMI program.

If a card reader is *not* the method of input chosen for student testing then the students usually take paper and pencil tests and enter their responses via the CMI program and the computer keyboard. This option, of course, consumes more computer time and may limit the use of the CMI package to a smaller number of students than would be possible with a card reader system.

Each CMI package has its own design and capabilities. Some systems will provide reports for parents listing the objectives mastered by their child over a certain period of time. *Instructional management systems* allow educators to enter local or state objectives and the tests used to determine the accomplishment of those objectives. Thus, it is possible to customize a CMI package for the unique needs of your own district, and for any subject area's learning objectives. Progress reports for students, groups of students, or classes of students can be obtained and utilized in order to better plan for the instructional needs of students.

To obtain full benefit from a CMI system, a *printer* is highly recommended because teachers can be provided with daily or weekly reports on student progress much more easily.

Some CMI systems come equipped with a set of ready-made objectives. The subject area objectives most commonly provided within these systems are elementary reading and math. Often these sets of objectives are taken from those which were used successfully in certain school districts over a number of years, and which have been revised until they have satisfactorily met the requirements of a school district. The CMI software automates the record-keeping process and is the computerized version of a criterion-referenced system for instructional management. CMI manufacturers will sometimes agree to customize the established objective list or the testing according to the needs of the school considering the purchase of CMI software.

Another type of management system not only includes objectives and mastery testing, but also provides drill and practice and/or tutorials related to each objective. In addition, teachers can easily ask the computer to generate personalized worksheets or tests for specific students or groups of students according to demonstrated needs. Other useful inclusions or options to a system may be sets of student workbooks, teacher's guides, and individualized learning prescriptions. Such prescriptions will not only list objectives yet to be mastered, but also may list the page numbers, locations, and titles of specific textual material, worksheets, workbooks, audiovisual aides, and other learning materials that would contribute to the mastery of those objectives. Again, some CMI manufacturers will customize these lists of learning materials according to the resources available in a particular school.

At least one math CMI system is directly linked and coordinated with a specific textbook series. This marriage of text and computer management capability may begin to occur for other major textbooks in the future.

We hope this description has given you an overview of CMI and its potential to make the organization of personalized instruction a less time-consuming and tedious task for educators. Because CMI systems tend to be the most expensive programs schools will ever purchase, great care should be taken in their selection. This means that packages should be reviewed and judged according to simplicity of operation ("user friendliness"), useful features included, educational applicability, and the instructional effectiveness of the objective hierarchy design. School districts that have used the system should be contacted because no management system can be judged fairly until it has been used in an actual school setting for a reasonably long period of time. Also, because most school districts are involved in Individualized Educational Progress (IEP) report generation, the management system's accommodation to the simplified writing of IEP's is an important time-saver for teachers and will help them to plan lessons according to recent data.

If drill and practice exercises or tutorials are provided, they should be judged with a critical eye. Algorithms and procedures introduced in the tutorials should mesh with teacher methods and opinions, and demonstrate acceptable techniques. They should also capture and hold the interest of student users.

As you may have noticed, there is a fine line between which programs are labeled "drill and practice," "tutorial," or "CMI," as they all may be written around a set group of objectives. A CMI package which includes tutorials and drill problems as well as pretesting and posttesting for objectives could very well be described as tutorial courseware with appropriate drill options and a complete student management system. Generally, however, a computer-managed instruction program may be larger and more expensive, contain a more extensive objective list, have greater reporting capability, and may be tied to textual or kit type materials that may be present in the classroom.

Dangers of CMI

Instructional management kits have been offered for a number of years, before the microcomputer's introduction to schools. Certainly, computers can make the enormous task of record keeping and finding appropiate materials for instruction easier and better organized. However, the dangers inherent in any totally individualized program are also present in CMI. The system should never be used as a complete instructional plan for all students. Discussions, experiments, discovery, peer learning, manipulation of concrete objects, art, music, and many other experiences and learning techniques have an important place in lessons. A CMI package does not absolve the instructor from planning lessons, but can help to personalize instruction, exposing students to objectives which will neither frustrate nor bore them. It will also eliminate some record-keeping tedium from teachers' lives.

Another danger lies in the *choice* of objectives upon which the program has been based. If the objectives do not closely match those of your district, or those you consider to be most important, the ability to customize the CMI package will be very important. Pretests and post-tests, of course, must test the objectives they are supposed to test, and they must be as valid and reliable as any paper and pencil test. Many educators would question the use of multiple choice or the short-answer format for the determination of mastery for some topics. As with any objective test, it is difficult to ask questions truly evaluating student progress for the learner goals of application and analysis.

More CMI packages exist for mathematics than for any other subject area because mathematics concepts tend to be better suited to objective-based learning than many concepts in other subject areas. In particular, CMI packages in the area of language arts must be used with extreme care. As many a writing teacher has noticed, teaching of grammatical subskills does *not* necessarily contribute to increased student writing skill. The computerized grammar lesson may be mastered by the student—but will those skills be remembered the next time a composition is written? Will the student see the need for written communication that demonstrates grammatical and mechanical correctness? Does the CMI allow the student the flexibility needed to interact with certain lessons at the optimum time for him or her personally?

Software written to increase reading and spelling skills is typically of a limited nature because an important part of learning in these areas requires *oral expression*. Unless *speech synthesis* hardware and accompanying spelling software is used to pronounce words, the testing of spelling words, for example, can be done only by flashing words on the screen, scrambling the words, or by using contextual clues so that the student knows which word is to be spelled.

Unless carefully integrated with other learning experiences, CMI software will not lead to optimum student growth. However, computerized CMI packages represent a practical use of technology, providing educators with a great deal of information and report-generating capability that can be used to better meet the needs of students. Again, it is suggested that extremely careful evaluation be made, and that user school districts should be contacted for advice based upon their experiences.

A Classroom Vignette

Kennedy High School offers special classes for those students who are demonstrating learning problems, and who have scored below certain levels on the yearly achievement tests in mathematics and reading. In the past, organization of instruction has been rather difficult for the resource room teachers. Class size has been increased during the past few years, and there is a wide range of ability, achievement, and learning difficulties among the students.

At one time, Title I funds made possible the purchase of a vast array of kits, workbooks, texts, learning materials, and trade books. However, locating useful materials for certain students and for certain objectives has been a time-consuming job, repeated frequently, and with varying rates of success. Often, teachers were not satisfied with the amount of time spent with individual students, and with the rather primitive way of deciding who should be grouped for the instruction of a specific objective. Criterion-referenced tests have been available, but locating appropriate tests at the right time, and correcting, evaluating, and recording the scores was a never-ending and tedious job. Too often, teachers were not able to perform this task consistently enough to be assured that planning would be based on the most recent data.

The generation of IEP reports was another burden upon the teachers, consuming time that could have been spent in more creative educational pursuits.

In February, several resource room teachers attended a local microcomputer conference and saw a demonstration of some particularly good CMI packages. Impressed by their discovery, the teachers approached Mr. Wilson, the high school principal, with their plan. They suggested that the package could also be used for general math and special education students, as well as for resource room teachers. At this point, they compiled a list of needs, and a search was made to find the best CMI package available for the unique needs of Kennedy High School.

Several CMI packages seemed to fit the list of requirements. The manufacturers were contacted and asked to give complete demonstrations to a committee consisting of involved teachers, the principal, and curriculum supervisors. In addition, the vendors were asked to supply the names, addresses, and telephone numbers of contact persons in districts who had used the CMI packages in a school environment, and had witnessed its operation, advantages, and disadvantages.

The selection process lasted for a month. This particular high school chose CMI systems for math and for reading which already included objectives and the pretests and posttests for those objectives. IEP information and individualized student worksheets can be generated easily and quickly. The math CMI system also included tutorial segments and practice stored on separate diskettes that could be accessed by students, when desired, using resource room microcomputers.

The company agreed to tailor the CMI packages so that certain objectives were eliminated, and a few objectives were moved to other positions in the learning hierarchy. More consumer math and reading comprehension objectives were to be added at some later date.

Eventually, the committee decided that for the first year, the resource room teachers would pilot the system, and that other classes could be added later, depending upon the performance of the CMI over the school year. A microcomputer, black and white monitor, disk drive, and card reader were purchased and placed in an easily accessed location. An aide was made responsible for the distribution and collection of tests, and for overseeing the operation of the microcomputer.

The task of customizing the CMI package to fit the needs of the school was a time-consuming process. Finally, however, the problems were resolved. An appropriate objective list was adopted, and classroom learning materials were matched to objectives. Additional tests were written when necessary.

During the pilot year, drill and tutorial modes allowed a unique kind of instruction to take place, one that motivated students who previously showed little interest in learning. In addition, the problem of an unwieldy collection of materials was solved. If a student's test indicated nonmastery of certain objectives, a prescription specifically referring to textbook or workbook pages, computer software, or to other learning materials present in the classroom was generated quickly. And it took only moments for teachers to interpret a computer report which suggested grouping for instruction according to those objectives not yet mastered and the achievement levels of students. Teachers found more time for individual conferences with students, and these conferences were judged to be even more valuable because specific objectives spotlighted by the CMI system were discussed and further understanding developed. Plus—and to the relief of many—fewer hours were spent with clerical tasks, and this additional time could be filled with planning useful learning activities for students.

PROBLEM SOLVING

Software of the problem-solving type requires student strategy and input. As the name suggests, a problem situation is presented by the software and the user must attempt to solve the problem. Concepts are not taught; instead, the student applies what is already known, learns from mistakes, and refines skill as s/he gains mastery of certain problem-solving techniques. In a way, a *simulation* could be described as a high-level problem-solving program because the user must assess situations and form strategies for successful completion of the simulation. Some problem-solving software could be described as "educational games."

"Bagels," a program available in slightly different formats and through several software houses, is a simple example of a problem-solving program. In this case, the problem to be solved strengthens logical thinking and understanding of place value. Students can choose the difficulty level by indicating whether they wish to guess a two-, three-, or four-digit number. Then the computer randomly selects the number. The student tries to guess the number in the least amount of tries possible.

After each guess, the computer will give certain clues as to whether any digits in their guess are in the secret number. If none of the digits are correct the computer will respond with the word BAGEL. If one digit is guessed correctly, but it is in the wrong place, the computer prints PICO. If one digit was guessed correctly *and* happens to be in the correct place, then the computer will respond with FERMI.

Let us assume that the computer has secretly chosen the number 287. You choose the number 345.

	Your Guess	Clue
1)	345	BAGELS (Nothing correct!)
2)	789	PICO PICO (2 digits are correct, but are in the wrong place)
3)	897	PICO FERMI
4)	197	FERMI
5)	687	FERMI FERMI
6)	287	YOU'RE RIGHT!

The clues must be interpreted and used to select the best guess possible during the subsequent turn. In the example above, a certain amount of logical thinking is apparent. The first guess's clue was BAGELS, meaning that *no* digits were correct. Therefore the digits 3, 4, and 5 were not guessed again. In guess (4) the clue logically indicates that it is the 7 that is totally correct, and that neither the digits 1 nor 9 are present in the computer-chosen number.

Another problem-solving program is called "Hurkle," also available through several software houses. "Hurkle" aids students in learning to use grids and number lines of various types. A furry little creature called a Hurkle hides behind the grid or number line. In the case of grids, the student indicates where the Hurkle is believed to be hidden by typing in the coordinate points of the guess. Unless the guess is exactly right, the computer will respond by giving directional clues, that is, North, South, East, West. The game continues until the Hurkle has been "uncovered."

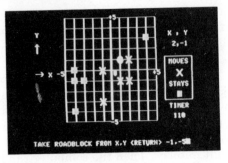

Figure 3-7
Bumble Plot by the Learning Company

Logical thinking aids successful playing of Hurkle, and students practice the use of coordinates to describe locations on the grid.

Other problem-solving programs allow the user to specify certain variable values, and then to witness the results of those variable assignments. For instance, *Log to Any Base* allows the student to specify a base 10 number and another base. Then the computer calculates the *log* of the number to the specified base. In this way, students may experiment with variable changes and relationships. Problem-solving software of this type can be found for science and mathematics classes, and can be considered as a *tool* for problem solving rather than a piece of CAI.

Although the most common software in the problem-solving category is math-oriented, other subject areas are represented as well. Some programs allow students to create new words by adding prefixes or suffixes to root words. Sentence diagramming problems can be presented. Cryptograms can be decoded, puzzles and riddles solved. Still other programs deal with transformational grammar exercises, where the student begins with a "kernel" sentence (noun and verb only) and expands the kernel in varying ways to create a list of sentences derived from the original kernel sentence.

One problem-solving program may be totally different in design and operation from another one; it is difficult to imagine a general definition that could cover all aspects of problem-solving software. A useful framework for furthering one's understanding of what problem-solving software really is may be to think in terms of *learner control*. In the programs Hurkle and BAGELS, there is little learner control given to the user beyond the ability to make logical guesses, one at a time. In programs allowing *full* learner control, the user decides exactly what he or she will do next, and can move freely from one activity to another. In the case of Gertrude's Secrets (spotlighted in the following vignette) learner control is so complete that a child can leave a puzzle without completely solving it, go work in another of Gertrude's "rooms," and come back later to solve the unfinished puzzle. Rocky's Boots, another program available from the Learning Company, illustrates the concept of complete learner control in problem-solving software appropriate for older students.

Other problem-solving software provides a moderate amount of learner control, or varied amounts of control for the different options offered by the program's "menu."

At best, problem-solving programs promote the development of systematic thinking patterns, and can also help students practice associated skills in a mode which is not traditional drill and practice and which may appear to be a game more than anything else. Good problem-solving software will transcend the boundaries of simple tutorial or practice software; it can be evaluated in terms of its uniqueness and its ability to fascinate students even as they are learning. For this reason, educators should be certain to locate and implement exemplary programs of this type, even though they may not readily match the objectives listed in a particular curriculum.

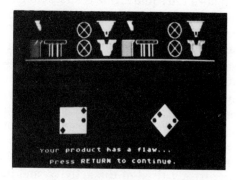

Figure 3-8a
The Factory by Sunburst Communications

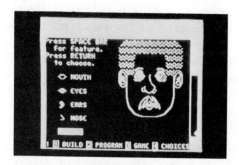

Figure 3-8b
Facemaker by Spinnaker Software

A Classroom Vignette

Mr. Green's second grade classroom has been working with attribute pieces of many different varieties. One set of manipulative attribute pieces contains three different shapes, and three different colors:

Attributes of Shape and Color
Shapes: Circles, squares, triangles,
Colors: Red, blue, yellow

As a whole class activity, children have been forming one-difference attribute "trains." Let's take a peek at what Diane is doing right now. She has placed a red circle on her desk. She knows that the next step will be to find an attribute piece that differs from the red circle *in only one way*. First she chooses a blue square and places it next to the red circle; but with a bit of thinking she decides that the blue square differs in two ways, not just one. So the piece goes back to the pile.

Then Diane spots a red square. She realizes that this piece matches the red circle in color, but that it does have a different shape. A smile lights up her face, because she knows that the next "car" of the train will be the red square: there is only *one* attribute different from the red circle.

Diane continues in a similar manner, making some mistakes, but is generally able to perform well. Mr. Green notes that Diane is making good progress, and will introduce a larger set of attribute pieces the next day to her and to some other children. These pieces will be described by *size* as well as by color and shape.

Terri and Judy have been having some difficulties with the assignment. They have already tired of the activity, and have shown little understanding. Several other students in the room have progressed to the point that they have mastered all the different assignments given to them.

Mr. Green decides that certain children in the classroom can particularly benefit by "Gertrude's Secrets," a program for the Apple IIe® microcomputer.* So he plans to have Terri and Judy run the program the next day. One of the other children, John, has already mastered the operation of the program and is quite a sociable, helpful little boy. Mr. Green will ask John to introduce Terri and Judy to "Gertrude's Secrets."

---

*Apple IIe® is a registered trademark of Apple Computer, Inc. "Gertrude's Secrets" is available from the Learning Company, 4370 Alpine Road, Portola Valley, California 94025. A color monitor or television is necessary for full use.

The next day, John and Judy visit the computer corner in the classroom, where the program is "booted up," ready to go. A small rectangle ☐ signifies where Judy is located on the screen. John helps Judy to practice picking up objects on the screen, and then putting them down again. This feat is accomplished by using four keys to move

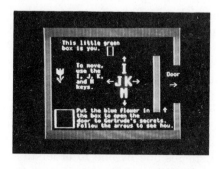

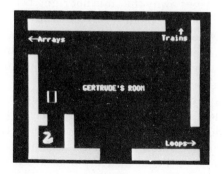

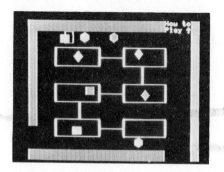

Figure 3-9
Gertrude's Secrets Screen Displays

her rectangle up, down, left, or right until the object is reached. Then the space bar is pressed, picking up the object. Now that Judy has the object in her possession, she can carry it around with her.

Mastery of this skill will now allow Judy to explore any of the rooms in Gertrude's domain. She moves her rectangle into the next rooms, following the pointing arrows.

However, there is now a problem. Gertrude, who is a goose, sits in a corner of the room that is rather hard to reach. Judy must use the movement keys in a manner allowing her to reach Gertrude and pick her up. But with a bit of additional practice, Judy does move her little rectangle to Gertrude, and picks Gertrude up by pressing the space bar. Now that Judy has Gertrude, she can carry her to another room, where a special game can be played. As soon as the next room is reached, Judy needs to let Gertrude fly away. This is accomplished by pressing the space bar. Gertrude goes away, but comes back with a surprise: a collection of shapes, in several different colors. Now Judy must pick up the shapes one by one in order to solve the "One-Difference Train" puzzle. When Judy places an incorrect piece in the train, she realizes right away that it is not right, because the piece falls down to the bottom of the screen. With John's advice, Judy continues to solve the puzzle. After a few tries, she begins to understand how a one-difference train must be made, and competently finishes the puzzle. She looks on proudly as the music plays, and Gertrude comes back in the room with a special treasure.

There are many other rooms to be visited, but now it is Terri's turn to visit Gertrude. This time, Judy helps Terri to get around in Gertrude's kingdom and to play the one-difference train puzzle.

Mr. Green checks in now and then and is pleased with Terri and Judy's progress and enthusiasm. He plans to use the program with most of the children in the room, using peer teaching to introduce them to traveling and solving puzzles in Gertrude's kingdom.

MICROCOMPUTERS FOR SPECIAL NEEDS

The use of microcomputers for instructional purposes applies to all students, regardless of any handicaps or learning difficulties they may have. In fact, CAI is eminently suitable for all situations where repetition and practice can lead to skill and understanding. The computer is an infinitely patient teacher, providing experiences and reinforcement as long as they are needed, in an individualized fashion. Whether students are placed in special education classes or mainstreamed into regular classrooms, this capability means that needs can be met more fully, and in a way that does not embarrass or frustrate.

For those who have good coordination, almost any piece of software on their educational level may be beneficial. However, it is sometimes the case that CAI requiring input of longer answers or manipulation of movement keys will be beyond the capabilities of some students. Consequently, when selecting software for these students the amount and type of input required should be considered. Answers should ideally consist of one or two keystrokes, and screen displays and instructions should be particularly clear.

Certain hardware additions can make input of answers easier. *Light pen* input will allow users to choose answers by touching the display screen with the pen at appropriate places. Light pens can not be used unless the software has been designed in such a way that it can accept that kind of input. Joystick or paddle input options can also contribute to ease of student response. Again, the software must include those response options.

Even the foregoing input possibilities may be beyond the physical capacity of some students. Consequently, special communication boards have been designed for connection to microcomputers. The student uses the alphabet and other characters on the much larger board instead of the computer's own keyboard (Figure 3-10). Thus input of

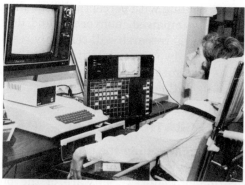

Figure 3-10
Students Using Different Communication Boards
(Courtesy of Frederick Jipson and
the Gompers Rehabilitation Center)

answers does not require fine motor coordination. In addition, some communication boards possess different *levels* for each character on the keyboard. This means that whole words or sentences can be input into a program by the student with one or two keystrokes. Communication boards vary in expense and capability. Electronics engineers and educational specialists continue to work on improving these boards and reducing the expense involved. At least one board has been created for wheelchair use, along with a miniature computer and video display unit.

For those who are not able to indicate answers and messages manually, other methods of input can be invented. A blink of the eye, touch of a nearby button, a head movement, and so on can enable the user to indicate responses. Generally, these modifications should be tailored to the needs of individuals, and much work is going on in this area of research and hardware design. Those who could neither respond verbally or with a keyboard will now be able to communicate with others in a way not possible just a few years ago. A whole new world will open to them.

Finally, software dealing with perceptual difficulties, and with the needs of blind, hearing-impaired, nonverbal, and deaf students has also been created. Ongoing research will certainly result in much specialized software and hardware availability.

Appendix I lists organizations and companies dealing with software and hardware inventions for special needs.

CURRICULAR INTEGRATION OF CAI

As you have seen through reading the classroom vignettes presented in this chapter, the different types of CAI lend themselves to different classroom integration procedures. Software of the purely drill and practice variety should not be used until some conceptual development has taken place. Tutorial software is most effective when students show varying levels of conceptual understanding, and it can provide for individual tutoring needs that may be difficult to consistently satisfy through traditional instructional arrangements. Computer-managed instruction, in its purest form, will test students on certain behavioral objectives and offer suggestions for instructional materials and grouping arrangements. Simulations and problem-solving programs typically require that students have gained certain skills and knowledge before using the program. Use of these two kinds of software will allow students to practice skills, develop strategies, and think logically; their decisions will actually determine the outcome of events.

The success of integration also depends upon the *quality* of the software selected and how it appeals to the intended user. (See Chapter

6, "Choosing Appropriate Software.") Software should not be used just because it is there. Although it is tempting to stock a room solely with inexpensive odds and ends, the result may be that a teacher does not have a ready means to integrate that software into the curriculum. One disk may include unrelated topics from several subject areas and directed toward widely varying grade levels. How many educators have the time and expertise to locate and sort through everything and come up with an effective combination that is easy for students to access and use? Would buying, or in some cases, creating carefully designed software actually amount to that much more expenditure in terms of time and money?

Every effort should be made to select *combinations* of software or courseware packages to suit the needs of the students in the classroom. To illustrate, a language arts teacher may begin by envisioning a certain combination of software packages:

1. Spelling drill and practice, several methods of presentation, capability to add new word lists.

2. Transformational grammar exercises.

3. Tutorials and practice with punctuation and capitalization. Teacher uses computer management system to designate specific lessons for individual students.

4. Tutorials and practice with Greek and Latin word parts. Teacher uses program to test students and assign the computerized lessons.

5. Vocabulary development, preferably a program possessing prepared vocabulary lists plus the capability for the teacher to enter new vocabulary lists.

6. Word processing (described in Chapter 4).

Once a determination of immediate needs has been made, then a search for software which fulfills those needs can be made. (See Chapter 6.) This job may prove to be difficult and sometimes software that exactly matches requirements may not be in evidence. Plans may need modification before purchase decisions can be made. But who knows? One of the software packages found may have capabilities that exceed the original expectations.

The skillful teacher will gradually learn how to interweave these packages into the language arts program. Computer-aided instruction should represent only one part of the total learning experience, and its effectiveness will be determined by whether well-designed software has been utilized at the optimum times for individual students. Later on, other software fitting into the instructional picture can be added to the collection, according to demonstrated needs.

Although the example illustrated the area of language arts, possible combinations of software for any subject area can be determined by a teacher familiar with software types and capabilities. Imagination can lead to successful implementation.

SUMMARY

Computer-assisted instruction is a term used to describe the use of computers for instructional tasks. Disks, cassette tapes, or cartridges containing CAI programs require only operational knowledge of microcomputers. Some distinct types of CAI are drill and practice, tutorial, simulation, computer-managed instruction, and problem solving. Any one piece of software can combine two or more of these approaches.

Drill and practice software allows learners to come in contact with facts, relationships, problems, or vocabulary until they are learned or until skill has been developed. Programs have been written for a great number of topics, from preschool to technical subjects. Tutorials, on the other hand, attempt to aid concept development by careful presentation of ideas, and, through feedback, help to students concerning their responses. Pretesting and posttesting may determine the placement of a student in a particular lesson belonging to a tutorial courseware package. Tutorials are designed in both linear and branching fashion. Though they can supplement the curriculum, computer tutorials represent only one mode for concept development, and they will never match the intuition of a human teacher.

Computer simulations allow students to experience real life events in the safety of their own classrooms. Decisions must be made which will affect the outcome of the simulation, so the student tends to become an involved and interested learner. Computer-managed instruction, in its purest form, offers no tutorials or drill and practice exercises, but through computerized testing on objectives determines the educational needs of students. Card readers are sometimes used to minimize data entry tasks. Results are stored and printed out on paper so that teachers can determine optimum grouping arrangements for instruction. Often the objectives are linked to books and other materials; this helps teachers locate appropriate learning materials for their students at the right time. However, CMI should not be the total learning package for students, but should be integrated with other useful learning activities.

Problem-solving software requires logical thinking on the part of students and assumes that some previous concept development has taken place first. The continuing development of logical thinking is an important goal for problem-solving software. It is helpful to note that some educators would call these "educational games."

Computer-assisted instruction comes in many styles and forms. It is important to acquire an ability to identify programs by their proper labels so that software purchase decisions can be made wisely and according to expressed needs.

Specially designed microcomputers are useful for students with special needs. Special hardware can allow those with hearing or speech difficulties to learn and be better able to communicate with others.

Finally, there are some important considerations when planning for the integration of software so that optimal learning potential is reached. These include determination of software type, appropriate procedure for integration, determination of quality software, and envisioning the *combinations* of software most effective for significant impact on the curriculum.

SUGGESTED READINGS

Archer, Doug. "Matching Functions of the Apple Computer to the Instructional Needs of the Learning Disabled Student." *Twentieth Annual Association for Educational Data Systems (AEDS) Convention Proceedings,* 1982, 1–4.

Bork, Alfred, and Jack A. Chambers. "Computer Assisted Learning in the U.S. Secondary/Elementary Schools." *The Computing Teacher* 8, no. 1 (September 1981): 50–51.

Dence, Marie. "Toward Defining the Role of CAI: A Review." *Educational Technology* 20, no. 11 (November 1980): 50–54.

Doerr, Christine. *Microcomputers and the Three R's: A Guide for Teachers.* Rochelle Park, N.J.: Hayden, 1979.

Edwards, Judith, et al. "Is CAI Effective?" *Association for Educational Data Systems Journal* (Summer 1974): 122–128.

Eisenkraft, Arthur. "Microcomputers in a Physics Curriculum." *Journal of Computers in Mathematics and Science Teaching* 1, no. 2 (Winter 1981): 9–11.

Esbensen, Thorwald. "Elevated Education Made Easy: Computers in Schools." *Personal Computing* 5, no. 10 (October 1981): 93–97.

Forman, Denyse. "Search of the Literature" (originally from *Instructional Use of Microcomputers: A Report on B.C.'s Pilot Project). The Computing Teacher* 9, no. 5 (January 1982): 37–51.

Holman, Elli. "Speech Peripherals Make Computers More Human." *Personal Computing* 5, no. 6 (June 1981): 19–20+.

Marks, Gary H. "Computer Simulations in Science Teaching: An Introduction." *Journal of Computers in Mathematics and Science Teaching* 1, no. 4 (Summer 1982): 18–20.

McConnell, Barry. "The Handicapple: A Low-Cost Braille Printer." *Creative Computing* 8, no. 10 (October 1982): 186–188.

McIsaac, Donald N., and Frank B. Baker. "Computer-Managed Instruction System on a Microcomputer." *Educational Technology* 21, no. 10 (October 1981): 55–59.

Noddings, Nel. "Word Problems Made Painless." *Creative Computing* 6, no. 9 (September 1980): 108–113.

Nomeland, Ronald. "Some Considerations in Selecting a Microcomputer for School." *American Annals of the Deaf* 124 (September 1979): 585–593.

Price, Robert V. "Selecting Free and Inexpensive Computer Software." *Educational Computer* 2, no. 3 (May–June 1982), 24–26.

Ragan, Andrew L. "The Miracle Worker: How Computers Help Handicapped Students." *Electronic Learning* 1, no. 3 (January–February 1982): 56–58, 83.

Spencer, Mima, and Linda Baskin. "Classroom Computers: Do They Make a Difference?" *Classroom Computer News* 2, no. 2 (November–December 1981): 12–15.

Watkins, Marley W., and Cynthia Webb. "Computer Assisted Instruction with Learning Disabled Students". *Educational Computer* 1, no. 3 (September–October 1981): 24–26+.

4

The Computer as a Tool
for Teachers and Students

INTRODUCTION

As the microcomputer gradually becomes a standard fixture in schools, businesses, and the home, we will begin to see increased public use of software to perform tasks previously accomplished through much less automated methods. In other words, computers can help us define and accomplish tasks for our own purposes as well as those that arise in our own personal work spheres. CAI is one effective way to use the computer as a tool for education, but it represents only a portion of all the possible uses for computers in society.

When today's children graduate from high school, we can safely predict that they will face a job market or collegiate situation quite different from that which faced their own parents after graduation. Many jobs will probably involve some use of computers. Creative application of computer power can, therefore, contribute to future job satisfaction and performance. Those high school seniors contemplating college will be faced with a radically changing environment for learning where computers are used to perform the most tedious and repetitious tasks, and where concentration on more major issues will contribute to higher levels of subject matter understanding. Since details can be handled by a computer, they will no longer tend to distract the learner from seeing a view of the whole.

It is no fluke that several major universities and colleges have begun to require a certain amount of computer knowledge as a prerequisite for freshman admission or for admission to certain graduate programs. This trend may grow rapidly as more college educators familiarize themselves with computer potential.

Seymour Papert, a professor at the Massachusetts Institute of Technology and the creator of a powerful computer language called Logo, has spoken of the role computers will play in the society of the future. In *Mindstorms* (1980), he says that computers can provide specialized mathematical or verbal environments for learning; we can use them in much the same way that we have learned to use pencils, in order to compute, write, and create.

The challenge inherent in any such goal must be to introduce computers into the educational setting, and then to familiarize students and educators with computer capabilities and operation until they are thoroughly confident and begin to *use the computer* as a *logi-*

of their own intelligence. This implies the appropriate
plications which will both improve their performance and
or more relevant and creatively demanding educational
students trained in such a manner leave schools and enter
the marketplace, their computer pencils will tend to become an integral part of their working environment. Those people aware and trained in applications which use the computer as a tool may also view the computer in a similar manner for many home applications, such as balancing checkbooks, keeping financial records, preparing tax forms, generating letters and other textual material, memo lists, appointment and birthday calendars, and so on.

Microcomputer access to informational services such as CompuServe and Videotext promise to change the entire nature of how we exchange information with one another. They will provide instant access to important data banks, current news, and textual resources, and will help users make decisions based upon the most current and accurate facts available.

People can use microcomputers to access national data bases such as ERIC and DIALOG. Library searches can be made by using key words describing the desired topic. Orders for microfiche or paper copies can be made, thus allowing users in rural communities to research topics without having to travel to a large city or university library.

Although full-fledged access to informational services through telephone lines may be beyond the financial and logistical constraints of today's schools, there is much to be said for at least developing some awareness among students. Even one microcomputer in the principal's office set up for communication with an informational service would be enough to demonstrate the idea to groups of students.

The use of computers as valuable tools in our lives should not be a forgotten aspect of computer knowledge, but should share the stage with CAI and programming instruction. Not every person will find CAI the most effective way to learn, and not every person will have the desire or ability to become an accomplished programmer. But nearly *everyone* will experience the computer as a tool in some way, whether or not this happens in the workplace, the home, a library or a recreation center. Schools planning for computer implementation would be wise to provide a proper environment for this kind of computer thinking.

Integration of applications that stress the computer as a tool should ideally cross all subject lines. This generally cannot be accomplished solely through a school computer room and personnel. No person is an expert on every aspect of every subject. A potent combination of teacher subject matter expertise and an accompanying knowledge of computer application possibilities will help students gain a techno-ability which may prove to contribute to the very quality of their lives.

This chapter will provide an overview of the functions that can be performed by computers in the educational environment. Some ideas pertain solely to use by teachers or administrators, and others have wide appeal for students as well. In any case, the possibilities invite exploration.

TESTING AND TEST BANKS

Would you like to have an aide at your disposal who compiles and duplicates tests, corrects them, records the grades, and then provides reports according to your wishes? How about an aide who can generate 10 forms of the same exam, but still sees that each exam form will have the same number of items testing each objective?

Sounds almost too good to be true, doesn't it? Yet this capability is at our disposal at this very minute. Computer software can be obtained which allows us to create a bank of test items classified under specified objectives. Computer testing on screen or on paper can be generated through the use of special software.

Not all testing software reaches quite this level of sophistication. Some do not accommodate for test banks of items, but allow the teacher to easily enter tests, and also serve as the means to *administer* tests to students. When the learner is ready to be tested, s/he goes to the computer, runs the appropriate test, and answers the questions by inputting responses into the computer via the keyboard. Of course, the computer grades the tests and will show the results in tabular or graphic format.

Other testing systems may require the presence of an optical card reader. Students mark their answers on computer cards; the card reader and testing program perform the subsequent functions.

An additional feature of some pieces of testing software is *commenting* capability. Students can ask the computer to record comments about specific questions. In this way, a teacher can obtain a listing of all comments for questions; examination of student comments helps the test designer to determine which questions need revision in some way. Commenting capability also means that a test may be designed to offer subjective as well as objective questions because essay type answers can also be input into the testing program. A welcome by-product will be better readability of student answers because they will be printed in typewritten form.

At the Educational Technology Center, University of California at Irvine, students in Personalized System of Instruction (PSI) courses for physics once took eight traditional written tests in order to indicate their mastery of the eight units composing the course. (See Bork 1981, pp. 165–67.) Students were required to take different forms of the same test until proving mastery of objectives. Of course, the logistics of any such testing arrangement can be difficult at best. Students need to know whether they have passed a particular unit test as soon as possible so that they can confidently progress to the next unit. Yet, due to understaffing problems, tests could not always be graded immediately. Graduate assistant proctors who performed the scoring process understandably had different opinions on how the tests should be graded. Because the grading was not uniform, the testing room atmosphere hectic at times, and grading sometimes delayed beyond what was optimal, student morale was affected. So the decision to switch to on-line computer testing was made.

The primary test designers of the computerized physics tests, Joseph Marasco and Stephen Franklin, did not employ the "test bank" idea, but rather created each unit test individually. The testing system still required that students demonstrate mastery of each unit's concepts by repeating the unit test until mastery level was obtained. Certain variables within the test questions changed for each repeated session, so that the test was different each time. In addition, the student was not permitted to take the same unit test again until at least twelve hours had passed; the testing program monitored this.

A course management system assisted the instructor to better judge the progress of students. For instance, a common problem in PSI courses is student *procrastination*. The course management system allowed frequent listing of student mastery levels so that warning notices and personal contact could be made with those students progressing too slowly.

Overall performance on tests indicated whether certain questions on the tests should be revised, or whether more specific attention should be paid to concepts very difficult for a class as a whole. These physics tests are rather special, however, because they are more than just tests. Students can request to view tutorial segments on specific ideas or problems before taking unit tests. Even while a test is in progress, an incorrect response may cause feedback in the form of small tutorial-like segments, giving immediate assistance to students showing lack of comprehension. Thus, the testing itself becomes a mode of learning and, most appropriately, has been given the name "interactive testing."

Finally, as was mentioned in Chapter 3, some CMI packages allow teachers to request tests based on certain objectives. In the case of mathematics tests, random generation of problems assures that no two tests are exactly alike.

Limiting Factors

Although computerized testing provides numerous advantages, some factors tend to limit its use. First of all, it may be more organizationally and economically feasible to give a paper and pencil test to 120 students taking the same test on the same day than to have them all report to a computer room. But as courses lean toward more individualized approaches to learning, computerized systems may be a practical answer to testing needs.

Computers are masters at grading objective tests, and they can be programmed to judge the accuracy of short-answer questions. But they may never be able to match the perception of a human teacher when evaluating essay type answers.

Another problem concerns *access* to computers. Obviously, an "interactive testing" mode, such as that at Irvine, will require a great deal of computer time.* So care must be taken that a realistic evaluation of microcomputer availability be made, and that specific arrangements are made for student testing hours.

Some test takers will, at least in the beginning, object to the fact that answers usually cannot be changed after they have been chosen. This is unlike traditional testing, where the student is free to go back, check answers, and change them if necessary.

In addition, how will the system preserve security? Will you require passwords of some kind so that students can access only their own tests? How can you be certain that students do not give a good and learned friend their passwords and receive a grade not reflecting their own work? Details of this nature and concerning test construction and operation must be considered carefully before opening a testing center in a computer room, or even within a classroom setting.

THE COMPUTER AS A CLASSROOM DEMONSTRATION MACHINE

The computer can serve as a flexible, portable audiovisual aid for teachers hoping to provide illustrations of ideas. This use goes far beyond demonstrations limited to concrete items and overhead transparencies. In some demonstration programs and according to the user's desire, substitution of certain variables results in an instant change on the computer screen. A specific and common example of an educational demonstration would be graphing (plotting) programs for linear, quadratic, trigonometric, and absolute value functions, conic sections, and so on. Merely by changing one variable in an equation (example: $2x + 3y = z$ to $4x + 3y = z$) the teacher can demonstrate vividly the relationship between the resulting graphic respresenations—without performing tedious and time-consuming point-by-point plotting. Thus, a variable can be changed many times and its resulting graph shown

---

*It may also require more memory than possessed by most microcomputer models available. The "interactive testing" at Irvine, California, was performed utilizing the large memory of a mainframe computer.

an equal amount of times, something that would be just too tedious to do with normal chalk and blackboard methods. Students, then, can concentrate on *relationships* between variables rather than on the plotting process itself.

In the area of science or social studies, the "World Clock" demonstration* allows students to see which parts of the world are dark or light during any hour of the day. It will also demonstrate the sun's effect on the earth during any day of the year, according to the earth's orbital position in relationship to the sun.

Still another demonstration type program illustrates celestial bodies and their relationship to the earth's position.

In the area of health education, a teacher can demonstrate life expectancy predictions by entering responses to computer questions. According to the responses, the computer will predict life expectancy for a particular person.

Biology teachers can integrate the use of demonstration software in lectures. For instance, one demonstration called the "Nucleic Acid Connection" illustrates the transcription and translation of DNA in chromosomes into mRNA and polypeptides. The program can also call up outline drawings of the principal nucleic acid bases.

Students in physics, math, art, and drafting classes may be interested in computer-generated three-dimensional figures, which may also have rotating ability.

At the elementary level, a teacher can choose to demonstrate various clock times, constellations, string art designs, and so on by the use of software and a microcomputer.

Demonstration software currently exists only for a limited number of topics. As more teachers begin to integrate microcomputers into the curriculum, many more demonstration type programs will be designed. But if the existence of a readily assessible series of graphs, tables, diagrams, pictures, or even musical compositions is desired, teachers can work closely with students to create them by programming, or through special graphics design or music software. Then the whole series can be brought under the roof of a single program for demonstration purposes; each screen display can be called up by the simple means of selection from a menu.

Use of computers in this mode need not be quite so formal. For instance, an English teacher may demonstrate sentence-expanding techniques on a computer screen rather than on the blackboard. Keyboarding, editing, and copying capabilities enjoyed by means of a microcomputer may make the demonstration less time-consuming and

---

*The "World Clock" is available from Compress, a division of Science Books International, Inc., P.O. Box 102, Wentworth, New Hampshire 03282, (603) 764-5831.

more constructive. The existence of a printer allows results to be put into permanent form, painlessly.

The screen display *size* may limit the amount of students who may see a particular demonstration. However, wide-screen technology already exists: Projection screen televisions can be interfaced with microcomputers so that the screen display can be viewed by an entire class—or lecture hall—of students. Although this option is ideal and rather exciting, the cost may be prohibitive and out of the reach of many classrooms and schools.

Several other options may enhance use of demonstration software. First, if more than one computer is available, the same demonstration could possibly be run on all of them. A more palatable arrangement may be to connect one or more large televisions or monitors to the microcomputer. The third option involves the use of computers in *networks* (see Chapter 7). The teacher's host computer allows downloading of the demonstration program into all the computers in the network. Or, by certain manipulations, the teacher's host computer screen display may be transferred to all other computers.

It is possible to interface computers with slide projectors in such a way that any particular slide can be shown to illustrate the speaker's point, regardless of its position in the slide group.

Looking toward the future, *videodisk* technology can allow the storage of a tremendous amount of moving and still pictures, speech, and other visual and auditory information on one video disk. Demonstration programs will allow teachers to access specific film, photographic, or graphic sequences at will. If the topic is the Rocky Mountains in Colorado, film segments can be called up immediately, describing these mountains in a way unavailable by other means, yet neatly integrated with the lecture or discussion session.

The thought of such a flexible system sends the imagination soaring. Yet it may be many more years before videodisks and videodisk players are present in enough numbers that they become common tools for teachers who wish to demonstrate ideas, concepts, information, procedures, and even feelings and moods.

WORKSHEET AND PUZZLE GENERATION

Educators have always customized worksheets and puzzles according to specific needs in the classroom. Because development of these materials takes a great deal of time and effort, teachers often opt for less applicable, but ready-made ditto masters or workbooks. Software houses have written programs that provide a ready *framework* for customized worksheets and puzzles. For example, if students need practice in the area of writing the correct, but irregular forms of singular nouns, the teacher can run a worksheet generation program, which provides step-by-step prompts allowing the input of information to be printed on the worksheet page. The program may begin with a menu:

1. Create a worksheet
2. Print a worksheet
3. Save a worksheet
4. Edit a worksheet
5. Load a worksheet

When creating a worksheet (1.), the program may ask questions similar to the following:

Subject area? <u>Science</u>
Do you wish a heading to be printed? <u>Yes</u>
What is the title of this worksheet? <u>Energy</u>
Other directions or comments to be printed? <u>No</u>
How many question? <u>20</u>

QUESTION FORMAT
  1. Multiple Choice
  2. Fill in the Blank
  3. Matching
Which one? <u>2</u>
Any worksheet directions? <u>No</u>
Do you wish to print a list of words to choose from? <u>Yes</u>

Type the first test item, including the word to be blanked out on the student worksheet:
1) <u>Temperature is a measure of the warmth or coldness of an object or</u>
     <u>substance with reference to some standard value.</u>
Which word or words should be left blank on student worksheet? <u>Temperature</u>

When a fill-in-the-blank type student worksheet is finally printed, a list of words to be selected will appear at the top of the page. The computer, of course, will list them randomly or alphabetically so that their position on the list is no clue.

Then prompts for the next nineteen questions will guide the teacher through all steps in a similar manner to the example above. Typographical errors can be erased easily by using the back arrow or delete key, depending upon the brand of microcomputer—no correction tape, fluid, or razor blades for this teacher. And after the questions have been completed, a good worksheet program will allow the teacher to correct any mistakes or to make any necessary changes.

Then the main menu appears again. The teacher selects (3.) for SAVE. The worksheet will now be stored on the diskette, under its subject heading, topic name, and a computer-selected identifying code. This will make later revisions quite simple; the teacher will be able to "load" an old worksheet and change the questions that need revision.

Printing out the worksheet for student use would be the obvious next step. This means that access to a printer is vital, though a printer does not necessarily have to be housed in the teacher's classroom. A centrally located microcomputer of the same brand interfaced to a printer can service the worksheet generation needs of quite a few teachers.

After selecting option (2.), PRINT, from the main menu, the computer prompts:

How many student copies should be printed? 10

Thus the teacher is saved from typing problems and from ditto machines. Depending upon the printer and the kind of paper it uses, the cost of printing can be less than the cost of dittoing.

Now the message appears:

How many answer sheets should be printed? 2

The printer produces two answer sheets, identical to the student worksheet, but with the blanks filled in with the correct answers.

Each worksheet generation program on the market has its own advantages, disadvantages, options, and organization. Some have far greater capabilities than others, and some are more difficult to use.

Puzzles of various types can also be created by purchasing appropriate software. Microcomputers can do the hard work involved in developing word search puzzles, for example. Perhaps a teacher wants children to be more familiar with words pertaining to the electricity unit in science class. A list is compiled. The word search puzzle software will ask the teacher to input worksheet format decisions and a list of vocabulary words to be included. Then the computer decides where the words should cross, and whether they should be printed horizontally, vertically, diagonally, forward, or backwards. The computer places nonsense letters in all empty spaces, so that the entire puzzle rectangle of letters is filled. Of course, the puzzle may be saved, edited, and printed out as many times as desired. Answer sheets can also be requested.

Crossword puzzles may also be designed by puzzle generation programs. Like word search puzzles, the computer searches the vocabulary words for matching letters and crosses them where appropriate. Prompts on the screen allow the puzzle creator to give a clue for each word involved.

When student copies are printed, the puzzle will be numbered and show only blank boxes; a list of clues will be printed on the bottom of the puzzle sheet. The answer sheet showing the correct answers can be easily obtained.

Some CMI packages include worksheet generation capability, based on the objectives chosen by the teacher according to individual student needs.

Worksheet and puzzle generators can be powerful tools for special needs in the classroom. Though teachers may be the main users of these programs, students can also be taught how to operate these programs and can create puzzles or worksheets for themselves and their classmates. The development of a crossword puzzle, for instance, requires students to provide clues which identify specific vocabulary words. This is a learning experience in itself.

Another kind of program will allow teachers to produce messages in block size or poster-sized letters. These can be used to decorate bulletin boards, dress up worksheets, and to print headings for student newspapers and magazines. Teachers will find such programs useful for many imaginative classroom applications.

SPECIAL SOFTWARE FOR READING

Readability Analysis

It is often beneficial to determine the reading level of textual material to be used with students. If some doubt exists as to the actual readability level of a particular trade book, for example, programs can be run that allow educators to input sample paragraphs from the material involved. Special formulas have been used by the author of the readability program that now allow the computer to indicate the readability level, such as "3.0."

When committees select new textbooks, great attention should be paid to readability level. It makes little sense to choose a fifth grade social studies text which is written on an eighth grade level. The time-consuming, normal readability determination process too often has been bypassed by textbook selection committees; teachers have been forced to rely on their own intuition and the readability level provided by the publisher. Readability software can greatly simplify the process; and, if the theory behind the formulas used to determine levels is accurate, then the computer-generated readability level will be useful for textbook selection decisions. Some parameters that may be checked in order to determine readability are average sentence length, average word length, and estimation of word difficulty.

Cloze Passage Generation

One helpful activity for developing reading comprehension skill is to have students fill in the missing words in reading passages. For instance, every tenth word may be blank, and the student must guess the identity of each missing word from the context of the sentence. A cloze program provides the framework for creation and printing of such passages. Text must be typed by the teacher or teacher aide, and blank frequency chosen (every five words, every eight words, and so forth). Of course, an accompanying answer sheet can also be printed to help in teacher evaluation of student work.

Vocabulary Placement

Vocabulary placement programs find a student's independent reading level quickly and without assistance from the teacher. Some software of this type has been validated through the testing of a large number of students who have also been evaluated through determinations from reading specialists. Most programs of this type available currently have a possible placement range of reading readiness through seventh or eighth grade.

Beyond viewing scores no teacher time is required, so programs of this nature can be a useful indicator of a student's independent reading level, particularly when large class size limits the amount of attention a teacher can afford to give to individual students. This information can help the teacher decide what grouping arrangements and learning materials may be best for students.

Memorization Aids

Some software is available which will help students memorize poems, quotes, speeches, scripts, and any other textual material desired. A series of prompts forces students to memorize phrase by phrase and will provide feedback as to the memorization accuracy. An accompanying outcome may be development of vocabulary and reading comprehension practice.

ADMINISTRATIVE DUTIES

Paperwork and record-keeping duties put a stranglehold on all educators at times, as does the careful process needed to record scores and compute grades. Now that microcomputer power is within reach, teachers can begin to think in ways that use the computer as a tool which can free them from the most repetitious and tedious tasks that must be performed. Not only will time and trouble be saved, but students will also witness the way teachers utilize their "computer pencils."

Grade Book

Programs of this type simulate an actual grade book, but have far more flexible and useful capabilities. Generally, a teacher would start by entering class lists for each class taught. If the same list of students will be used for a variety of subject areas, as in many self-contained classrooms in elementary schools, this computer can do the repetitious copying of names for all subject areas to be recorded.

When entering a set of grades for tests, quizzes, homework, and so forth, the grades will be stored along with the appropriate student names. Weight values are usually assigned to each of the scores, so that a quiz, for example, will represent a less important portion of the final grade than an exam. With a special computational formula, the computer figures out grade averages—not just at report card time, but during any day of the year when the teacher, a student, or a parent wishes to determine achievement level.

Other features may include a report-generating capability that summarizes the performance of an individual, a small group, or a class. Often, statistical summaries are available as well, showing the mean, standard deviation, and graphical representation of performance. New students may be added to rosters, and on all subsequent listings they will appear in neat alphabetical order, not at the *bottom* of the roster as is usually the case when using manual record-keeping methods. Of course, student records can be deleted when appropriate. Some programs also allow a teacher to list all missing homework assignments for students in a class, a feature which can provide daily reports and help teachers keep track of potential problems. Also, good grading programs will allow teachers to correct data entry mistakes, to enter grades for late assignments, and may even allow teachers to insert comments about a particular student's performance. Some grade book programs provide capability for report card preparation; usually these are designed for use by an entire school, not just by one individual classroom. A handy feature in certain packages is the use of *light pens* rather than keyboarding to enter grades. This can appreciably speed up the data entry process.

Attendance

If a teacher wishes to keep private records of the students' attendance, this can often be done directly through the use of the gradebook programs mentioned above. The whole school generally must be involved in a regular, computerized attendance-reporting system for the optimal time-saving effect; plus these attendance-keeping systems are usually too expensive to be purchased for each individual classroom.

At least one system coordinates with a school's grade-reporting system so that attendance over a certain amount of time can be automatically printed when student report cards are generated and printed by the computer. Summary reports may include total absences, excused absences, unexcused absences, and so on. According to the school's unique needs, certain categories can be defined, determined, and totaled. For instance, if a total of unexcused absences for girls in gym classes for all high school students is needed, the school office may request this report through the attendance-keeping software.

State Departments of Education may require teachers to keep attendance, find totals, and even use certain computational formulas in order to complete necessary governmental forms. The computer can do this automatically; teacher record keeping would include only the task of taking attendance, collecting excuses, and entering this data into the attendance program. In some cases even these tasks can be lifted from the teacher by having clerical workers in the school office do the actual data entry. If teachers take attendance on special computer cards, then a *card reader* can cut down the amount of data entry time required to a considerable extent.

Software of this type allows for convenient review of attendance data by principals and counselors. Reports can be generated for each class roster indicating those students who have not returned to school with excuses from parents or doctors, so that teachers can more easily keep track of required attendance duties.

Naturally, the choice of attendance-keeping software should be primarily the decision of school administrators and should take into account ease of reporting for teachers, and the kind of reports required by the state's Department of Education and the federal government.

Library Circulation Software

The circulation of book, magazine, and audiovisual material can be monitored by software which keeps track of borrowed items, listing student or teacher name, title, author, catalog number, and due date. A microcomputer system can replace or complement the usual record-keeping arrangements and can even print out overdue notices and lists of overdue books. When individuals put in requests for

Figure 4-1
Microcomputer in Media Center

books currently in circulation, this information can be stored and help librarians to identify the books when returned and see that they are held for the person who requested them.

Even classrooms possessing small libraries of trade and informational books, as well as other educational materials that sometimes must leave the classroom, can benefit by such a record-keeping arrangement, because it allows easy day-to-day tracking of the whereabouts of all borrowed material.

Development, Maintenance, and Reporting of Individual Records

Programs of this type are especially applicable to special education requirements. They may allow easy input of testing data and anecdotal information. The generation of IEP documents, summary reports, and letters to parents may be greatly simplified. Data sort capability provides a way for educators to obtain listing of pupils who have selected characteristics in common; this option can be valuable for some tasks that need to be performed, such as determining optimum grouping arrangements for instruction.

In some cases record-keeping software includes ready-made lists of objectives for certain subject areas and may allow for additions and deletions from the lists.

What is the difference between record-keeping software and computer-managed instruction? The label that best describes the aim of the system should be used. A program designed primarily for IEP report maintenance and generation will tend to employ some aspects of CMI, but only those that directly contribute to reporting performance. In addition, a greater range of reporting and data-handling ability may be possessed by record-keeping software.

WORD PROCESSING

A phenomena in today's business world, word-processing software allows written communication of all sorts to be easily generated, proofread, printed, and revised. Gone are the days when revisions of a paper or manuscript entailed many long typing sessions and many big headaches. With the power of word processing at our disposal, working hours can be saved which would normally be devoted to repetitious typing tasks.

Because most businesses use word-processing machines or microcomputers possessing word-processing software, it is fast becoming a necessity that business education classes prepare students for the atmosphere and demands of modern offices. Job opportunities for those trained on word-processing equipment will be much greater than those available for students merely trained on typewriters. But even if you are *not* a business education teacher the potential uses for word processing in schools may surprise you.

For the uninitiated, a description of word-processing capabilities is warranted. The *computer screen* serves as the blank sheet of paper, and the text is typed using the computer keyboard. The first draft of a letter or essay can take as much time to enter using a word processor as it would to type it on an electric typewriter. But if the typist tends to make a lot of mistakes, word-processing power will result in a better product in a decreased amount of time. Why?

For many word-processing programs, insertion and deletion of characters, words, lines, and even paragraphs can be done with the touch of one or two keys. This means that even those mistakes uncorrectable by normal typing methods can be easily done with a word processor.

The *word wrap* feature allows the typist to enter long paragraphs without ever pressing the return key. The computer makes certain that no word exceeds the right-hand margin, automatically bringing words that are too lengthy down to the next line. Thus, absolutely no attention needs to be paid to margin limitations when entering text. This is a great time-saver because hyphenation decisions need not be made and the touch typist can concentrate on reading the material to be typed.

Some authors feel that their word processors are invaluable tools in the actual *composition* process, allowing them to delete unwanted sentences as they write and replace them at will and with the greatest of ease.

At invervals, and after a piece of writing has been completely entered, the user *saves* it by a special command. This means that the work will be saved on a *storage diskette* and can be recalled whenever needed in the future.

A word-processing system is of little value unless a *printer* is available because the natural outcome has to be words printed on paper, so that others can read the written material. For some applications, dot matrix or thermal printers will serve the purpose. However, when the outcome should resemble that provided by regular electric typewriters, a letter quality printer is necessary. (See Chapter 1 for more information on printers.)

Now, let's assume that a five-page composition has been originally entered, checked on the screen, revised, and then saved on a diskette under the file name of COMP2. A copy of the composition is printed on paper. Over the next day, the author proofreads and revises the composition as s/he normally does. This is where a word-processing program can make a tremendous difference: no laborious retyping is required, and the author can make revisions with no thought of how difficult a correction may be for the typist. The user calls the piece of writing from the storage diskette; this usually is done by a simple command like holding down the CONTROL key while pressing the L key (for LOAD), and then by indicating the name of the file which contains the composition to be revised (like COMP2).

The writing will now reside in the computer's memory, and it will also remain on the storage disk. The author (or typist) is now free to make deletions, insertions, paragraph moves, and so on. The word wrap feature insures that adding or deleting sentences and words will not interfere with correct paragraph and margin format after revisions are done. In addition, titles can be automatically centered, and both margins can be *justified* when the composition is printed on paper.

Newspapers normally justify columns. This means that both right and left margins of the column are even, not jagged in appearance. The word-processing program does this by putting extra spaces between words so that each line ends at the same right-hand position on the paper.

Now that all changes have been made, the user can save his work, including the corrections, and print the revised manuscript, complete with pagination. A letter-perfect copy will be produced, unmarred by correction fluid or erasure marks.

The implication for business education classes is obvious, but only represents *one* of the possible applications in schools. First of all, teachers, administrators, and other school personnel can make personal use of such software for letters, writing of all sorts, and for the design of educational materials. Files of student names, parent addresses, and so on can be easily made; whenever mailings, distributions, listings, or labels are needed, they can be easily printed out—no laborious typing or writing. As one gains proficiency with a word processor's operation, many different applications will come to mind, according to specific needs.

Students will find that use of word-processing software can greatly add to their productivity and the quality of the final draft of writing. Junior high and senior high classes may employ word-processing techniques, but simple word-processing programs have been used for grade levels as low as the first grade.

In Junior and Senior High Schools

Business education classes, as previously mentioned, can benefit greatly by exposure to word-processing capabilities. But the transcription of writing assignments may be required in other classes as well. The most obvious job would be to compose and edit writing assignments for English and journalism classes. As currently practiced, English teachers receive first drafts from students which may or may not be legible, read them, and then make comments which pinpoint strengths and weaknesses of the paper. Quite. often, the revision process comes to a dead stop at this point because rewriting by the student and rereading by the teacher is a time-consuming problem. But if student work is saved on disk, revisions can be done quite painlessly, and will therefore encourage students to continually improve writing assignments. When word-processing methods are employed, work can be revised to student satisfaction, and because it will be produced in typewritten form, can be more easily read by others.

If a group of networked microcomputers is available, or enough monitors are hooked up to a single microcomputer, an entire class can

Figure 4-2a
Word Processing Room in High School

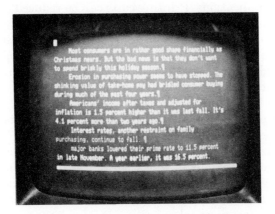

Figure 4-2b
Close-up of Word Processing Screen

view a completed composition and express positive comments and constructive suggestions for improvement. The English or journalism teacher can zero in on specific writing skills, changing word usage or sentence and paragraph structure at will and with great ease—all within full view of the class. In this way the teacher demonstrates vividly how the editing and revision process can be performed. Although this process is common to many adults, some students have the mistaken impression that good writers are able to produce perfect work the first time they write. If they are able to witness an adult writer actually in the process of composition and revision by seeing what is happening on a computer screen, they will begin to understand that even good writers must revise their work many times until the desired product has been obtained. Word-processing capabilities allow a composition to be "tailored" until it exactly reflects what the author is trying to communicate.

Similarly, students can learn to compose using the special capabilities of a word processor. In one approach, an outline of the topic to be written about is entered, then printed out and revised. Then step by step, students can turn the outline into a full composition. The first step may be to add topic sentences; then to add supporting ideas and details under the topic sentences; and so on . . . according to the kind of writing to be accomplished. How is this different from handwritten or typewritten approaches to composition? Ideas can be added whenever and wherever necessary, and without need to retype. Extraneous words and sentences as well as outline comments can be deleted easily. Using word-processing capabilities, the final composition is created through a kind of continuous evolution. Elementary as well as secondary students can benefit by this approach to composition.

Student newspapers can use word-processing technology to produce quality publications. Printing costs can be reduced by using word processors to justify margins and to produce photo-ready copy.

Reports and research papers required by social studies and science classes can be typed and revised using word-processing equipment. Quality should improve because a student will be much more likely to make first and second revisions before a paper is finally printed and handed in to the teacher.

One is tempted to ask at this point: how can students find enough computer time to generate assignments in this manner?

Obviously, most schools today do not have enough microcomputers to accommodate all students who wish to use them. Word processing consumes more time than many other computer applications, and it will therefore not be practical for widespread use until more microcomputers are present in schools.

Where should students do their word-processing work? In individual classrooms? Computer rooms? Media centers? When planning a school's total computer program, word-processing uses and needs should be seriously considered in the light of the potential benefits, and time scheduled for those students who wish to write in this manner.

Another problem occurs when students do not know how to type; they will be frustrated and use far too much computer time. It is recommended that those using word processors first build their typing skills. This can be accomplished through personal or business typing classes already offered by schools. Also, many good computer tutorials in touch typing do exist and can meet some of the training needs of students.

As more microcomputers are purchased for homes, students may elect to do word processing at home. There is a considerable advantage when home computers are identical to ones housed at local schools. That way, a student can carry his or her work to school on a diskette and use school printers to produce final copies.

In Elementary Schools

Some teachers have been experimenting with word processing in the elementary schools and have noted a great rate of success. Children who previously refused to rewrite stories and reports, because the job involved laborious handwriting and/or erasures, now look forward to the task of revision. Corrections are easily made, and in addition, the final product is in a form easily shared with others. If children are convinced that their work is communication, then they will also be convinced that their work must be written in such a way that others can understand their meanings. Capitalization, spelling, punctuation, and grammatical mistakes can now be viewed as roadblocks to communication. Unclear sentences and poor paragraph organization also block communication. The ease with which revisions can be done encourages children to improve their work, and it allows the teacher to hold meaningful individual writing conferences. In fact, the conference can actually take place at the computer, with the teacher or student trying out different ways to express ideas, and to organize the story. Mechanical and grammatical mistakes can be discussed and corrected immediately.

For younger children, teacher use of word processing can replace the blackboard or poster paper when taking story dictation in a language experience approach to reading and writing. At times, specific composition skills can be highlighted, leading to greater student understanding of the writing process. For instance, the role of topic sentences can be demonstrated as an element very important in reading comprehension.

An additional benefit to all this will be easy compilation of student

Focus: The Bank Street Writer

Teachers experimenting with the notion that word-processing software can be a useful tool for writing activities in the classroom have done so with word-processing software originally designed for the needs of businesses and adult authors in mind. Documentation accompanying these packages is difficult for older students to understand, and way beyond the reading comprehension level of the average elementary school child. Thus the teacher must learn the word processor's operation and then train students, building instructional materials along the way. Despite this, experimenting teachers have reported productive results (Judd, 1982; Gula, 1982).

Acknowledging certain limitations for widespread use of more complicated word-processing packages in the classroom, researchers from the Bank Street College of Education and other experts developed and field-tested a *word processor* for young writers, called the Bank Street Writer (BSW).

What makes the Bank Street Writer different from the usual?

The operation of the BSW is easy to learn and requires little memorization of commands, since various operations are selected from a menu appearing at the top of the screen, in the editing mode. On the flip side of the diskette is a good tutorial program for teachers and students learning to use the BSW. Thus, training teachers and students is a less complex procedure.

The BSW may be loaded into more than one computer at one time. (This is also true for some adult-oriented word processors.) Students save their work on storage diskettes.

Students may safely share the same storage diskette. The filing system for textual material is such that students indicate a special password when saving or loading text, thus assuring that others cannot access their text and make unauthorized changes. Adult-oriented word processors do not usually provide this option because sharing storage diskettes is unnecessary.

Students can select to print out drafts in rough copy or final copy, answering computer prompt questions about format.

Teacher and student manuals are provided. Ideas for the BSW's use in the classroom are included.

Bank Street Writer marks a new generation of text editors designed with the needs of students in mind. It is likely that others will appear as time goes on. The school package for the BSW is available from Scholastic, a distributor of educational software (see Appendix A for address).

work for bulletin board displays, books, magazines, and newsletters. Previously, such publications entailed rewriting and more rewriting by students, or much teacher typing. It is no surprise that student publications at the elementary level have been few and far between. Word-processing capabilities can change all that because students' final products will be typewritten and in a form easily laid out for newspapers or magazines. Students begin to feel as if they are in a kind of grown-up work world, where growth and productivity are important and attainable. They can be proud of the work they have accomplished; they can be convinced that writing is indeed a real and valuable kind of communication. Such attitudes insure that writing skills steadily improve.

As in the secondary level, typing skill makes a difference. Although a hunt-and-peck style of typing may be acceptable for short stories and reports, longer jobs can be frustrating if no skill in typing exists. Again, computer tutorials in typing are available, and they may be an ideal way to help children (and teachers) to learn this skill. Some typing programs possess a gamelike format that attracts students and helps them gain skill rapidly.

Typing skill will not only help students who use word processors, but it can also be important for programming classes as well, allowing students to concentrate on program statement construction and logic rather than on typing details. This tends to allow programming skill to grow more rapidly. And it is also true that students entering the job market may be working with microcomputers or computer terminals. A comfortable familiarity with the keyboard can only be of benefit.

A Classroom Vignette

Mrs. Adams' fourth grade classroom has decided to produce a school newsletter. The children show great excitement because they know

Figure 4-3
Bank Street Writer Screen Display

what they produce will be read by the whole school *and* by their own parents. A brainstorming session results in many good ideas. Several editors are chosen and made responsible for various components of the newsletter.

All the children will be reporters, and follow up ideas according to their own or the editor's wishes. Teachers and children in other classrooms are interviewed. Topics for articles to be printed in the first issue include "The Fifth Grade Field Trip to the Museum of Natural History," "The Care and Feeding of the Second Grade Pet Hamster," "Ideas for Simple Programs in BASIC," "Favorite Recipes from Mrs. White's Collection," and so on.

The editors look at each report as it is written and sometimes make revision suggestions. Mrs. Adams oversees the whole operation and offers advice when needed. She looks at the rough drafts in order to note the *kinds* of mistakes made, so that skill teaching can follow—in small groups, a large group, or individual writing conferences.

Finally, all reports and columns have been finalized and printed out. The children determine what headings and headlines will be used. When larger type is needed for headlines, the children produce them with special lettering software.

Then, a small group of children works with Mrs. Adams to lay out the newsletter and to integrate artwork and other kinds of illustrations. Eventually, the children will become so proficient at layout that little teacher supervision will be needed. When the newsletter layout has been completed, photocopies and ditto masters are made. Copies are duplicated and then distributed to the other classrooms and to parents.

What has all this accomplished? The children have written *for a purpose,* revisions were cheerfully done, and children contributed their unique talents to the team effort in order to reach the desired goal. A lot of incidental skill learning has occurred and will contribute more toward improvement in writing ability than a raft of English workbook pages. Mrs. Adams has taken note of skill deficiencies and is planning future lessons accordingly. But most importantly, the children take pride in their work, and they do not view writing as a laborious task totally unrelated to their lives.

STATISTICAL STUDIES

Statistical software exists for most brands of microcomputers that may be considered for purchase by schools and should greatly simplify research into various topics, particularly in the subject areas of social studies and science, though certainly not *limited* to those areas. Of course, we first must believe that statistics does hold a rightful place in the curriculum. Quite a few educational councils have stated their consensus that statistical analysis can add a new dimension to learning, and create much interest and involvement on the part of students.

Statistical reasoning can be directly compared to the kind of procedures followed when performing scientific experiments. A hypothesis is made; data must be collected in an organized manner. Tables, graphs, and charts will illustrate findings; according to the results one must be able to describe, interpret, and draw conclusions. Repeated experiences of this nature will help students move toward the stage of formal operations in their cognitive development.

The microcomputer will aid in accomplishing these goals, and much more complicated and detailed projects may be tackled due to the famous "number-crunching" power it possesses. Not only will the computer add large columns of numbers with ease, it will also use special formulas (algorithms) which are traditionally utilized to compute statistical measures. At elementary and even senior high level, these algorithms and how they were derived need not necessarily be clearly understood by all students. The important thing is that students understand the reason for using a certain statistical measure and know what information that measure can provide.

A Classroom Vignette

During a rather heated class discussion, Mr. Noonan's senior political science class brought up some relevant and interesting questions concerning the relationship between political party affiliation and age. John and several other students argued that older people tended to be Republican and younger people were more often members of the Democratic party.

Mary and other classmates argued that there was very little or no correlation. Still other class members agreed that there was a correlation in the country as a whole, but not in the locality where the high school was located. The rest of the class had no strong opinion one way or another, but suggested that some kind of poll be taken and some kind of comparison made.

Mr. Noonan appointed a committee to plan and organize a poll. It was decided that each student visit other classes in the building during the political science period. A form was designed so that students giving information for the poll could confidentially indicate their parents' and/or grandparents' political affiliation and age.

Once the form was designed and revised until acceptable, enough copies were made to include a sample of 1,000 people.

The polling project was reported to the school office. The principal approved of the idea and suggested that the poll could be taken on the following Monday, during the fifth period, as suggested.

On Monday the poll was taken, with only a few minor problems occurring. Those participating in the poll were warned only to list certain information. For instance, if a student had no idea of the age of his grandfather, then his grandfather was not to be included in the poll.

Once the data had been collected, the committee checked forms to eliminate those which were obviously jokes, such as

Party Affiliation	Age
Nudist party	99
Republican party	2

Then the process of data entry could proceed. Volunteers from the class took turns on the microcomputer after school, entering the data collected via a statistics software package. Once this was completed, a graph showing correlation between age and percentage of those in the Republican party was generated by the computer. A similar graph showed the correlation between age and percentage of those in the Democratic party.

Results showed quite conclusively that there was a correlation between age and percentage of those belonging to the Republican or Democratic parties. The correlation between Democratic affiliation and age was −0.7, showing that as age increased, the percentage of people affiliated with that party decreased. The correlation between Republican affiliation and age was +0.82, showing that as age increased, so did the chance of affiliation with the Republican party (correlation values range anywhere from −1.0 to +1.0).

The committee felt that the poll was a success and that more experiences of this type would contribute much to their reasoning abilities and to learning. When the whole class convened again, results were discussed and areas for further research were suggested. Randy thought that the poll should be compared to statewide and nationwide figures, if possible. Such a comparison would entail some research and knowledge of various informational sources. Some other students felt it would be interesting to go to an organization such as the League of Women Voters to get public data which would help determine whether the correlation found in the student poll matched official data and findings. Although little class time would be devoted to these ideas, several students had become so interested that they decided to research and write the required political science research paper on related topics.

THE MICROCOMPUTER AS A LABORATORY INSTRUMENT

Use of the microcomputer as a laboratory instrument is an exciting application for many of those involved in science education. In addition, certain vocational-training programs may benefit from using the microcomputer in this manner.

Advantages

In the past, the use of computers for this purpose was singularly impractical. Time-sharing systems involving large computers and computer terminals do not readily lend themselves to direct interfacing with laboratory experiments. Because the time-sharing computer determines *when* data should be read from any particular terminal, it is very difficult to allow for the precise timing required for accurate laboratory measurements. In regard to public schools, only large school systems may own their own large computers and even then they may be housed in a building other than the high school. Therefore, the issue is further complicated by the need to transmit data over telephone lines (Tinker 1981, p. 94).

Because the difficulty and expense involved with use of large computers makes it highly impractical for science classes in secondary schools, teachers are then limited to experiments which can be performed through human gathering of measurement data. If a school is fortunate, certain laboratory instruments can be substituted for human measurement. But even one of these instruments may cost more than the total price of a microcomputer, including the additional hardware needed to convert data to signals the microcomputer can read and use in order to make needed calculations.

Some experiments that have been performed using the computer in this manner can be done by human measurement. One famous application, the cooling curve experiment, can be done by gathering repeated thermometer readings and then plotting the data obtained. However, this can be a tedious and boring task, especially when it must be repeated several times. Interface with a microcomputer allows this data to be read automatically and continually. And even better, the computer can take readings thousands of times per second, allowing events which last a very short time to be measured and studied.

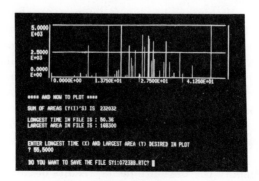

Figure 4-4
Screen Display of Data Collected through
Computer Interface with Laboratory Experiments

Microcomputers can show results of experiments in many forms. Data can be continually displayed in large lettering on one or more video display screens. Thus a large class can easily view data. The measurement data can be sent through calculation sequences and the results also displayed on the screen. Data can be displayed as a table, a graph, a CRO type trace, and so forth (Laramie 1980, p. 36).

So far, various individuals and organizations have designed hardware and supporting software that simplifies the use of the microcomputer as a laboratory instrument. And, it is hoped that continued research in this area will enable teachers untrained in electronics to make use of some small subset of the possible applications. Even science teachers at the elementary level may someday be able to utilize the microcomputer as a laboratory instrument, as the appropriate hardware and software increases in simplicity of design.

There is an additional advantage to all this. Modern science labs in industry, research, and in universities are now beginning to use microcomputers for the collection of data. Many commercially available microcomputers serve the purpose quite well, including the Apple,® TRS-80,® PET,™ and some small, inexpensive computers like the KIM,™ AIM,™ and SYM.™ All these microcomputers are based on a 6502 chip. Microcomputers based on other chip designs have possibilities as well, but the bulk of development and research done concerning the computer-as-instrument, particularly for educational application, does involve the 6502 chip (Tinker 1981, p. 102).

Students with scientific interests will benefit by learning how to use the computer as a laboratory instrument because they will probably be dealing with microcomputers during college and when entering the job market as scientists and researchers.

Analog to Digital Conversion

At the heart of all this are hardware components that allow analog measurements (such as temperature, pressure, and movement) to be converted to the digital form (or signal) understood by computers. Most microprocessors deal with eight-bit binary numbers, called bytes, most ranging from 0 to 255. Therefore, the analog to digital converter accepts physical measurements (input) which are processed by a transducer and support circuits; this input is then mulitiplied or divided so that they conform to the range of 0 to 2.55 volts. A *computer program* determines how often a measurement should be taken. At this point, the measurements are converted to digital form, and the computer can immediately display the measurements, results of calculations based on the measurements, or can store the results in memory or on a diskette for later recall (Laramie 1980, pp. 348–49).

Researchers have developed hardware and software of this particular type; but it is not useful for all applications. Other special interfaces have been designed and are available from several sources.

Laboratory Equipment Microcomputers Can Replace

A computer such as the Commodore 64 can be purchased by schools for less than $700, including the video display. There are also small computers like the KIM that come in kit form for as little as $150, not including video display. Even *one* computer can be a valuable addition to a science laboratory. Microcomputer cost efficiency has been described in the *School Science Review,* a British publication (Laramie 1980, p. 350). Laboratory equipment is listed that a microcomputer can replace, and can even outperform in some cases:

1. A four-channel data memory

2. An oscilloscope with screen

3. A demonstration voltmeter or ammeter

4. An electrometer (charger measurer)

5. A wattmeter

6. A joulemeter

7. Millisecond accuracy timer

8. Velocity and acceleration measurer

Sample Applications

The Technical Education Research Center (TERC) is a nonprofit educational research and development corporation located in Cambridge, Massachusetts. Over the past few years, TERC has developed several applications for microcomputers in laboratories. In fact they now offer a workshop and accompanying information and learning packages that will help put interested science teachers in the right direction.

A list of applications TERC has developed can help give a more specific description of current capabilities of computers used as a tool in the science laboratory (Tinker 1981, pp. 95–97):

1. Counter-timer

2. Integrated Circuit testing

3. Function generator

4. Fourier synthesis

5. Transcient recorder

6. Fourier analysis

7. Radioactive half-life experiment

8. Pulse height analysis

9. The computer of average transcients (measures seismic waves: earthquakes)

10. Linear dynamics

11. Rotational dynamics

The Future?

A world of possibilities is now open to us, involving the computer as a tool in the greatest sense of the word. We need to see additional research and development of educational applications, including more user-friendly hardware and software. Curriculum materials that integrate use of the computer-as-instrument must be developed and tested in actual classrooms, then distributed for the use of others.

At present, it is perhaps unrealistic to expect science teachers with little or no background in electronics to buy interface kits, assemble them, and set up the whole system. This could result in a lot of frustration because if it so happens that the experiment does not work, exactly *who* does the teacher ask for help? Proper training and resources are essential.

TOOLS FOR MUSIC

The role computer-assisted instruction can play to strengthen student achievement in music theory topics has been discussed in Chapter 3. However, another and most exciting development over the past few years has been the invention of *music synthesizers* for microcomputers.

Synthesizers have been around for a number of years, but have been driven by larger computers. Access was largely denied to the

Figure 4-5
Music Synthesizer System
(Courtesy of Alpha Syntauri Corp.)

average person because these synthesizers are expensive, complicated, and located only at certain locations around the country. The microcomputer has changed all that, making the prospect of home use and use by educational institutions a fascinating possibility.

Microcomputer music synthesizers have many different designs and possess different levels of capabilities. One arrangement that is very popular is to combine a pianolike keyboard with music synthesizers and the microcomputer. Accompanying software allows for simplicity of operation. Other systems do not possess a keyboard, so the musical notation and the creation of instrumental voices must be done via the computer's regular keyboard.

When using a music synthesizer, one *creates* a piece of music, complete with a number of different *voices* that can represent various musical instruments. Users can create instruments by controlling pitch and amplitude. Special effects can be created in much the same way. Once instruments or voices are designed, a musical composition for each voice can be entered into the computer's memory by playing the keyboard like a piano. Tempo, note sequence and duration, and other important elements of music can be determined. During and after the composition process, music can be played back through the computer, and in some cases, through stereo speakers. Compositions can be stored on diskettes and can be retrieved at any time.

If the composer plays back a composition, and feels that its tempo is too fast, the tempo can be changed until satisfactory, and without having to reenter the composition. Some music synthesizer arrangements allow the composer to select backup rhythms to accompany the music.

Students in music composition classes attempting to write music for orchestras will find that microcomputers allow them to experiment and change musical arrangements in a way not possible before. It will not be necessary to play a piano and *imagine* what the music will sound like when played by an orchestra. Rather, the microcomputer can be used to simulate the true sounds of an orchestra. Eventually, low-cost music synthesizers may even allow musical arrangements to be printed in readable form for orchestra members, a great time-saver for school orchestra directors.

Music teachers interested in the benefits that such equipment may bring to their own lives and to the lives of their students may wish to contact the National Consortium for Computer Based Music Instruction (NCCBMI).* This organization publishes a quarterly journal and offers consultation for new users of computer-based music instruction.

---

*For information about the National Consortium for Computer Based Music Instruction (NCCBMI), write to Fred Hofstetter, Music Department, University of Delaware, Newark, Delaware 19711.

COMPUTERS AND ART

The use of the microcomputer as a tool in artistic endeavors promises to be an important part of the future. Advances in computer graphics capabilities have led to its use in many fields, from cartoon animation to engineering. Computer graphics may even be considered a brand-new art form bound to make spectacular advances during the next few years. Computer capabilities can free the artist from much of the drudgery of artistic production so that s/he can concentrate on creativity.

Computer-aided design (CAD) is a fast growing industry that has carried the design of automobile parts, circuit boards, tools, bridges, and homes to new heights of sophistication. The laborious sketching needed to produce a blueprint can be replaced by computer graphics capability; and what's more, details of the blueprint can be changed until they exactly meet the company's or customer's needs with no redrawing.

A student wishing to explore the field of computer art has quite a few options from which to choose. First, specialized computer commands through a computer language such as BASIC or Pascal can be used to create pictures and graphics designs. But this is rather difficult to learn, and it requires a lot of patience and superior programming techniques. A second option involves the purchase of special graphics software which eliminates the need for programming knowledge. By using the keyboard, designs can be drawn in many colors and with various sizes and textures of brush strokes. Other graphic software allows line designs only, but may still offer the use of color. Truly useful packages allow designs to be stored away on disk to be used in programs later, or to be printed on paper with special printers that can produce in color. There are programs that allow the user to create three-dimensional shapes, and to rotate them in space. Animation software allows figures to move across the computer screen, a capability that can add much interest to computer-assisted instruction programs.

Special hardware additions to a microcomputer can make artistic design an even simpler process. One can draw on a device called a *graphics tablet* with a magnetic pen, and the design drawn will appear on the video display screen. The artwork can be saved on a diskette and be used in computer programs. An additional feature of a graphics tablet is the ability to draw on the tablet to create a design, then *shrink* the design in order to produce very detailed work. Software may accompany the graphics tablet; this generally makes operation less confusing and provides more options.

Another kind of board uses a double-jointed arm resembling a small-scale drafter's pantograph. The user lightly moves the arm around in order to create artwork in whatever colors are desired. Extra features may include options for moving, rotating, shrinking, or ani-

Figure 4-6a
Graphics Created by Programming and Mathematical Equations

Figure 4-6b
Screen Displays of PAINT,
Created by the Capital Children's Museum

mating drawings. In some cases, the artist or graphics designer can change colors until the perfect combination is found.

We hope this section has given you some idea of the current state of microcomputer art. Businesses that make a living on drafting and design are now finding that to stay competitive they must use computers; otherwise they will not be able to meet the specifications requested by their customers, who desire the flexibility to change designs when necessary. Students who learn to use computer graphics capabilities will find a ready market for their skills. Teachers may wish to team with talented students to create interesting computer-assisted instruction. And there will certainly be those who wish to experiment with computers as a new mode of artistic expression. Who knows what the future will bring?

COMPUTER PROGRAMMING AND MATH-RELATED SUBJECTS

The microcomputer as a tool in mathematics and mathematically related topics in various subject areas has received much attention and is currently a common application of computing at the secondary level. Algorithms utilized to solve mathematical problems can be translated into computer language. The very process of translation encourages students to think through the steps involved in solving a problem. To take a simple example, let's translate a problem into the BASIC language:

Maria has a bookcase with 2 shelves.
Each shelf has 8 books.
If she orders 3 more books, how many books will she have in all?

```
10 Let S=2          (Number of shelves)
20 Let C=8          (Maria's original collection)
30 Let B=3          (books on order)
40 Let T = S*C + B
50 Print "Maria will have";T;"books when she receives the books she ordered."
99 End

RUN

Maria will have 19 books when she receives the books she orders.
```

The above problem is so simple that it seems like a very trivial job for a computer. But it does illustrate the way a computer program can be used to solve all kinds of problems, even those using larger numbers and involving more computations, all of which should be performed in a particular order. Careful attention to the sequence of an algorithm leads to greater understanding. In addition, the variables can be changed easily, and the results of that change can be witnessed immediately, allowing students to see mathematical relationships by solving many different problems with the same algorithm.

Mathematics and computer languages have always been compatible partners. Both rely heavily on the use of algorithms. Computer languages possess many special functions useful in mathematics, like SIN, COS, ABS (absolute value), MAT (Matrix algebra), LOG, and so on, which can be used effectively in solving higher-level mathematical problems. Proofs for geometry expressed in computer language can be self-checked, because the logical ability of computers is unsurpassed.

Another interesting area in computer math involves the use of computer graphics to teach mathematical ideas. Students write programs which demonstrate changes in variables for certain functions and their effect on the computer-generated designs.

Although past efforts have mostly been geared toward senior high, there is no reason why even elementary students cannot learn to solve simple story problems with computers. Concentration can rest on the procedure used to solve a problem rather than on the actual calculations required. Because a single program can be designed to accommodate many different kinds of problems, students will be encouraged to think about and solve a larger amount of problems than when only paper and pencil were available. The special computer language called Logo (see Chapter 5 for description) encourages students to use mathematics to create geometric shapes, pictures and animation; thus, children begin to view mathematics in such a way that both its usefulness and beauty are seen.

Gifted students will benefit more by mathematical thinking required by programming than by doing many long pages of division problems. Growing competence should naturally contribute to progress in higher mathematics once these students reach junior high and high school.

The postulates and identities are vividly demonstrated when programming problems in computer language, as is the idea of representing unknown quantities with symbols and using equations.

Math and science teachers interested in the idea of computer mathematics and mathematics CAI may wish to contact the Association for Computers in Mathematics and Science Teaching. The association publishes a quarterly journal which offers many valuable ideas and resources for this interesting aspect of computers in education.*

SUMMARY

The use of computers as valuable tools in our lives should not be a forgotten aspect of computer knowledge, but should share the stage

---

*For information on *The Journal of Computers in Math and Science Teaching,* write to P.O. Box 4455, Austin, Texas 78765.

with computer-assisted instruction and programming instruction when planning for a total computer-related curriculum in the schools. If students experience the computer in this function, they will graduate with a comfortable knowledge of the computer's ability to help them with the most tedious and time-consuming tasks they may encounter when at work or at home.

Teachers and other school personnel can lighten their administrative duties by the use of special software. Tests may be designed, then given to students through computer testing. Some systems even grade the tests and produce reports showing mastery of objectives or percentage of questions correct. The computer can be used as a classroom demonstration machine that can provide illustrations of ideas and relationships between variables. Worksheet and puzzle generation programs allow teachers to easily create interesting and timely learning materials, specially tailored to classroom needs. Software that may be helpful for reading teachers includes readability programs, cloze passage generation, and vocabulary placement programs. Grade books can be kept electronically rather than manually; grade averages can be calculated automatically and on any day of the year. Attendance-keeping software decreases the amount of teacher time spent on daily and quarterly reports and allows the school office to request reports on designated categories, which can contribute to smoother operation of many necessary tasks. Library circulation programs help media centers and even individual classrooms keep track of materials in circulation. The development, maintenance, and reporting of individual records can be simplified.

Word-processing programs can contribute much to the school setting. Teachers, administrators, and other school personnel can use word processing to produce letter-perfect copy in many writing duties, such as letters, manuscripts, and learning materials. Mailing lists, listings, labels, and so on may be made without laborious retyping. Students, too, will benefit by knowledge of word processing. Use of such software is becoming common in the business world; word-processing training can add to the quality of business education. Students can compose and edit writing assignments for all their classes. An English or journalism teacher can demonstrate the editing process vividly to students. Publications can be more easily produced.

On the elementary school level, children using simple word-processing programs will be encouraged to revise and edit their work. Because the final writing will be in typewritten form, newsletters and magazines can be compiled with much greater facility than was previously possible.

Statistical studies encourage students to look at facts and relationships in a more organized and logical way. Software currently available allows for more lengthy and complicated research into topics of interest than would be possible with manual methods. Graphs, tables, and other statistical displays can be easily generated.

The microcomputer may also be used as a laboratory instrument that can take many measurements per second, then automatically display readings and make calculations with the information read. This capability eliminates the tedium necessary to perform certain experiments, and it may even allow some activities to take place in the classroom which would otherwise be impossible or impractical.

Music can be composed and played by special music software and hardware systems, allowing students to simulate sounds of an orchestra and then to edit the tempo, notation, and instruments wherever desired. Graphics software and hardware allows drafting and design students to create blueprints, other design projects, and animation in a way not possible before the invention of computers. Beyond practical applications, computer art is indeed a new mode of artistic expression.

Finally, computer-programming techniques have always mixed very well with mathematical problem-solving situations. Algorithms can be translated into computer language and solved with lightning speed. A special computer language called Logo encourages even elementary school students to use mathematics in such a way that its relevancy and beauty are appreciated.

Quite a few possibilities have been described in this chapter, but with some imagination and further research, one can find other ways that computers may be used as a tool in an educational setting. Most importantly, students who become accustomed to the computer as an important tool in their lives may improve the very quality of their lives in the future.

REFERENCES

Bork, Alfred. *Learning with Computers*. Bedford, Mass.: Digital Equipment Corp., 1981.

Gula, Robert J. "Beyond the Typewriter." *Classroom Computer News* 2, no. 5 (May 1982): 31–33.

Judd, Dorothy. "Word Processing in the Classroom: Is it Really Practical?" *Educational Computing Magazine* 2, no. 3 (May 1982): 18–19.

Laramie, J. R. J. "A Useful Microcomputer Interface that Makes a Computer Cost-Effective." *School Science Review* (December 1980): 348–351.

Papert, Seymour. *Mindstorms: Children, Computers, and Powerful Ideas*. New York: Basic Books, 1980.

Tinker, Robert F. "Microcomputers in the Teaching Lab." *The Physics Teacher* (February 1981), 94–105.

SUGGESTED READINGS

Badiali, Bernard. "Micros Make Time for Readability." *Educational Computer* 2, no. 5 (September–October 1982): 26, 76.

Barth, Richard. "The Handicapped Educational Exchange." *Educational Computer* 2, no. 2 (March–April): 48–49.

Bell, Kathleen. "The Computer and the English Classroom." *English Journal* 69 (December 1980): 88–90.

Bradley, Virginia N. "Improving Students' Writing with Microcomputers." *Language Arts* 69, no. 7 (October 1982): 732–743.

Clark, Dennis. "Plotting N-Space Cubes." *Creative Computing* 8, no. 7 (July 1982): 148–161.

Davidson, Ned J. "Verse Weaving: A Challenge for All Ages." *Creative Computing* 8, no. 7 (July 1982): 166–172.

DiGiammarino, Frank. "Text Editing." *Classroom Computer News* 2, no. 2 (November–December 1981): 32–33.

Friedman, Batya. "Art and the Computer: A Computer Art Course." *Creative Computing* 8, no. 7 (July 1982): 97–99.

Hooper, George A. "Computerize Your IEPs." *Classroom Computer News* 2, no. 2 (November–December 1981): 34–37.

Kellisch, Frederick J. "Computer Graphics on a Shoestring." *Instructional Innovator* (September 1981): 19–21+.

Levine, Carl. "Electronic Information: An Introduction to What Lies Ahead." *Electronic Learning* 2, no. 1 (September 1982): 66–69.

Malsam, Margaret. "A Computer First for an Elementary School: Microcomputer Replaces Card Catalog." *Educational Computer* 1, no. 3 (September–October): 40–41.

Meuer, Leonard T. "Special Education Management System Using Microcomputers." *Educational Computer* 2, no. 3 (May–June 1982): 12–13.

Miller, Charlotte M. "Computer Graphics: An Art Medium in Lights." *Creative Computing* 8, no. 7 (July 1982): 86–90.

Peelings 3, no. 6 (July–August 1982). Entire issue devoted to the reviews of ten word processors for the Apple II.

Pogrow, Stanley. "Administrator's Notebook: Microcomputing Your Paperwork." *Electronic Learning* 2, no. 1 (September 1982): 54–59.

Price, Samuel T., and Larry M. Dillingham. "Using a Microcomputer to Manage Large Files of Instructional Pictures." *Twentieth Annual Association for Educational Data Systems Convention Proceedings*, 1982.

Saltinski, Ronald. "Microcomputers in Social Studies: An Innovative Technology for Instruction." *Educational Technology* 21, no. 1 (January 1981): 29–32.

Sell, Nancy J., and Thomas E. Van Koevering. "The Energy-Environment Simulator as a Classroom Aid." *Journal of Computers in Mathematics and Science Teaching* 1, no. 2 (Winter 1981): 20–22.

Smith, David A. "Using Computer Graphics to Teach Mathematics." *Journal of Computers in Mathematics and Science Teaching* 1, no. 4 (Summer 1982): 24–27.

Wiggins, Thomas. "Utilization of the Apple Microcomputer for the Generation of Matching-Type Examination Questions." *Educational Computer* 2, no. 4 (July–August 1982): 32–33.

5 Computer Languages for Microcomputers

INTRODUCTION

Microcomputer users who wish to learn how to program their computer systems must begin by learning a *computer language,* a language of symbols and commands that allows humans to interact with computers. The process of learning a computer language is similar to learning any foreign language; it requires study and practice.

There are several ways for the microcomputer user to learn programming languages. Many helpful and informative books have been published that help microcomputer users teach themselves to program in a computer language. These books and other teaching materials are available at computer retail stores as well as popular bookstores. Another way to learn a computer language is to study programs published in computer-related periodicals. Many users begin by modifying programs included in computer journals; by altering programs, they learn the fundamentals of the programming languages in which these programs are written. Those wishing to study programming languages in a more structured environment may choose to enroll in a course offered by a local university, technical school, or community college.

The first step in learning a computer language is deciding which language to study. Basically, computer languages fall into two general categories: *low-level languages* and *high-level languages. Low-level languages* allow the programmer to address the computer directly in a language that it can immediately understand. Low-level languages may also be referred to as *machine languages* or *assembly languages.* Although low-level languages were used for many years, programs written this way are long and tedious. On the other hand, *high-level languages* must be interpreted by the computer's CPU so that the computer can execute the instructions it is given. High-level languages allow the programmer to write instructions for many different machines. In addition, high-level languages are simpler to understand and easier to use than are low-level languages.

As computers have gained popularity, many high-level languages have been developed. Not all of these have survived, however. Among those languages that are widely used today are BASIC, Pascal, COBOL, FORTRAN, and other special-purpose languages such as Logo and Pilot that have been designed for use in an educational setting. Each of these languages possesses certain qualities that makes it more suitable for some applications than for others. The nature of the work that a computer will perform determines in large part which computer language is most appropriate.

BASIC

BASIC, or Beginners All Purpose Symbolic Instruction Code, was designed for use in teaching beginning programmers to write instructions for computers. Consequently, it is relatively simple and does not include some of the complex features of other languages. BASIC is especially popular with microcomputer users because it requires less space in the computer's memory than do other high-level languages.

BASIC is made up of approximately twenty commands that instruct the computer to perform various functions. In spite of its relatively simple structure, though, BASIC can be used to create surprisingly powerful programs.

There are two disadvantages of writing programs in BASIC. First, there are many kinds of compilers or interpreters that translate BASIC instructions into machine-readable code. Hence, a program written in BASIC for use on one computer may have to be rewritten before it can be used on another computer. Second, BASIC does not always contain the structures necessary to perform structured programming, a popular modern programming method.

PASCAL

Pascal is a computer language named in honor of Blaise Pascal, a seventeenth-century French mathematician whose work during the preindustrial era proved influential in computer technology. Pascal was developed in the 1960s and gained popularity as a beginning computer language because of its relatively simple structure. Many universities introduce computer science students to Pascal as a first language because it provides an excellent foundation for learning other more complex languages.

Programs written in Pascal, like those written in BASIC, are easy to understand, to use, and to debug. Like COBOL, Pascal includes different sections for dividing a program into segments, allowing for easier programming. The design of the Pascal language encourages structured programming techniques.

Pascal combines the simplicity of BASIC with the more powerful capabilities of COBOL. However, it is not suitable for highly sophisticated programming applications. It is useful for the beginning programmer who does not wish to perform complex scientific applications.

COBOL

COBOL, or Common Business-Oriented Language, was developed for use in commercial applications. As computers were accepted into the field of business, computer scientists recognized the need for a programming language that would take into consideration the unique requirements of business applications. COBOL was the result.

A major advantage of COBOL is that a program written in this language can be run on any computer system that supports COBOL. COBOL is also relatively easy to write and to understand. It is an excellent language to use for writing files, a major application of computer capability in a commercial setting.

COBOL does have several disadvantages, though. Many programmers consider COBOL inconvenient because instructions tend to be less concise than instructions written in some other languages. Also, COBOL requires a large amount of main computer storage. It does not lend itself easily to structured programming, which is becoming increasingly popular. In spite of these disadvantages, COBOL is used on from 70 to 90 percent of all mainframe applications.

FORTRAN

FORTRAN, or Formula Translation, was developed by IBM in the late 1950s for use in scientific and mathematical applications. The primary quality of FORTRAN is that it allows for easy writing of mathematical formulas. It has been used widely in scientific settings. Space technology, for example, has been greatly enhanced by the use of FORTRAN, which allows for fast and precise mathematical calculations.

Because of FORTRAN's complex nature, it is not a suitable first computer language for the beginning programmer. It is not particularly suited to business applications because it is inconvenient for writing files and handling alphabetic data and printed reports. Used for the specific applications for which it was designed, FORTRAN is an extremely expedient programming language.

LOGO

In addition to the widely used programming languages already discussed, a number of other special-purpose computer languages have been developed in recent years. Many of these languages have been designed for use in the educational setting. Logo is one such language that allows even young children to interact with computers without extensive training beforehand.

Logo was developed by a research group headed by Seymour Papert in the Artificial Intelligence Laboratories at the Massachusetts

Institute of Technology. Influenced by the educational theories of Jean Piaget, Papert set out to design an environment in which children could learn to program computers while studying mathematics. Papert holds that the computer is a vital tool in teaching mathematical concepts to children as young as three years of age.

Logo allows users to manipulate images on a video screen, or command actual computerized objects. Perhaps its greatest advantage is

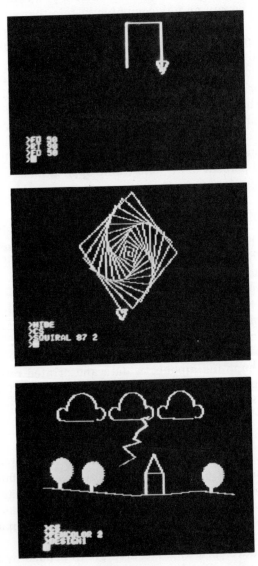

Figure 5-1
Logo Graphics

that it lays the foundation for the assimilation of increasingly complex computer languages while providing children with a positive and reinforcing early computer experience.

PILOT AND OTHER AUTHORING LANGUAGES AND SYSTEMS

Authoring languages and systems allow educators to *author* CAI in a simpler manner than would generally be possible when using a computer language such as BASIC. These packages are complete in themselves, and they require a less extensive knowledge of computer hardware and data handling than do traditional computer languages.

Two distinct categories exist: *authoring systems* and *authoring languages.*

No programming knowledge is needed to create CAI with authoring systems. The user answers a series of prompts that allow desired text and questions to be inserted. Possible correct and incorrect responses are then entered, so that when a lesson is run, the student's answers can be evaluated, and appropriate feedback presented. Each piece of CAI created by an authoring system follows a predesignated pattern; the framework of the authoring program limits the kind of screen displays that the student will eventually see when running the CAI. However, the simplicity of authoring systems allows teachers to quickly create CAI which employs textual displays, questioning, and feedback.

Some authoring systems allow only *textual* displays. Others provide means of creating diagrams, graphs, and pictures, an addition which can improve the quality of the CAI.

Authoring languages, on the other hand, provide more flexibility. The *user* creates the framework of the program by the use of program statements, in much the same way as when using BASIC and other programming languages. Though a variety of authoring languages exist, for the sake of detail, only Apple Pilot will be described here. (See Appendix C for a listing of other authoring systems and languages.)

Apple Pilot requires a 48K Apple II Plus Computer and two disk drives; no language card is necessary. After the CAI has been programmed, only one disk drive and the lesson diskette are needed to run the program. Apple Pilot possesses its own computer language, one designed to meet the special needs encountered when writing CAI. The operation of four editors must be mastered for full utilization of Pilot's capabilities.

All program statements are entered by means of the *Lesson Text Editor.* These statements serve to organize the lesson's textual, pictorial, and auditory elements. Most text or questions that will appear in the computer lesson will be entered through this editor. The performance of the lesson can be tested and "debugged" through a special testing procedure option within the lesson text editor. Correction of program statements will also be done through this editor.

A very short sample lesson segment follows:

*BEGIN	(Label for this part of lesson)
TH:What is your name?	(This will appear on student's screen when lesson is run.)
A:N	(Computer stores student name in memory.)
T:	(Blank line will appear when lesson is run.)
*QUES1	
T:What term describes the process by :which plants make their own food?	
M:photosynthesis, photosinthisis	(Acceptable responses to question)
T:	
TY:That's right.	(If student matches either answer above, this message will appear.)
TN1:Please try again.	(If student answers question inaccurately only once, this message will appear.)
W:5	(Pause of five seconds)
JN1:QUES1	(Lesson will return to original question.)
TN:PHOTOSYNTHESIS is the process :by which plants make their own food.	(After second unsuccessful attempt to answer question, this statement will appear.)

What is your name? JEFF

Now, Jeff, what term describes the process by which plants make their own food?
photosynthesis

That's correct.

If Jeff answers correctly (that is, his answer *matches* one of those words shown after the M: statement), the message "That's correct!" will appear. If he answers incorrectly, then another message will appear, such as "Please try again." A second incorrect response may cause a lesson segment to appear which introduces the term "photosynthesis."

The second editor, called the *Graphics Editor,* allows for the creation of pictures, maps, and other visual aids that may illustrate concepts the lesson is intended to develop. The author uses either certain keys on the computer keyboard, or game paddles in order to draw lines. Desired colors are chosen simply by using the number keys on the keyboard; each color has a special one-digit number code. Additional features include the ability to automatically draw boxes, frames, circles, ovals, and to fill in line drawings with color.

Special sets of characters, such as a larger alphabet or mathematical symbols, can be designed by entering the *Character Set Editor.* Pictures may also be created in this editor by coding certain designs and calling up those codes through the Lesson Text Editor.

A final editor allows composition of songs and sound effects, and then allows an author to store them in sound files on diskette. These files can be called up for auditory information and for reinforcement purposes during a student-run lesson.

Although Pilot was originally created for use by educator-authors, it has also been effectively used by students, who are attracted by the ability to create graphics and musical compositions to accompany their programming efforts.

Advantages of Pilot

Pilot does allow teachers with little knowledge of computer hardware to create CAI, complete with interesting visual and auditory elements. Busy teachers rarely have time to learn the complicated programming and computer operation techniques necessary to create full-fledged, effective CAI in languages like BASIC, Pascal, or machine code.

An *Animation Tools* package can be purchased that allows moving graphics to occur within a lesson, an interesting addition to many kinds of CAI. A more recent offering from Apple, *Super Pilot,* boasts some features that the original Apple Pilot lacks: animation, faster display of visual information, an already-designed set of larger alphabetic and numeric characters, and an optional record-keeping system for storing information about students' performance.

Versions of Pilot and other authoring languages are available for most microcomputers popular in schools today.

Disadvantages of Pilot

Once the operation of the editors of Pilot (or any authoring system or languages) has been mastered, there is still much to be learned and accomplished. The lesson may revert to only a series of questions and answers unless the author knows something about good instructional design and wise integration of graphics and sound. In the case of authoring languages, programming skill is needed. Creating any piece of good CAI requires much time and determination; many teachers may not be able to find the time and energy necessary. And although authoring languages may have many capabilities, those capabilities do have limitations. A plan for a certain screen display may be difficult or even impossible to produce through authoring languages.

Although authoring systems and languages can certainly meet some CAI needs and serve a useful purpose, limitations and requirements should be considered as well. If possible, those wishing to use the more complex authoring systems or languages should seek formal training of some type.

6 Choosing Appropriate Software

LOCATING SOFTWARE

This book has provided information about the kinds of software that may be considered for educational purposes, but where does one go to actually look at enough software to be able to choose that which is applicable to a particular situation, educationally sound, and easy to use? The first idea that comes to mind would be to visit local computer stores. However, most computer stores do not possess much variety in the way of educational software. This is not surprising because computer stores may rely on the business trade for most of their income, and therefore stock mostly business-oriented software. Still, if you are considering purchase of software, local computer stores would be a good starting point in the review process and will allow you to see some examples of computer-assisted instruction. Those interested in word-processing, art, or music software may find a ready stock of those items in stores as these products find a place in businesses and in homes. In addition, some software originally meant for entertainment or business purposes may serve a useful purpose in educational settings. For instance, most adventure games require that users read in order to solve a mystery; a creative teacher of reading could utilize a game of this type to interest students and to build reading comprehension skills.

In some parts of the country, computer stores that stress software over hardware are appearing. They carry many pieces of software, some of which are educational in nature, and provide several micro-computers so that customers can review software. *Computer clubs* have been organized which require annual membership fees, and in return allow members to review and use software owned by the club. Micro-computers housed in the club's headquarters allow software to be run on location, and staff members train members in proper use of the software. Again, depending upon the composition of the club member-ship, the amount of educationally oriented software may be limited.

The local university or college may possess a software library and microcomputers. You may be able to visit and to review those items in your area of interest. In addition, try to locate instructors and other knowledgeable persons in the field of educational computing. They may be valuable sources of information and can give advice that may make your software search less time-consuming and more productive.

In larger cities, and even in some rural settings, microcomputer user's groups have been organized. Members share programs, ideas, resources, and opinions. Be sure to find out which members share your interest in education. Try not to let excessive "computer talk" dampen your enthusiasm. Teachers and other school personnel need not know complicated computer engineering terms to use software wisely in a classroom setting. A limited knowledge of computer terms, however,

Figure 6-1a
Software Shelf in Store

Figure 6-1b
Customer Uses Stock Market Program at
Computer Time/Software Rental Business

will assist you in obtaining and understanding information. Usually, asking at the local computer store or calling a microcomputer manufacturer's home office will yield the location and contact person for the nearest user group.

Other ways to find and review software locally may be possible.

1. Attend educational computing conferences. Quality software may be demonstrated; you can obtain brochures and catalogs, and meet possible contact persons.

2. Take an educational computing class. One may be offered at a local college or university.

3. Contact the state Department of Education for information on software. In addition, you may be able to find out what kind of computers are in certain school districts. Then contact administrators and teachers in those districts to discuss your software needs. They may have very definite opinions and suggestions.

4. Contact microcomputer users in your own school district. If some groundwork has already been laid, why not make use of it?

5. Look for workshops stressing microcomputers in education.

6. There may be a computer-using educators' group in your area.

7. Contact software houses or representatives from educational publishing companies located near you. Usually they will be happy to demonstrate their offerings.

Contacting Software Houses

Numerous software houses exist that deal in educational software. In addition, several educational publishing and supply companies have begun to offer software for sale. Advertisements for software also appear in educational journals and magazines. But, as you might suspect, the advertisements do not always give a clue as to the *value* of the software described. Unfortunately, teachers have been known to purchase software without seeing it first, and then have been very disappointed in the product. In some cases, software houses do not have a return policy to the purchaser's benefit, and they may refuse to replace disks or tapes that do not run properly, or to refund money when the software appears to have little value.

A reasonable first step in deciding which software houses to contact would be to look at an educational software directory for the particular brand of microcomputer you will be using. If no microcomputer has been chosen, then, of course, you will have to locate directories for all brands under consideration. Sometimes computer stores will stock educational software directories. These books generally do not attempt to provide any kind of review information, but merely list prices, ordering instructions, and describe available software for specific purposes. A perusal of a directory can add a lot to your knowledge of software for a particular brand of microcomputer, though you still will have no way to judge quality. See Appendix A for software directories and review publications.

Once you have located some possibilities through the directories, you may wish to send away for catalogs and brochures from various companies.

You will find that several software houses and educational publishers do offer a thirty-day guarantee. This means that software can be purchased via purchase order, money order, check, or credit card; if the software does not meet your expectations, it can be returned for full credit.

If a school district wishes to conduct an organized search for software, it may sometimes be possible to request software review copies. Policies for different companies vary. Some organizations will not send software for review purposes. Others may consider it if they are assured that the software will not be "pirated," and a person with administrative status takes full responsibility for its safety and speedy return.

A word of caution: good software requires much hard work and monetary expenditure for development. Understandably, the creators of software do not wish their offerings to be copied because they will have everything to lose if their programs proliferate illegally. If software authors fail to make a profit for all their hard work, they will have to stop spending their time writing software. This would be a great loss to all of us, for the future of educational computing depends upon the continuing improvement of computer-assisted instruction and other useful software. Educators should emphasize their aversion to such unethical behavior.

Books and other print materials often cost less to buy from a bookstore than the costs that xeroxing would entail. Software, on the other hand, can be copied for only the price of a diskette or cassette tape and will resemble the original exactly. Most companies have *copy protected* their offerings, adding certain program statements which make unauthorized copying much more difficult. Particularly in educational settings, where chalkdust, student mischief, and other factors can contribute to appreciable loss of disks and tapes, the inability to easily make backup copies can be unnerving and costly. Some software houses try to deal with these difficulties by charging a small amount of money and replacing the unusable item with a good copy.

The whole question of electronic robbery has not yet been settled; many problems remain that seem almost unsolvable. In the meantime, we can protect ourselves and the rights of software houses by refusing to use unauthorized copies, and by providing security for software collections.

Obtaining Software Review Information

The search for appropriate software can be simplified when an effort is made to find out what others have said about quality and applicability. Repeated favorable reviews of a piece of software indicate that many users have found that software to be worth its price and find it educationally applicable and sound.

Where can these reviews be found?

First, magazines like *Electronic Learning, Educational Technology, Computing Teacher, Creative Computing, CUE Newsletter, Electronic Education, Classroom Computer News, Educational Computer, Infoworld, Instructor, Microcomputing,* and *The Apple Journal of Courseware Review* all provide reviews of educational software. You can find more information on these magazines in Appendix A.

As a productive starting point, you may wish to subscribe to *The Digest of Software Reviews: Education,* c/o School & Home Course-Ware, Inc., 1341 Bulldog Lane, Suite C, Fresno, California 93710. This publication abstracts reviews found in magazines and journals so that for any one piece of software, up to ten different opinions are represented. For those educators who have little or no access to magazine collections, this publication will provide a lot of information which might be unobtainable any other way.

Second, correspondence with organizations specializing in software review can help in the search process. Again, you may refer to Appendix A for addresses and other details. A project called Microsift has been funded by the federal government to review software and to disseminate findings. Microsift publishes a newletter which can keep educators up to date on project activities. Courseware reviews will be published by several sources, including RICE (Resources in Computer Education), an informational service which can be accessed through library computer services or through a microcomputer.*

Third, contact with universities or colleges may yield some useful information on particular pieces of software.

Fourth, a growing trend for computer centers in some areas is to hire sales representatives or consultants with educational backgrounds. Naturally, these people will have a special interest in educational software for the brand of microcomputer they are selling, and they will also realize that knowledge and demonstration of good software possibilities makes their brand more attractive to schools.

---

*For information about RICE, write or call RICE—Northwest Regional Educational Laboratory, 300 SW Sixth Avenue, Portland, Oregon 97204, (503) 248-6800.

Free and Inexpensive Software

It is possible to obtain free, public domain, software from several sources. Be on the lookout for news of completion of funded projects, and should the software meet your needs, contact project directors for information on how to obtain copies.

An organization called Computer-Using Educators (CUE) in conjunction with the San Mateo County Office of Education in California has organized a public domain software collection, under the name "Softswap." Diskettes for each of the most commonly used microcomputers in schools are available. The only cost to you would be the price of the diskettes used to carry the programs back to your school district. You can make as many copies of the diskettes as you wish, as long as the copies are not sold for profit. "Softswap" also offers these diskettes by mail order, at a minimal cost.

Educational computing magazines will frequently publish leads on the acquisition of free or inexpensive software. Teachers and administrators seriously interested in building their school's software collections would be wise to subscribe to magazines and to follow up promising leads. Remember, though, programs available through public domain may have uneven quality and can not be counted on to adequately provide for the total software needs of a school.

EVALUATING SOFTWARE

When reviewing and evaluating software, it will be necessary to keep some kind of permanent records that organize information for later referral. In some cases, evaluation of software will be informal and require less written information. When an entire school, committee, or school district approaches the task of software selection, a more formal mode of record keeping will be appropriate.

At present, software written for one particular brand of microcomputer will not run on other brands of microcomputers. Thus, educators who have access only to one brand of computer usually must limit their investigation to software written for that particular brand. If the school has not yet chosen which microcomputers will be purchased, an assessment of desired applications should be made; then a thorough search must be conducted for the system which best suits those needs. Software and hardware can not be considered separately. A beautifully designed microcomputer system available at low cost may be almost useless unless a reasonable variety of software has been written specifically for that system. Experts agree that software should be considered first; at that point evaluation of hardware should begin.

It is also true that certain software meant for a particular microcomputer can not be used unless that machine has a certain amount of *memory capacity*. Many educational and administrative packages require memory of 48K or greater. Thus, it becomes necessary to choose software that can run on the memory configuration available on the school's computers. Memory capacity can be upgraded on most microcomputers; if it soon becomes apparent that the 16K capacities of a school's hardware possessions severely limits the variety of software available, it may be advisable to consider the purchase of additional memory.

Sometimes a microcomputer possesses color display capabilities. If a school owns computers with color capabilities, but has only black and white monitors for visual display, extra attention must be paid in the selection of software. If color is a requirement for proper use of the software, than that software will not be appropriate for use with black and white monitors.

Similarly, software written for computers possessing certain hardware additions can not be chosen for systems without those additions. For instance, some software requires the presence of a printer, a card reader, disk drive, cassette recorder, or speech synthesizer.

The foregoing illustrates the critical importance of finding and recording information about the software's memory and hardware requirements. Even when hardware choices have not yet been made by a school district, knowledge of these requirements can help to realistically evaluate the total cost for purchase of a flexible microcomputer system which can truly meet the needs of a school.

Reviewing software is definitely a subjective process, one that can be compared to reviewing books, magazines, or films. Each person has his or her own personal likes and dislikes which will flavor perception and result in disagreements between those involved in choosing software. It is quite possible that one teacher will rave over a particular

Figure 6-2
Teachers Reviewing Software

piece of software, and another teacher will disapprove of its methodology or format. For instance, there is a computer drill and practice program that involves a slot machine effect. Some people find the program motivating and productive; others totally disapprove of any software that smacks of gambling, even though no actual monetary betting takes place.

Similarly, teacher and student opinions can vary widely. Though a teacher may find a particular program to be educationally sound and relevant for classroom purposes, some students may be totally unmotivated and unimpressed when using the program. So, ideally, some effort should be made to have students "test drive" software under serious consideration.

It is helpful to identify software by a specific label, that is, drill and practice, tutorial, simulation, problem solving, demonstration, and so on. When the expected applications require a certain type of program, then the label becomes extremely important when making decisions.

Not all software can or should be evaluated by the same set of criteria. A simple vocabulary drill program can not be judged by the same criteria as a computer simulation, for instance.

When a school expects to keep careful software evaluation records, it is important that a software review sheet be utilized so that records are consistent and easily compared. Simplicity can be a plus as it will encourage teachers and other persons involved in review to completely record information. Different types of review sheets can be designed, according to the situation. An in-service software review session for teachers may require a shorter review form than the form an official software selection committee may need. In view of the variety of software review form needs, several kinds are included in this chapter. Even so, a school district may need to tailor a form in order to adequately represent criteria for its unique needs.

First a series of four software review forms will be presented for the areas of drill and practice, tutorial, simulation, and word processing. They are formal in nature and would only be used in some situations. Each characteristic mentioned in these checklist forms will be described.

A written evaluation type of form and a short one-page checklist appear at the end of this chapter, along with suggestions for their use.

Software Review Forms, Full Checklist

PROCEDURE: Because various types of software for educational applications require unique sets of criteria, forms reflecting that need will be presented in this chapter. Refer to pages 140–143 as you read the following explanation of form usage.

Each criteria should be given a **weight** according to its relative importance. The weight factor can range from 0 to 5, though you can select to use a greater range of values. If selecting a weight factor of 0 for a certain criteria statement, you indicate that the criteria has *no* importance for your purposes. (Even if that criteria has the top rating of 5, for example, when it is multiplied by the weight factor of zero, the total point value for that statement will be 5 × 0, or zero.) A weight factor of 1 indicates that the criteria has only a small amount of value, and a weight factor of 5 would show that the criteria has a large amount of value for your purposes.

It is usually best to decide on weight factors first, then decide on rating values without reference to the value of the weight factors. In certain situations, teacher reviewers may be given checksheets that do not contain information on the weight factor values which have previously been determined by the software selection committee.

Rating values range from 0 to 5. A rating of zero indicates that the criteria is not at all applicable to the particular piece of software being reviewed. A 1 indicates low satisfaction of the criteria. And of course, a 5 represents the top rating value possible.

After all the ratings have been done, the rating factors are multiplied against the weight factors to determine a total score for each criteria under consideration. The total score for the whole checksheet can be ascertained. That score can be divided by the total points possible (sum all the weight factors and multiply by 5) in order to find a percent rating for that particular piece of software—like 79 percent, 95 percent, and so on. If several teachers review the same piece of software the scores can be compared or averaged.

Notice that several blanks are included in each section of characteristics. This allows educators to tailor the reviews by adding criteria statements not already included in the checksheet.

The following checklist type of software evaluation forms would normally be used only for formal, thorough selection procedures, when specific criteria must be evaluated, and will not be applicable for more informal review sessions. Novice reviewers, however, may benefit by being trained in the checklist method. In this way, certain criteria can be highlighted and understood. Then later on, these reviewers will be more able to intelligently complete review sheets which have no checklists and require written evaluations.

These evaluation sheets can also be used without determining point values. The headings "Rating," "Weight," and "Total" can be changed to "Excellent," "Satisfactory," "Poor," and "Not Applicable."

An identifying information section heads each evaluation form. The type of microcomputer, memory capacity needed for the running of software, storage medium, and other details can be entered quickly.

Then space is provided for a brief description of the program under evaluation.

Possible criteria relevant in the review process have been grouped under four main headings:

- Characteristics: Program Operation and Documentation
- Characteristics: Student Use
- Characteristics: Instructor Use
- Characteristics: Content

The last page of the form allows a summary of the evaluation to be briefly stated, and a percent rating determined. Reviewers can indicate their personal recommendations for purchase or nonpurchase of software under evaluation, as well as any other comments they feel should be included in the review.

Immediately before the statement that asks for the reviewer's final recommendation, you will see a request to describe the BACKUP POLICY. Usually you can find this information by reading documentation accompanying the software. Sometimes the software house does not make its policy clear. If this is so, then it is highly recommended that this information be ascertained before purchase of software. What are acceptable backup policies? It is hard to make perfect generalizations about this matter, and "acceptable" can vary according to expense of the software and the proposed users. You may wish to think about these common policies.

1. **Software comes with a master disk and a backup disk included in the original package.** This is usually acceptable. An even better arrangement for the consumer would be the possibility of sending the master disk *or* the backup disk back to the software house for replacement. Don't expect this to happen for free, though. You will usually be charged $10 or more to replace a disk.

2. **Software comes only with one disk (no backup).** In these cases, you must ask yourself: will I be able to do without the disk long enough for it to be replaced by the software house? Again, expect to pay a replacement fee.

3. **Software comes with only one disk (no backup).** However, a card inserted in the regular package allows you to "register" as an owner, and sometimes also results in a backup disk being sent to you. Usually an acceptable arrangement, since your registration allows you to ask for replacements. Check details carefully. And don't forget to send in the registration card.

4. **One disk, *no* replacement policy.** In most cases it is impractical to purchase software when only one disk is sent, and the policy is to reject all requests for replacement. If the software cost $50, and after only a few weeks of use, it becomes inoperable, then of course the situation is frustrating and wasteful. A possible exception to this rule would be in the case of software that is very inexpensive, that is, $20 or less.

5. **Software is not copy protected.** Usually the software house's policy will allow you to make your own backup copies, though not an unlimited amount. Check documentation for more information regarding this policy. This, of course, is excellent for the consumer since he or she can make backup copies as needed, and will not ever have to replace the software. However, this kind of arrangement necessitates that whoever receives the disk must immediately make a backup disk and store it in a safe place.*

The Identifying Information, Brief Description of Program, and Characteristics: Program Operation and Documentation sections are similar for the drill and practice, tutorial, and simulation forms, and will be described for all forms below. The word-processing review form is unique and will therefore be described separately.

The sections "Characteristics: Student Use," "Characteristics: Instructor Use," and "Characteristics: Content" vary according to the type of software; terminology and reviewing procedure will be described for each one in the descriptions accompanying each software review form.

Identifying Information Sections

Subject Area: What general subject area? Reading? Spelling? Science?

Microcomputer: Identify the brand and model of microcomputer for which the software has been written. If hardware has not yet been chosen for a district, you may wish to indicate if the particular piece of software under consideration is available for more than one brand of microcomputer.

Topic(s): What topics in the general subject area are covered? Sometimes only one topic has been included. Frequently, more than one topic is covered; if so, these should be clearly indicated. In the

---

*We have used the term "disk" in this discussion, but cassette tapes and even ROM cartridges may need some backup arrangement.

general subject area of mathematics, for instance, one piece of software may include the topics of place value, addition, and subtraction.

Requires___K of Memory: A microcomputer must possess a certain amount of memory in order to run a particular piece of software. Required memory should be indicated in the documentation accompanying the software, or on the diskette or tape. If a school's computers have only 16K of memory, it may be the case that many pieces of software under consideration *will not run* on those computers.

Grade Level (estimate):   Documentation accompanying software usually indicates what grade levels will benefit from its use. However, teachers may not always agree with the manufacturer's estimate. Therefore, it is suggested that reviewers indicate their own personal estimations of appropriate grade level use.

Program Name, Author, Publisher, Copyright Date, Publisher Address: This may be important information if it is decided that the software should be purchased. If the manufacturer has *coded* the offerings, the code should be indicated as well, for ordering purposes.

Storage Medium: Indicate by a check mark what form of storage has been utilized—tape cassette, cartridge, or diskette. You may wish to circle and check the kind of storage you have reviewed, and check the other storage forms that are available for purchase from the company.

Storage Medium: Tape Cassette ___√___ Cartridge _____ Diskette __(√)__

Type of Package: Sometimes only one diskette or tape represents the entire package, but other times a courseware package will include several diskettes or tapes. This should be indicated clearly.

Price: This piece of information is not only needed for ordering purposes, but also for final evaluation of a particular piece of software's worth. One drill and practice program may be superior to another, but if its price is ten times as much, its worth should be judged in light of that fact. Similarly, a tutorial costing $11.95 may have some shortcomings, but may still be a good possibility for purchase in light of its reasonable price.

Reviewer's Name: The educator reviewing the software indicates his or her name in this blank.

Application(s) Under Consideration: If the software is being reviewed for one or more particular classroom purposes, this can be clearly indicated.

Additional Hardware Required: Sometimes a piece of software requires extra hardware or hardware modifications. For instance, a printer or speech synthesizer may be needed for proper utilization of the software. In some cases, a special chip or memory board may be required.

Additional Software Required: Occasionally a piece of software cannot be run unless you also purchase a special program which allows its use.

Possible Grouping Arrangements: Using the software instruction documentation, and your creativity and classroom experience, indicate what ways the software might be used in a classroom setting. To illustrate, some simulation software requires that small group arrangements be utilized.

Special Format: This information will vary greatly according to what type of software is under review. For instance, a tutorial program may include drill and practice segments, game sequences, a management system, and/or tests. (Special format options will be described for each form presented.)

Brief Description of Program

Evaluators will describe software briefly, so that others can quickly assimilate the most important design and content elements of the software.

Characteristics: Program Operation and Documentation

These characteristics describe the actual operation of the software, and allow reviewers to indicate opinions of the documentation accompanying the package. The characteristics included on the drill and practice, tutorial, and simulation forms are identical:

1. Allows user to correct typing errors. When a student or teacher uses the software package, can mistakes be corrected? It can be frustrating when programs do not allow this. You can check this criteria by typing in answers, then using the back arrow key or delete key to see if errors can be erased, allowing users to input the answers exactly as wished.

2. Documentation available and clearly written. Though software under review may use the same microcomputer, each one may be *operated* in a different manner. Why? It is entirely up to the person creating the software as to how answers will be indicated, how programs can be accessed, and so on. Unless very clear instructions are included in the package, teachers and students will find that operation of the package may require much too much guesswork.

3. Clear, nicely formatted screen displays. A computer should not be used merely as an electronic textbook or workbook. When viewing the computer's video display screen, students should not be subjected to large passages of glaring text. The format of the display should make the reading of the information presented as pleasant as possible. Graphics, sound, underlining, double spacing, pointing arrows, larger printing, color, boldface, and a reasonable amount of flashing words or numbers can help students *attend* to the task desired. On the other hand, overuse or misuse of such capabilities can be distracting and cause unnecessary eyestrain. Other questions to be considered: do textual statements merely flash on the screen, or do they appear in a manner that contributes to readability? Has some attention been paid to the position of graphics and textual elements on the screen? Is it necessary to scan each screen display to find what must be read or answered next? Is there a screen-by-screen display, or does text roll along (scroll) in an irritating manner?

4. Incorrect selection of commands or keys does not cause program to abort. Poorly designed software may allow improper key selection to cause the program to stop in midstream. For instance, if a question requires a YES or NO answer, and the user answers with another word, number, inadvertent keystroke, or enters nothing, does the software answer with a beep, message, or refusal to accept the answer? Or is the program stopped in its tracks, with some esoteric error message printed on the screen? This event frustrates the user, and generally requires that the lesson be started all over again.

5. Menus and other features make the program "user friendly." The best software allows the user to proceed through a carefully constructed sequence of events with a controlled vocabulary. If reference to documentation must be constantly made to operate the program, then teachers and students using the program will find its operation much harder to master. Depending upon the design of the software under consideration, *menus* may be an important feature contributing to "user friendliness." Just as one can select a food item from a restaurant menu, various options concerning a lesson may be selected from menus displayed on the computer screen. Both the level of simplicity and the method used to *select* options desired determine the user friendliness of menu construction.

6. *Instructions can be skipped if already known.* It is often the case that a program or lesson within a program will be used more than once. Although the presentation of special instructions may be vital for first-time users, second-time users may find it unnecessary to read instructions again. Good software allows users to indicate their preference in this regard.

7. *Uses correct grammar, punctuation, and spelling.* Believe it or not, some software sold does not follow proper grammatical rules in its textual statements and may contain a number of spelling or punctuation errors. Although some errors of this nature can be ignored in certain situations, there are some cases where even one bad error would cause educators to recommend that the software not be used with their students.

8. *Clear and useful summary of program operation provided.* A short summary of operation may be included in either the program itself or in the accompanying documentation, or both. Some elements that may be discussed are how to load the program, answer questions, delete mistakes, select from menus, and "quit" the program, among others. Inclusion of such a summary may be vital for easy use of the software for teachers and students. If a summary is not provided, then one may be forced to wade through pages of documentation, hoping to locate the most vital information.

9. *Loading instructions clear: program easy to load.* Software documentation should include instructions on how to load the program into the computer's memory from the appropriate storage medium, that is, cassette tape, disk, or cartridge. Some programs are "turn key," that is, once the program is loaded, the title of the program will appear and the user need not do anything but view instructions, and perhaps, choose from menus. Other software, once loaded, will present a nearly blank screen to users, with no instructions provided as to what must be done next. Sometimes, even the documentation will fail to tell what should be typed in next! If software is not of the "turn key" variety, then at the very least, the documentation's instructions for operation should *clearly state* the necessary procedure.

10. *Bug-free: program runs properly.* Part of this was discussed in number 4; that is, improper keyboarding should not cause the program to drop off to nowhere land. However, "bugs" can also be mistakes in the programming logic or program statements themselves. Even one stubborn bug can ruin an otherwise excellent program. For instance, if

a student answers incorrectly for a third time for a particular question, and an "error message" appears indicating that there was some mistake in the program, this means that the lesson comes to a halt, and there will be nothing to do but to start the lesson all over again. One or more problems of this type can make a piece of software almost useless. Software manufacturers distributing such software usually will be quite interested to hear of any bugs found by users, so that errors can be corrected in all software sold in the future.

11. Uses computer capabilities well. An important question must always be asked about educational software: does this software achieve a level of sophistication that a text or workbook could not? Are the special abilities of the computer used wisely and for benefit of the user? Is too much computer time wasted while students sit and figure answers on paper? Does the program provide learning experiences that could not be achieved in any other way? As one reviews a variety of software, it will be seen that calculators or worksheets with answer keys could easily substitute for some software. An effort should be made to find those examples of educational software that add a new dimension to the learning process.

12. Accepts abbreviations for common responses (i.e., Y for YES). Obviously, not all users will be familiar with the keyboard, or possess touch-typing skills. Time and effort can be saved by allowing users to abbreviate responses that may be required often. Also, the addition of an extra space or punctuation mark in the response should not cause the program to ask the user to retype the response.

13. Operation of program does not require user to turn computer on and off. Unfortunately, some poorly designed programs cause users to be "backed into corners" with no way to escape, or continue! The only way to proceed may be to remove the disk, turn the computer off, and then reload the same program disk (or cassette) again. This is not a laudable feature.

14. Readability of text appropriate for intended user. Although a topic may be appropriate for a particular grade level, the text may require a higher degree of reading ability than is common on the grade level. This criteria should be judged according to the reading abilities of the intended users. For example, addition may be an appropriate topic for first graders, but if the explanations are written on a fourth-grade level, then the children will not be able to operate the program without teacher intervention.

15. and 16. Other criteria. The software evaluation committee or individual reviewers may feel that other, specific criteria should be included. Spaces 15 and 16 allow for easy addition of these criteria.

HOW TO EVALUATE DRILL AND PRACTICE SOFTWARE

For description of the Identifying Information section, Brief Description of Program, and Characteristics: Program Operation and Documentation, see pages 127–132.

Identifying Information, Special Format

Some drill and practice programs make heavy use of game format. This approach to learning can contribute to more interesting practice with greater student involvement. The inclusion of a student management system may be desirable for some purposes because this system may allow teachers or computerized testing segments to designate skill areas a particular student should practice, and it will allow for the recording and reporting of performance information about each student.

Another special format involves inclusion of "tutorial helps." Although the program may be primarily drill and practice in nature, repeated difficulties with particular kinds of problems may serve to call up tutorial segments that attempt to explain concepts or algorithms.

Characteristics: Student Use

These characteristics focus on the software's strengths and weaknesses concerning student use. Particular attention should be paid to how these criteria are weighted. For instance, the criteria "Student control over selection of lesson" may have little weight for a teacher who wishes to completely control student drill and practice assignments.

1. Requires no computer knowledge. It is usually the case that software will be of more value if students can load and operate without teacher intervention, and without lengthy training sessions. The language within a program should be carefully controlled, with little or no use of phrases like "boot the disk," and so forth.

2. Does not require student reference to manuals. Although there may be situations when student reference to manuals would be reasonable, or even contribute to learning, for the most part a program is of more value when all instructions appear on the screen and are easily understandable to the students. One exception to this might be when students are provided with workbooks and are asked to refer to certain pages containing diagrams, maps, pictures, or stories.

3. High student involvement. Includes all the elements that make a drill and practice session interesting for a student and not merely a series of boring questions. High student involvement may mean that the student can compete against his or her own scores or against the scores of other students. Sometimes more than one student can play at the same time. Practice may be enhanced by involvement in stories, or by the addition of graphics. A good drill and practice program encourages a student to run the program over and over again until skills have been learned.

4. Provides student with summary of performance. After a drill and practice session ends, students should be provided with information about their performance, either in percent, tabular, or ratio form. This can contribute to student motivation, and it also may provide a means by which records can be kept when no computerized management system exists.

5. Shows no racial, sexual discrimination, and so forth. Software materials, as well as all classroom learning materials, should not demonstrate bias of any type.

6. Effective feedback for correct responses. Positive reinforcement should motivate students and should never be condescending in manner. Use of a student's name in feedback can be attractive, if not overused. Sometimes the repetition of the correct answer in the feedback can serve to imprint correct responses in the student's mind. In addition, the use of nonverbal feedback can be very effective, that is, sound effects, graphics displays, winning points, and so on.

7. Effective feedback for incorrect responses. Negative feedback should contribute to the learning process and should not hurt students' feelings. Remarks like "Don't be foolish, try again" have no place in lessons, and may even cause student refusal to use the program again. In some situations, it is good for feedback to include tutorial helps, or to refer a student to his or her teacher. An inobtrusive beep, or a simple message of "Incorrect. Please try once more," may be adequate feedback. Clearly, this requires subjective evaluation on the reviewer's part, but usually it soon becomes apparent which programs are most effective in this regard.

8. Positive reinforcement more attractive than negative reinforcement. For best results in learning, the reinforcement given for correct responses should be more attractive than that given for incorrect responses. Otherwise, students will purposely answer incorrectly, hoping to see an attractive display they would not see for correct responses. For example, when correct answers are treated only to the feedback "Very good," and incorrect answers show an interesting hairy monster, students will probably answer incorrectly so they can see another monster.

9. Encourages cooperation. Some programs encourage cooperation between students in order to solve the presented problems. This can add to motivation and social interaction. This, however, may have little weight for situations when it is desirable for only one student to use the program at a time, or when a management system records performance data.

10. Student control over rate of presentation. The student should be allowed to read information at his or her own reading rate. Nothing is more frustrating than when necessary text disappears before it has been assimilated by the student. This problem is commonly solved by the use of messages like "Press the space bar to continue." Another feature concerning rate allows students to choose the timing of problem presentation. For instance, it may be valuable to let students select how fast math facts are presented. This way, students with less mathematical ability can compete with those possessing greater ability, and the software has an increased range of applicability. As competence increases, students can also choose to increase rate of presentation, thus adding practice for greater automaticity. It should be mentioned, however, that in some cases teachers would prefer to control presentation rate themselves and not leave selection up to the student.

11. Student control over sequence of lesson. At times, it is desirable that the students choose particular drill and practice exercises within a lesson, according to their individual needs.

12. Student control over selection of lesson. If a menu is provided, students can choose which lesson to do during a practice session. Users may feel more comfortable when they have some input into what kind of problems will be presented than when they are totally controlled by the program. If there is no management system included, ability to select lessons will add to greater flexibility and easier integration into the curriculum.

13. Student can select to go back and review previous frames of information. This is a useful feature in certain situations. For example, if after trying to answer a question, the student decides that he or she did not understand the instructions, it will be useful to go back to the previous screen display to review the instructions.

14. Student can select various styles of presentation. Because students may prefer varying modes and styles of presentation according to their own individual learning styles, the ability to select different ways of practicing skills and concepts can be a plus. To illustrate, in a spelling program some students may prefer to practice spelling by unscrambling words. Others may have an aversion to such exercises, but do enjoy identifying words by the context of a sentence. Still others may much prefer to practice words by using a game–like practice exercise.

15. and 16. Other criteria. These blanks allow educators to add criteria they feel should be considered in the software evaluation procedure.

Characteristics: Instructor Use

These criteria will focus on the needs of the instructor. Almost any piece of software will be more valuable when certain elements make life easier for the instructor, and allow the software to be used in varying situations.

1. Instructional objectives clearly stated. Objectives should be stated in the software or accompanying teacher materials. This will help teachers to plan the most effective use of software.

2. Easily integrated into curriculum. This is a general statement which may be evaluated by looking at the entire software package and judging whether it will be of substantial value as related to the curriculum. Accompanying student and teacher materials may help integration. Also, consider whether the topic or topics presented truly fit into lesson plans, or are really trivial in nature.

3. Teacher can change rates and difficulty of material. This option can be very important because students with varying degrees of talent will be able to use the same software.

4. Ability to change lists, that is, vocabulary, spelling, and so forth. When evaluating software one must consider its range of usefulness in the classroom. A program with a limited spelling list will cease to be useful when most students have learned the included words. Thus, the ability to change spelling lists, vocabulary lists, types of math problems, and so on can help to make a piece of software valuable throughout the whole year, not just for a few weeks.

5. Random generation of problems contributes to usefulness of program. If questions are presented in a preplanned sequence, students may begin to answer questions correctly because of their *order,* not because the skill or fact has really been learned. If questions are selected randomly, order will give no clue to the answer.

6. No need for instructor to assist users. A good drill and practice program should be planned well enough and written clearly enough that students do not need to ask for help from the instructor. There may be many instances where the instructor's time must be spent with a group of students; constant disturbance from computer-using students can be detrimental to learning. Also, if computers are housed in the media center or a computer room, the student may not be near his or her own instructor.

7. Useful teacher manual and/or accompanying materials provided. Some software comes with no extra materials for the instructor. Teacher guides and integrated learning materials (textual, filmstrip, workbook, and so forth) can greatly add to the value of the software and can provide many creative ideas for classroom integration. Software with accompanying teaching materials is often referred to as *courseware*.

8. Suggested lesson plans. The teacher's manual may suggest plans for lessons which use the software for drill and practice purposes. When rating this characteristic, judge the quality of the lesson plans, as well as the fact that they have been included in the software package.

9. Suggested grouping arrangements. Advice of this type may add to the usefulness of the software and allow more students to benefit than would otherwise be possible.

10. Useful student workbook provided. The inclusion of special student workbooks may contribute to the value of software and may also allow for more individualized learning. Reference to pictures and other material in workbooks may help to increase student understanding. In addition, if students can complete questions in workbooks and then enter answers into a computer program, computer time will be saved, and more students will be able to benefit from the use of software.

11. Useful blackline/ditto masters provided. Again, this feature can contribute to easier integration of software into curriculum, and it can maximize the usefulness of computer drill and practice.

12. Interesting follow-up activities and/or projects suggested. Although these criteria are not applicable to some drill and practice software, the existence of such suggested activities in accompanying teacher manuals can help teachers plan for student application of knowledge.

13. Management system easy to use and flexible. Of course, if the drill and practice program contains no management system, and management is not desired by instructors considering use of the software, then this criterion should have a weight of zero. Should it be of significance, evaluators should attempt to figure out the organization and operation of the management system, and then judge its simplicity and capabilities. Try adding students, deleting students, assigning lessons (in some cases), and viewing reports of performance. Does the management system help instructors to assign appropriate exercises for particular students, or to pretest students so that they can be placed in lessons for which they truly have need?

14. Provides whole class summaries of performance. Are reports provided that help the instructor plan for skill teaching for individuals and small groups? How much might these summaries help the instructor when evaluating student performance? Again, this has meaning only when a management system is included.

15. Other educational materials suggested or provided. Materials may be provided with the package, permitting additional experiences not available through the computer, and sometimes allowing experiences with concrete objects. Also, it may be helpful to the instructor when the teacher's manual suggests other textual, pictorial, or concrete materials that may add to the total learning experience.

16. Software does not require intermittent operation of disk drive or cassette recorder. A drill and practice program which can be loaded and used without need to operate a disk drive or cassette recorder during a lesson will allow instructors to load the same program into two or more microcomputers present in the classroom. Thus more than one student station can use the program at the same time. (Note: Check with software house to ascertain the legality of this arrangement.)

17. and 18. Other criteria. Spaces for additional criteria important for selection.

Characteristics: Content

1. Follows sound educational techniques. Does the program use techniques of which you personally approve? In mathematics, this may mean that the problem format meets your satisfaction, and that any tutorial segments have used proper algorithms that match your teaching methods. You may also disapprove of a particular format for answering questions, or the method students must use to respond.

2. Follows sound educational theory. This measures the software as a whole, taking in the elements beyond technique only. Are students expected to make impossible mental leaps? Is some effort made to go from concrete examples to the more abstract? Are facts organized in such a way that students can form a schema for better understanding and retention?

3. Accurate content. Obviously, the content of the program should be totally accurate, or else the students will learn incorrect information or skills.

4. Amount of learning justifies time spent by users. Is the content trivial, or of a more essential nature? Do students spend huge amounts of time on the program with little gain in useful skills?

5. Appropriate use of color. Sometimes use of color can greatly add to the effectiveness and attractiveness of drill and practice software. But at other times switching from one color to another, or using unrealistic colors can actually be detrimental.

6. Appropriate use of graphics and/or animation. As with color, software can be enhanced by the use of pictures, maps, diagrams, or moving figures. Animated displays for positive reinforcement purposes can be especially attractive and add extra student motivation. If graphic displays interfere with student task concentration, reinforce the wrong behaviors, or slow down the program too much, then they are considered to be inappropriately used.

7. Appropriate use of sound. Little beeps and musical selections can add to student interest, and they can be a good way to tactfully indicate when answers are correct or incorrect. On the other hand, overuse of sound can interfere with concentration, or even with the class as a whole. A loud rendition of "For He's a Jolly Good Fellow" can be disturbing when the rest of the class is involved in quiet activities. Particularly well-designed software will allow a student or teacher to choose whether sound will be used or not.

8. Accomplishes stated objectives. Does the student truly accomplish the stated learning objectives? Does the exercise depend far more on coordination, typing skill, and luck than on the actual skill to be learned? Will the student be able to apply what has been learned to subsequent tasks?

9. Sequence of lesson and instructions logical and clear. Does the sequence of the lesson make sense? Can instructions be understood by the average student? Does one statement follow logically from preceding statements?

10. and 11. Other criteria. These are spaces to add any additional criteria desired when evaluating software.

Drill and Practice Software Evaluation

Subject Area _____ Microcomputer _____

Topic(s) _____

Requires ____ K of memory   Grade Level (estimate) _____

Program Name _____ Author _____

Publisher _____ Copyright Date _____

Publisher Address _____

Storage Medium: Tape Cassette __ Cartridge __ Diskette __

Type of Package: Single Program __ Part of a Series __ Other _____

Price _____ Reviewer's Name _____

Application(s) under consideration _____

Additional Hardware Required _____

Additional Software Required _____

Possible Grouping Arrangements: Individual __ Small Group __

    Large Group __ Other _____

Special Format: Educational Game __ Arcade Game __ Management System __

    Tutorial Helps __ Other _____

Brief Description of Program:

Characteristics: Program Operation and Documentation

	Rating	Weight	Total
1. Allows user to correct typing errors	____	____	____
2. Documentation available and clearly written	____	____	____
3. Clear, nicely formatted screen displays	____	____	____
4. Incorrect selection of commands or keys does not cause program to abort	____	____	____
5. Menus and other features make the program "user friendly"	____	____	____

6. Instructions can be skipped if already known ____ ____ ____
7. Uses correct grammar, punctuation, and spelling ____ ____ ____
8. Clear and useful summary of program operation provided ____ ____ ____
9. Loading instructions clear; program easy to load ____ ____ ____
10. Bug-free: program runs properly ____ ____ ____
11. Uses computer capabilities well ____ ____ ____
12. Accepts abbreviations for common responses (i.e., Y for YES) ____ ____ ____
13. Operation of program does not require user to turn computer on and off ____ ____ ____
14. Readability of text appropriate for intended user ____ ____ ____
15. _____ ____ ____ ____
16. _____ ____ ____ ____

Total Program Operation/Documentation Score: ____ ☐

Characteristics: Student Use

	Rating	Weight	Total
1. Requires no computer knowledge	____	____	____
2. Does not require student reference to manuals	____	____	____
3. High student involvement	____	____	____
4. Provides student with summary of performance	____	____	____
5. Shows no racial, sexual discrimination, and so forth	____	____	____
6. Effective feedback for correct responses	____	____	____
7. Effective feedback for incorrect responses	____	____	____
8. Positive reinforcement more attractive than negative reinforcement	____	____	____
9. Encourages cooperation	____	____	____
10. Student control over rate of presentation	____	____	____
11. Student control over sequence of lesson	____	____	____
12. Student control over selection of lesson	____	____	____
13. Student can select to go back and review previous frames of information	____	____	____
14. Student can select various styles of presentation	____	____	____
15. _____	____	____	____
16. _____	____	____	____

Total Student Use Score: ____ ☐

Characteristics: Instructor Use

	Rating	Weight	Total

1. Instructional objectives clearly stated
2. Easily integrated into curriculum
3. Teacher can change rates and difficulty of material
4. Ability to change lists, that is, vocabulary, spelling, and so forth
5. Random generation of problems contributes to usefulness of program
6. No need for instructor to assist users
7. Useful teacher manual and/or accompanying materials provided
8. Suggested lesson plans
9. Suggested grouping arrangements
10. Useful student workbook provided
11. Useful blackline/ditto masters provided
12. Interesting follow-up activities and/or projects suggested
13. Management system easy to use and flexible
14. Provides whole class summaries of performance
15. Other educational materials suggested or provided
16. Software does not require intermittent operation of disk drive or cassette recorder
17. _____
18. _____

Total Instructor Use Score:

Characteristics: Content

	Rating	Weight	Total

1. Follows sound educational techniques
2. Follows sound educational theory
3. Accurate content
4. Amount of learning justifies time spent by users
5. Appropriate use of color
6. Appropriate use of graphics and/or animation
7. Appropriate use of sound
8. Accomplishes stated objectives
9. Sequence of lesson and instructions logical and clear

10. _____

11. _____   _____ _____ _____

_____   _____ _____ _____

Total Content Score: _____   ☐

Evaluation Summary: (Main strengths and weaknesses, and so forth)

Total points for all characteristics: ☐

Total points possible: ☐
(Add all weights and multiply by 5 to determine total points possible)

Percent Rating: _____ percent

Describe Backup Policy:

Backup policy is: acceptable __ not acceptable __

Recommendation: Worth the price __ Do not purchase __
                     Can recommend only if certain changes are made __

HOW TO EVALUATE TUTORIAL SOFTWARE

For description of the Identifying Information section, Brief Description of Program, and Characteristics: Program Operation and Documentation, see pages 127–132.

Identifying Information, Special Format

Tutorials attempt to provide learning experiences leading to concept development. In addition, drill and practice exercises for concepts are usually provided, either in game sequences or regular presentation of problems. A tutorial lesson or group of lessons may also include a management system which tests students for optimum placement in lessons and provides a record of student performance. Some attempt should be made to determine whether the tutorial is linear or branching, because the approach may determine applicability in the classroom. See pages 43–45 for an explanation of these two terms.

Characteristics: Student Use

These characteristics focus on the software's strengths and weaknesses concerning student use. Particular attention should be paid to how these criteria are weighted; for instance, the criteria "Student control over selection of lesson" may have little weight for a teacher who wishes to completely control student assignments or wants the management system to determine lesson selection.

1. Requires no computer knowledge. It is usually the case that software will be of more value if students can load and operate without teacher intervention, and without lengthy training sessions. The language within a program should be carefully controlled, with little or no use of phrases like "boot the disk," and so forth.

2. Does not require student reference to manuals. See explanation on page 133.

3. High student involvement. Includes all the elements which make a tutorial session interesting for a student, and not merely a series of boring textual statements and questions. Ideas should be expressed in an interesting way. Students should interact often, and their interactions should not be contrived, but useful.

4. Provides student with summary of performance. A tutorial can contain both "embedded questions" and regular tests in order to determine student progress. Students can, perhaps, receive results of final tests on objectives, expressed either in terms of "Mastery/Non-Mastery" or percent. However, some tutorials provide no test grades to students. Progress through the segments of the tutorial serve to indicate an individual's progress, a sufficient motivation in many respects. Take a look at the tutorial as a whole. Overuse, underuse, or unwise use of summary information are all poor traits. Summaries of performance can be recorded by the student on special record sheets, in cases where no management system is provided.

5. *Shows no racial, sexual discrimination, and so forth.* Software materials, as well as all classroom learning materials, should not demonstrate bias of any type.

6. *Effective feedback for correct responses.* Positive reinforcement should motivate students and should never be condescending in manner. Feedback should be varied; students soon tire of phrases like "Super!" when predictable and repeated often. Use of a student's name in feedback can be attractive, if not overused. Sometimes the repetition of the correct answer in the feedback can serve to imprint correct responses in the student's mind. In addition, the use of nonverbal feedback can be very effective, that is, sound effects, graphics displays, and so on. Tutorials should be designed so that students are not penalized for minor typing mistakes and use of synonymous words.

7. *Effective feedback for incorrect responses.* Negative feedback should contribute to the learning process and should not hurt student feelings. Remarks like "Don't be foolish, try again" have no place in lessons, and may even cause student refusal to use the program again. An inobtrusive beep, or a simple message of "Incorrect. Please try once more," may do the job of feedback well. At their best, tutorials will search incorrect answers to determine *what kind* of mistake is being made, then offer feedback specifically meant to clear up that particular kind of mistake. When a student has not yet answered correctly after two or three tries, then the program should state the correct answer or offer reteaching sequences.

8. *Positive reinforcement more attractive than negative reinforcement.* See explanation on page 134.

9. *Encourages cooperation.* See explanation on page 134.

10. *Student control over rate of presentation.* The student should be allowed to read information at his or her own reading rate. Nothing is more frustrating than when necessary text disappears before it has been assimilated by the student. This problem is commonly solved by the use of messages like "Press the space bar to continue."

11. *Student control over sequence of lesson.* At times, it is important that students choose whether to practice or to view portions of a lesson. The student can also benefit from tutorials that allow him or her to access "help" sequences at will.

12. Student control over selection of lesson. If there is no management system included, ability to select lessons from a menu will add to greater flexibility and easier integration into the curriculum. This will also allow the student to review previous lessons at will.

13. Student can select to go back and review previous frames of information. Tutorials are enhanced by this ability. When a student does not know the answer to a question, referral back to the previous frame of textual and graphic information may add to comprehension.

14. Student can select various styles of presentation. See explanation on page 135.

15. Length (time) of lesson appropriate. Length of lesson should be appropriate for the age, ability, and characteristics of the students using the tutorial. A third grader's attention span may preclude the use of long tutorial lessons.

16. and 17. Other criteria. These blanks allow educators to add other criteria they feel should be considered in the software evaluation procedure.

Characteristics: Instructor Use

These criteria will focus on the needs of the instructor. Almost any piece of software will be more valuable when certain elements make life easier for the instructor and allow the software to be used in varying situations.

1. Instructional objectives clearly stated. Objectives should be stated in the software or accompanying teacher materials. This will help teachers to plan the most effective use of software.

2. Easily integrated into curriculum. This is a general statement which may be evaluated by looking at the entire software package and judging whether it will be of substantial value as related to the curriculum. Accompanying student and teacher materials may help integration. Also, consider whether the topic or topics presented truly fit into lesson plans, or are really trivial in nature. Can the tutorials be used without much teacher intervention, so that students needing enrichment or review can accomplish the task by themselves?

3. Random generation of problems contributes to usefulness of program. This statement describes several features that tutorials can have. If a student must repeat a tutorial sequence, it may be appropriate to use a different example than was originally given. Associated practice exercises usually benefit by random generation or selection of problems.

4. No need for instructor to assist users. A good tutorial program should be planned well enough and written clearly enough so that students do not often need to ask for help from the instructor. There may be many instances where the instructor's time must be spent with a group of students; constant disturbance from computer-using students can be detrimental to learning. If computers are housed in the media center or a computer room, the student may not be near his or her own instructor.

5. Useful teacher manual and/or accompanying materials provided. Some software comes with no extra materials for the instructor. Teacher guides and integrated learning materials (textual, filmstrip, workbook, and so forth) can greatly add to the value of the software and can provide many creative ideas for classroom integration.

6. Suggested lesson plans. The teacher's manual may suggest plans for lessons which integrate the use of computer tutorials. When rating this characteristic, judge the *quality* of the lesson plans, as well as the fact that they have been included in the software package.

7. Suggested grouping arrangements. Advice of this type may add to the usefulness of the software and allow more students to benefit than would otherwise be possible.

8. Useful student workbook provided. The inclusion of special student workbooks may contribute to the value of software, and it may also allow more individualized learning. Reference to pictures and other material in workbooks may help to increase student understanding. In addition, if students can complete questions in workbooks and then enter answers into a computer program, computer time will be saved and more students will be able to benefit from the use of software.

9. Useful blackline/ditto masters provided. Again, this feature can contribute to easier integration of software into curriculum and can maximize the effectiveness of tutorials on an individualized basis.

10. Interesting follow-up activities and/or projects suggested. The existence of such suggested activities in accompanying teacher manuals can help teachers plan for student application of knowledge.

11. Management system easy to use and flexible. See explanation (# 13) on page 137.

12. Provides whole class summaries of performance. See explanation (# 14) on page 138.

13. Other educational materials suggested or provided. See explanation (# 15) on page 138.

14. When reentering program, student begins at appropriate spot. Some tutorials will record the place a student left a lesson. The next time that student returns to the tutorial, he will automatically begin in a logical starting place and will not be required to repeat the lesson. This will only apply to those tutorials possessing management systems of some kind.

15. Software does not require intermittent operation of disk drive or cassette recorder. See explanation (# 16) on page 138.

16. and 17. Other criteria. These are spaces for additional criteria important for selection.

Characteristics: Content

1. Follows sound educational techniques. Does the program use techniques of which you personally approve? Do you agree with the logic employed when introducing concepts? Is the student forced into memorizing definitions or rules with little real concept development? If utilizing an algorithm (such as in division problem computation), does the program closely match the method of instruction used in the classroom? Are multiple choice or matching questions overused or used improperly? Sometimes short answers are the best way to have students respond to questions. "Dialog" with the computer can have a good effect on student interest and achievement, and it can prevent good guessers from progressing through a lesson without having learned.

2. Follows sound educational theory. This criteria measures the software as a whole, taking in the elements beyond technique only. Are students expected to make impossible mental leaps? Is some effort made to go from concrete examples to the more abstract? Are facts organized in such a way that students can form a schema for better understanding and retention? Do questions test understanding beyond the level of facts? Will students apply their knowledge in new situations?

3. Accurate content. Obviously, the content of the program should be totally accurate, or else the students will learn incorrect information and skills.

4. Amount of learning justifies time spent by users. Is the content trivial, or of a more essential nature? Do students spend huge amounts of time on the program with little gain in knowledge or useful skills?

5. Appropriate use of color. Sometimes use of color can greatly add to the effectiveness and attractiveness of tutorial software. But at other times switching from one color to another, or using unrealistic colors can actually be detrimental.

6. *Appropriate use of graphics and/or animation.* See explanation on page 139.

7. *Appropriate use of sound.* See explanation on page 139.

8. *Accomplishes stated objectives.* Does the student truly accomplish the stated learning objectives? Will the student be able to apply what has been learned to subsequent tasks?

9. *Sequence of lesson and instructions logical and clear.* Does the sequence of the lesson make sense? Can instructions be understood by the average student? Does one statement follow logically from preceding statements?

10. *and 11. Other criteria.* These are spaces to add any additional criteria desired when evaluating software.

Tutorial Software Evaluation

Subject Area _____ Microcomputer _____

Topic(s) _____

Requires ____ K of memory   Grade Level (estimate) _____

Program Name _____ Author _____

Publisher _____ Copyright Date _____

Publisher Address _____

Storage Medium: Tape Cassette __ Cartridge __ Diskette __

Type of Package: Single Program __ Part of a Series __ Other _____

Price _____ Reviewer's Name _____

Application(s) under consideration _____

Additional Hardware Required _____

Additional Software Required _____

Possible Grouping Arrangements: Individual __ Small Group __

    Large Group __ Other _____

Special Format: Game sequences __ Drill and Practice sequences __

    Management System __ Pretests __ Posttests __ Linear __

    Branching __ Other _____

Brief Description of Program:

Characteristics: Program Operation and Documentation

	Rating	Weight	Total
1. Allows user to correct typing errors	_____	_____	_____
2. Documentation available and clearly written	_____	_____	_____
3. Clear, nicely formatted screen displays	_____	_____	_____
4. Incorrect selection of commands or keys does not cause program to abort	_____	_____	_____

5. Menus and other features make the program "user friendly" _____ _____ _____
6. Instructions can be skipped if already known _____ _____ _____
7. Uses correct grammar, punctuation, and spelling _____ _____ _____
8. Clear and useful summary of program operation provided _____ _____ _____
9. Loading instructions clear; program easy to load _____ _____ _____
10. Bug-free: program runs properly _____ _____ _____
11. Uses computer capabilities well _____ _____ _____
12. Accepts abbreviations for common responses (i.e., Y for YES) _____ _____ _____
13. Operation of program does not require user to turn computer on and off _____ _____ _____
14. Readability of text appropriate for intended user _____ _____ _____
15. _____

_____ _____ _____ _____
16. _____

_____ _____ _____ _____

Total Program Operation/Documentation Score: _____   [   ]

Characteristics: Student Use

	Rating	Weight	Total
1. Requires no computer knowledge	_____	_____	_____
2. Does not require student reference to manuals	_____	_____	_____
3. High student involvement	_____	_____	_____
4. Provides student with summary of performance	_____	_____	_____
5. Shows no racial, sexual discrimination, and so forth	_____	_____	_____
6. Effective feedback for correct responses	_____	_____	_____
7. Effective feedback for incorrect responses	_____	_____	_____
8. Positive reinforcement more attractive than negative reinforcement	_____	_____	_____
9. Encourages cooperation	_____	_____	_____
10. Student control over rate of presentation	_____	_____	_____
11. Student control over sequence of lesson	_____	_____	_____
12. Student control over selection of lesson	_____	_____	_____
13. Student can select to go back and review previous frames of information	_____	_____	_____
14. Student can select various styles of presentation	_____	_____	_____

15. Length (time) of lesson appropriate ___ ___ ___

16. _____

17. _____ ___ ___ ___

_____

Total Student Use Score: ___ ☐

Characteristics: Instructor Use

	Rating	Weight	Total
1. Instructional objectives clearly stated	___	___	___
2. Easily integrated into curriculum	___	___	___
3. Random generation of problems contributes to usefulness of program	___	___	___
4. No need for instructor to assist users	___	___	___
5. Useful teacher manual and/or accompanying materials provided	___	___	___
6. Suggested lesson plans	___	___	___
7. Suggested grouping arrangements	___	___	___
8. Useful student workbook provided	___	___	___
9. Useful blackline/ditto masters provided	___	___	___
10. Interesting follow-up activities and/or projects suggested	___	___	___
11. Management system easy to use and flexible	___	___	___
12. Provides whole class summaries of performance	___	___	___
13. Other educational materials suggested or provided	___	___	___
14. When reentering program, student begins at appropriate spot	___	___	___
15. Software does not require intermittent operation of disk drive or cassette recorder	___	___	___
16. _____			
17. _____	___	___	___

Total Instructor Use Score: ___ ☐

Characteristics: Content

	Rating	Weight	Total
1. Follows sound educational techniques	___	___	___
2. Follows sound educational theory	___	___	___
3. Accurate content	___	___	___

4. Amount of learning justifies time spent by users   ____ ____ ____
5. Appropriate use of color   ____ ____ ____
6. Appropriate use of graphics and/or animation   ____ ____ ____
7. Appropriate use of sound   ____ ____ ____
8. Accomplishes stated objectives   ____ ____ ____
9. Sequence of lesson and instructions logical and clear   ____ ____ ____
10. _____   ____ ____ ____
11. _____   ____ ____ ____

Total Content Score: ____ [ ]

Evaluation Summary: (Main strengths and weaknesses, and so forth)

Total points for all characteristics: [ ]

Total points possible: [ ]
(Add all weights and multiply by 5 to determine total points possible)

Percent Rating: ____ percent

Describe Backup Policy:

Backup policy is: acceptable __ not acceptable __

Recommendation: Worth the price __ Do not purchase __
Can recommend only if certain changes are made __

HOW TO EVALUATE SIMULATION SOFTWARE

For description of the Identifying Information section, Brief Description of Program, and Characteristics: Program Operation and Documentation, see pages 127–132.

Identifying Information, Special Format

Occasionally simulation type software will also include short tutorial lessons or drill and practice segments. Simulations can be integrated into the curriculum by assignment of teams who will compete with each other. These features can be identified in the special format section.

Characteristics: Student Use

These characteristics focus on the software's strengths and weaknesses concerning student use.

1. Requires no computer knowledge. See explanation on page 133.

2. Does not require student reference to manuals. See explanation on page 133.

3. High student involvement. Are students involved to the point that they "experience" the simulation? Do they care about the outcome?

4. Provides student with adequate summary of performance. Sometimes it makes sense to provide a summary of performance, especially for those simulations dealing with economics topics like running a business. At other times, it is enough for the student to know he or she has found gold in Alaska, or has traveled safely across the Oregon Trail.

5. Shows no racial, sexual discrimination, and so forth. Software materials, as well as all classroom learning materials, should not demonstrate bias of any type.

6. Encourages cooperation. This is an important element of many software simulations. Students form teams that compete against each other. Working together as a team results in better performance.

7. Student control over rate of presentation when appropriate. The student should be allowed to read information at his or her own reading rate. Nothing is more frustrating than when necessary text disappears before it has been assimilated by the student. This problem is commonly solved by the use of messages like "Press the space bar to continue."

8. Length (time) of simulation appropriate. Length of simulation should be appropriate for the age, ability, and characteristics of the students involved. Does the program require more time than would be appropriate for the learning involved? Does it take a long time for certain segments of the simulation to run?

9 and 10. Other criteria. These blanks allow educators to add other criteria they feel should be considered in the software evaluation procedure.

Characteristics: Instructor Use

These criteria will focus on the needs of the instructor. Almost any piece of software will be more valuable when certain elements make life easier for the instructor and allow the software to be used in varying situations.

1. Instructional objectives clearly stated. Objectives should be stated in the software or accompanying teacher materials. This will help teachers to plan the most effective use of software.

2. Suggestions for integration into curriculum. This is a general statement which may be evaluated by looking at the entire software package and judging whether it will be of substantial value as related to the curriculum. Accompanying student and teacher materials may help to suggest possible ways to wisely integrate simulation software.

3. Prerequisite skills for students indicated. Certain skills should have already been taught and practiced *before* a simulation can be used to its best advantage. The teacher's manual should indicate what skills are expected, so that lacking concepts can be developed before use of the software.

4. No need for instructor to assist users. See explanation (#6) on page 136.

5. Useful teacher manual and/or accompanying materials provided. Some software comes with no extra materials for the instructor. Teacher guides and integrated learning materials (textual, filmstrip, workbook, and so forth) can greatly add to the value of the software and can provide many creative ideas for classroom integration. Simulation can be particularly enhanced by accompanying teacher and student materials and manuals.

6. Suggested grouping arrangements. Advice of this type may add to the usefulness of the software and allow more students to benefit than would otherwise be possible.

7. Useful student workbook provided. The inclusion of special student workbooks may contribute to the value of software. Reference to pictures, graphs, maps, and other material in workbooks may help to increase student understanding and performance.

8. Useful blackline/ditto masters provided. Again, this feature can contribute to easier integration of software into curriculum and can maximize the effectiveness of the simulation.

9. Interesting follow-up activities and/or projects suggested. The existence of such suggested activities in accompanying teacher manuals can help teachers plan for student application of knowledge. A good simulation often captures the imaginations of students and will encourage them to do research.

10. and 11. Other criteria. These are spaces for additional criteria important for selection.

Characteristics: Content

1. Realistic simulation of events. Although no computer program can exactly simulate a real life event, there are some that do a better job than others. Student decisions should result in realistic outcomes. The entire format of the program should reflect a reasonable attempt to be accurate and contribute to student learning.

2. Valid formulas used to compute outcomes. Often, documentation accompanying the simulation will show the formulas used to compute various outcomes, based on certain variables entered by the student. Check for validity.

3. Accurate content. Obviously, the content of the program should be totally accurate or else the students will learn incorrect information.

4. Appropriate use of color. Sometimes use of color can greatly add to the effectiveness and attractiveness of simulation software. But at other times switching from one color to another, or using unrealistic colors, can actually be detrimental.

5. Appropriate use of graphics and/or animation. Simulations can be enhanced by use of pictures, maps, diagrams, or moving figures. Animated displays can be especially attractive and add extra student motivation. If graphic displays interfere with student task concentration, reinforce the wrong behaviors, or slow down the program too much, then they are considered to be inappropriately used.

6. Appropriate use of sound. Sound effects and musical selections can add much to student interest and can be a good way to tactfully indicate when answers have been entered in the wrong format. On the other hand, overuse of sound can interfere with concentration, or even with the class as a whole. A loud rendition of "For He's a Jolly Good Fellow" can be disturbing when the rest of the class is involved in quiet activities. Particularly well-designed software will allow a student or teacher to choose whether sound will be used or not.

7. Accomplishes stated objectives. Does the student truly accomplish the stated learning objectives? Will the student be able to apply what has been learned to subsequent tasks?

8 and 9. Other criteria. These are spaces to add any additional criteria desired when evaluating software.

Simulation Software Evaluation

Subject Area _____ Microcomputer _____

Topic(s) _____

Requires ____ K of memory   Grade Level (estimate) _____

Program Name _____ Author _____

Publisher _____ Copyright Date _____

Publisher Address _____

Storage Medium: Tape Cassette __ Cartridge __ Diskette __

Type of Package: Single Program __ Part of a Series __ Other _____

Price _____ Reviewer's Name _____

Application(s) under consideration _____

Additional Hardware Required _____

Additional Software Required _____

Special Format: Drill and Practice sequences __ Tutorials __ Team effort __

   Other _____

Brief Description of Program:

Characteristics: Program Operation and Documentation

	Rating	Weight	Total
1. Allows user to correct typing errors	_____	_____	_____
2. Documentation available and clearly written	_____	_____	_____
3. Clear, nicely formatted screen displays	_____	_____	_____
4. Incorrect selection of commands or keys does not cause program to abort	_____	_____	_____
5. Menus and other features make the program "user friendly"	_____	_____	_____

6. Instructions can be skipped if already known _____ _____ _____
7. Uses correct grammar, punctuation, and spelling _____ _____ _____
8. Clear and useful summary of program operation provided _____ _____ _____
9. Loading instructions clear; program easy to load _____ _____ _____
10. Bug-free: program runs properly _____ _____ _____
11. Uses computer capabilities well _____ _____ _____
12. Accepts abbreviations for common responses (i.e., Y for YES) _____ _____ _____
13. Operation of program does not require user to turn computer on and off _____ _____ _____
14. Readability of text appropriate for intended user _____ _____ _____
15. _____
    _____ _____ _____ _____
16. _____
    _____ _____ _____ _____

Total Program Operation/Documentation Score: _____

Characteristics: Student Use

	Rating	Weight	Total
1. Requires no computer knowledge	_____	_____	_____
2. Does not require student reference to manuals	_____	_____	_____
3. High student involvement	_____	_____	_____
4. Provides students with adequate summary of performance	_____	_____	_____
5. Shows no racial, sexual discrimination, and so forth	_____	_____	_____
6. Encourages cooperation	_____	_____	_____
7. Student control over rate of presentation when appropriate	_____	_____	_____
8. Length (time) of simulation appropriate	_____	_____	_____
9.			
10.	_____	_____	_____

Total Student Use Score: _____

Characteristics: Instructor Use

	Rating	Weight	Total
1. Instructional objectives clearly stated	___	___	___
2. Suggestions for integration into curriculum	___	___	___
3. Prerequisite skills for students indicated	___	___	___
4. No need for instructor to assist users	___	___	___
5. Useful teacher manual and/or accompanying materials provided	___	___	___
6. Suggested grouping arrangements	___	___	___
7. Useful student workbook provided	___	___	___
8. Useful blackline/ditto masters provided	___	___	___
9. Interesting follow-up activities and/or projects suggested	___	___	___
10. _____			
11. _____	___	___	___

Total Instructor Use Score: ___   [   ]

Characteristics: Content

	Rating	Weight	Total
1. Realistic simulation of events	___	___	___
2. Valid formulas used to compute outcome	___	___	___
3. Accurate content	___	___	___
4. Appropriate use of color	___	___	___
5. Appropriate use of graphics and/or animation	___	___	___
6. Appropriate use of sound	___	___	___
7. Accomplishes stated objectives	___	___	___
8. _____			
9. _____	___	___	___

Total Content Score: ___   [   ]

Evaluation Summary: (Main strengths and weaknesses, and so forth)

Total points for all characteristics: ☐

Total points possible: ☐

(Add all weights and multiply by 5 to determine total points possible)

Percent Rating: _____ percent

Describe Backup Policy:

Backup policy is: acceptable __ not acceptable __

Recommendation: Worth the price __ Do not purchase __
                      Can recommend only if certain changes are made __

HOW TO EVALUATE WORD-PROCESSING SOFTWARE

For description of the Identifying Information section, see pages 127–129. The Brief Description of Program should include information highlighting the operational requirements and special features of the word-processing package.

Characteristics: Program Operation and Documentation

The only criteria to be evaluated in a word-processing program are those concerning the operation of the program and the written material accompanying the package. Most word processors have been designed for general public use. Teacher and student materials are not usually included, and there is no *content* involved. When evaluating these criteria, always keep in mind the abilities and needs of the potential users. For some applications, certain criteria listed below will have no importance.

1. *Allows user to easily correct typing errors.* Most word-processing programs allow mistakes to be erased easily. But if several commands must be used to erase even small mistakes, then the word processor will be harder to use.

2. *Documentation available and clearly written.* The manuals should clearly describe the operation of the package and all its special features.

3. *Documentation provides index and table of contents.* Without a handy index, users may be forced to read a lot of unnecessary information just to locate one particular command.

4. *Clear, nicely formatted screen displays.* Any textual displays should be easy to read and understand. When entering or editing text, it is helpful for a heading to appear at the top of the screen, giving important information.

5. *Incorrect selection of commands or keys does not cause program to abort.* Although a user may end up losing some words or paragraphs, or even a file,* by using incorrect commands or by pressing keys inadvertently, this should not cause the program to stop running. If this happens, the work currently in the computer's memory will be lost, and the word-processing disk or tape will have to be loaded again.

6. *Menus and other features make the program "user friendly."* Menus provide a way for users to easily change format of text, load or

---

*When saving text, one gives that text a *file* name, and the text is saved on a diskette. Later, that file can be loaded into the computer's memory to be revised and/or edited.

save files, or print out the textual material. The language employed should be understandable, and the method used to select from the menu should be sensible and easy to learn. Another feature that may contribute to the smooth operation of a word processor would be the ability to access "help" screen displays, which will list and describe commands used for certain purposes.

7. *Uses correct grammar, punctuation, and spelling.* The menus and other written information within the program should use correct grammar, punctuation, and spelling.

8. *Clear and useful summary of program operation provided.* The documentation will sometimes provide a page or card of summary information about commands and other features of the word processor. This will help the user to operate the program without constant reference to manuals. In addition, when there are *many* different commands to learn, a template which fits over the computer keyboard and indicates which keys are used for what purpose, can provide help to the new user.

9. *Loading instructions clear; program easy to load.* There should be clear instructions for loading the word-processing program and loading textual files that have been stored on disk or tape. The process itself should not require an inordinate amount of steps.

10. *Bug-free: program runs properly.* Mistakes in the word-processing program logic, or in the program statements themselves can cause the program to stop running and may cause loss of textual files.

11. *Uses computer capabilities well.* Is production of written work speeded up by using the word processor? Or are so many problems added that using a typewriter would be a simpler procedure?

12. *Accepts abbreviations for common responses (i.e., Y for YES).* It is time-saving when programs allow users to abbreviate responses used often.

13. *Operation of program does not require user to turn computer on and off.* The program should be organized in a way that allows users to return to a menu of the word-processing program, choose to do another job or to QUIT the program in an orderly fashion.

14. *Commands easy to learn.* In most cases, it is better to use a word processor which can be operated with a minimum of different commands. The commands should make sense (that is, to SAVE a textual file, the command CONTROL S would be the easiest to remember).

15. *Keys chosen to perform operations located wisely on the keyboard.* Keys used to delete sentences or paragraphs of information

should be located at a place that is not easy to touch inadvertently. Some word-processing programs locate all keys used to *insert* characters and lines and so forth toward the top of the keyboard, and all keys used to *delete* characters toward the bottom of the keyboard. As you become familiar with a word-processing package, you will be able to judge whether the arrangement is sensible.

16. Allows paragraphs to be deleted quickly and easily. This feature contributes to editing ease.

17. Allows words, sentences, and paragraphs to be moved quickly and easily. This is an extra feature which adds usefulness to the word-processing package. How simple is it to identify which paragraph needs to be moved, and then to move it to the correct spot within the text?

18. Possesses "word wrap" feature. Only the least sophisticated word processors lack this feature. The word-processing program allows the user to type away with no concern as to where the right-hand margin is; if there is not enough space for the last word being typed on a line, then that word is automatically brought down to the next line, at the left-hand margin. Therefore, no hyphenation decisions are required. In most word-processing programs, the user presses the RETURN key only when indicating the end of a paragraph, or when typing lists of information. The word wrap feature allows subsequent editing (insertions, deletions) to be done without damaging paragraph format.

19. Protective features help user avoid loss of word-processing files. Nothing is worse than a word processor that constantly allows you to lose textual files. Although the user is ultimately responsible for naming, saving, and loading files in such a way that this does not happen, a word processor can provide certain check features to avoid some problems of this nature. For instance, when selecting the "delete file" option from a menu, the word processor should require that the whole file name be typed and may even ask the question "Are you sure?"

20. Superscripting and subscripting available and easy to use. Mathematical and scientific papers may require a good deal of superscripting and subscripting. Most word processors can not handle the typing of equations, which may require many levels of half spacing from the main typing line. Research reports also require a way to superscript or subscript numbers, for indication of footnotes and notations. Be aware, however, that it is often the *printer* that determines whether this can be done, and what commands must be used. For many purposes, superscripting and subscripting ability is not of importance.

21. Cursor movement becomes automated with practice. The cursor is usually a small, lighted arrow indicating your location within the text appearing on the screen. The keys used to move the cursor should be sensibly chosen, and eventually their use should become fully automatic. If the microcomputer possesses up, down, right, and left arrows on the keyboard, these are good choices for cursor movement.

22. Underlining capability easy to use. Does your word processor allow words to be underlined? Is it easy to learn how to underline, and does this process involve as few steps as possible?

23. Text can be justified easily. Justification means that both the text's left-hand and right-hand margins will be straight, not jagged as when using a regular typewriter. Newspapers use justified text. Look into the word processor's ability to do this.

24. Upper-case and lower-case letters. Only the least sophisticated word processors can not produce lower-case as well as upper-case letters when printing work on paper. Sometimes a word processor screen will show capital letters in what is called "inverse video" (black letters on white background), and lower-case letters in regular capital letters; but when the text is printed on paper, regular lower-case and upper-case letters will appear. Also, is the regular SHIFT key used to capitalize letters? Or does one have to go through a series of steps just to capitalize? This requirement, of course, will cut down on typing speed.

25. Can easily switch between single and double spacing. There are many instances when a report or story may require variable single or double spacing. One example would be when one desires double spacing for regular paragraphs and single spacing for lists. How does the word processor handle this need?

26. Entire width of text can be seen on the video display screen. Many microcomputers common in schools possess video display screens that show only 40 characters per line. Yet, when printing textual material on paper, we usually wish lines to consist of 60 or more characters. Some word-processing packages handle this problem by having users move the cursor from the left-hand to the right-hand margin in order to see the entire 60-character line of text. Only *part* of the line (40 characters) will be seen at once. Check also: Does the word-processing program allow text width to be changed as it is viewed on the screen and when it is printed on paper?

27. Loading, saving, and printing files a simple procedure. Typing and editing text is only part of the word processor's capabilities. Users should also be able to SAVE their work, so that some time in the future they can again access the work, edit it, then print it out in revised form. Word-processing work is usually saved on diskette or cassette tape, depending upon what microcomputer and word-processing software you are using. Each letter or essay would be saved under a different *File Name,* so that later you can identify the file you want to work with, and LOAD it back into the computer's memory. In addition, when reviewing any word-processing program, you should see how easy it is to actually PRINT out your work on paper.

28. Search and replace features. Existence of these features allows the user to (a) input a key word in order to access the part of a file which needs revision, (b) replace mispelled words easily, and (c) insert "markers" (such as $ @) in text when originally typed, and then automatically replace those markers with words or expressions that are difficult to type.

29. Automatic pagination. Does the word-processing program allow the user to request pages to be numbered when printed? How easy is it to use this feature?

30. Mail merge capability. When it is important to produce a number of copies of a letter or form, addressed to different individuals, and perhaps containing certain variable statements, the ability for a word-processing program to merge letters and addresses together will be an important time-saver. This is accomplished with great difficulty in some word-processing packages. Some packages have a companion *Mailer* software package which makes the procedure quite simple.

31. Use of word-processing program does not require intermittent access to master word-processing diskette or tape. Some word-processing programs can be loaded into a microcomputer, then removed and loaded into another one. This means that the same master diskette can be used for two or more microcomputers within a classroom. Only a student storage diskette would be needed, in order to store word-processing textual files. (Note: Check with software house on legality of this arrangement.)

32. and 33. Other criteria. These are spaces to add additional criteria important to you.

Word-Processing Software Evaluation

Microcomputer _____ Requires _____ K of memory

Program Name _____ Author _____

Publisher _____ Copyright Date _____

Publisher Address _____

Storage Medium: Tape Cassette __ Cartridge __ Diskette __

Price _____ Reviewer's Name _____

Application(s) under consideration _____

Additional Hardware Required _____

Additional Software Required _____

Brief Description of Program:

Characteristics: Program Operation and Documentation

	Rating	Weight	Total
1. Allows user to easily correct typing errors	_____	_____	_____
2. Documentation available and clearly written	_____	_____	_____
3. Documentation provides index and table of contents	_____	_____	_____
4. Clear, nicely formatted screen displays	_____	_____	_____
5. Incorrect selection of commands or keys does not cause program to abort	_____	_____	_____
6. Menus and other features make the program "user friendly"	_____	_____	_____
7. Uses correct grammar, punctuation, and spelling	_____	_____	_____
8. Clear and useful summary of program operation provided	_____	_____	_____

	Rating	Weight	Total
9. Loading instructions clear; program easy to load	_____	_____	_____
10. Bug-free: program runs properly	_____	_____	_____
11. Uses computer capabilities well	_____	_____	_____
12. Accepts abbreviations for common responses (i.e., Y for YES)	_____	_____	_____
13. Operation of program does not require user to turn computer on and off	_____	_____	_____
14. Commands easy to learn	_____	_____	_____
15. Keys chosen to perform operations located wisely on keyboard	_____	_____	_____
16. Allows paragraphs to be deleted quickly	_____	_____	_____
17. Allows words, sentences, and paragraphs to be moved quickly and easily	_____	_____	_____
18. Possesses "word wrap" feature	_____	_____	_____
19. Protective features help user avoid loss of word-processing files	_____	_____	_____
20. Superscripting and subscripting available and easy to use	_____	_____	_____
21. Cursor movement becomes automated with practice	_____	_____	_____
22. Underlining capability easy to use	_____	_____	_____
23. Text can be justified easily	_____	_____	_____
24. Upper-case and lower-case letters	_____	_____	_____
25. Can easily switch between single and double spacing	_____	_____	_____
26. Entire width of text can be seen on the video display screen	_____	_____	_____
27. Loading, saving, and printing files simple procedure	_____	_____	_____
28. Search and replace features	_____	_____	_____
29. Automatic pagination	_____	_____	_____
30. Mail merge capability	_____	_____	_____
31. Use of word-processing program does not require intermittent access to master diskette or tape	_____	_____	_____
32. _____	_____	_____	_____
33. _____	_____	_____	_____

Total Program Operation/Documentation Score: _____ ☐

Evaluation Summary: (Main strengths and weaknesses, and so forth)

Total points for all characteristics:

Total points possible:
(Add all weights and multiply by 5 to determine total points possible)

Percent Rating: ____ percent

Describe Backup Policy:

Backup policy is: acceptable __ not acceptable __

Recommendation: Worth the price __ Do not purchase __
Can recommend only if certain changes are made __

Review, Written Variety

;hers have become practiced software evaluators and are the criteria that should be judged for particular kinds of the written variety of review form may be preferred. One possiuic format allows for rapid indication of identifying information and evaluation of the software using a 1 to 10 scaling. Only the description of program operation and structure and personal evaluation will be in written form.

The identifying information section of the written review form is completed similarly to the preceding long checklist forms in this chapter. For the "Description of software and written evaluation" section, reviewers may wish to write a description of the software's operation and lesson sequences, then discuss the software's strengths and weaknesses under the main headings of program operation and documentation, student use, instructor use, and content.

This form can also be used in workshop sessions as a quick indicator of software value.

Software Review, Short General Checklist

Obviously, there is a lot to be said for using a short checklist in certain situations. Teachers may not always have time to complete complicated forms, so short checklists will encourage them to consistently record information when reviewing software. Also, it may be wise to use a short form in order to do quick, initial reviews of software, weeding out those offerings that are unsuitable or which obviously lack sound educational techniques. This form can also be used in workshop sessions when little time is available for more complete evaluations.

The leading section of this form includes less information. This will save time for reviewers and make a one-sided form possible. A new category, "Library Identifier," has been added. In cases where teachers review materials in a workshop setting, each piece of software under consideration can be given a library identifier code of some sort. That way teachers need not waste time hunting up addresses, or wading through documentation to find out additional hardware needs, and so forth.

The evaluation checklist includes criteria summarizing each of the characteristics sections included on the longer checklist forms.

Characteristics: Program Operation and Documentation

1. Smooth program operation
2. Good documentation
3. Screen displays attractive and clear
4. Creative use of computer capabilities

Characteristics: Student Use

5. Handles student responses wisely
6. High student involvement
7. Format encourages students to use program more than once
8. Provides students with summaries of performance

Characteristics: Instructor Use

9. Provides teacher with student performance records
10. Classroom applicability
11. Teacher's manual, learning materials, etc., provided

Characteristics: Content

12. Educationally sound
13. Wise use of color and sound
14. Wise use of graphics and/or animation
15. Accomplishes stated objectives

If any of these criteria are not fully understood, refer to the criteria descriptions for the long checklist forms.

Microcomputer Software Review

Subject Area _____ Microcomputer _____

Topic(s) _____

Requires _____ K of memory   Grade Level (estimate) _____

Program Name _____ Author _____

Publisher _____ Copyright Date _____

Publisher Address _____

Storage Medium: Tape Cassette __   Cartridge __   Diskette __

Type of Package: Single Program __   Part of a Series __   Other _____

Price _____ Reviewer's Name _____

Application(s) under consideration _____

Additional Hardware Required _____

Additional Software Required _____

Possible Grouping Arrangements: Individual __   Small Group __

    Large Group __   Other _____

Instructional Techniques: (Check all applicable descriptions)

    Drill and Practice __   Tutorial __   Simulation __   Arcade Game __

    Educational Game __   Problem Solving __   Management System __

    Other _____

	Yes	No	Unknown
1. Teacher's guide included	_____	_____	_____
2. Manual included	_____	_____	_____
3. Worksheets included	_____	_____	_____
4. Lesson plans suggested	_____	_____	_____
5. Follow-up activities suggested	_____	_____	_____
6. Written for other microcomputers? Which ones?	_____	_____	_____

Price? _____   Your opinion: Is this software worth its price? _____

Overall Rating (10 indicates highest rating):   1 2 3 4 5 6 7 8 9 10

Description of Software and Written Evaluation:
(Advantages and disadvantages for instructor and student, smoothness of program operation, quality of documentation and other materials, ability to integrate program into curriculum, potential uses, and so forth)

Is backup policy acceptable? _____
Describe:

Short Checklist for Software Evaluation

Name of Program _____ Library Identifier ____

Topic/Subject _____ Publisher _____

Storage Medium: Tape Cassette __ Disk __ Cartridge __

Brand of Microcomputer: Apple II Plus __ Atari __ TRS-80 Model III __

    Radio Shack Color Computer __ Pet __ Texas Instruments __

    Other _____

Instructional Techniques: (check all that apply)

    Drill and Practice __ Tutorial __ Simulation __ Problem Solving __

    Game __ Management System __ Other _____

Evalution Checklist:

	SA	A	D	SD	N/A
1. Smooth program operation	—	—	—	—	—
2. Good documentation	—	—	—	—	—
3. Screen displays attractive and clear	—	—	—	—	—
4. Creative use of computer capabilities	—	—	—	—	—
5. Handles student responses wisely	—	—	—	—	—
6. High student involvement	—	—	—	—	—
7. Format encourages students to use program more than once	—	—	—	—	—
8. Provides students with summaries of performance	—	—	—	—	—
9. Provides teacher with student performance records	—	—	—	—	—
10. Classroom applicability	—	—	—	—	—
11. Teacher's manual, learning materials, etc., provided	—	—	—	—	—
12. Educationally sound	—	—	—	—	—
13. Wise use of color and sound	—	—	—	—	—
14. Wise use of graphics and/or animation	—	—	—	—	—
15. Accomplishes stated objectives	—	—	—	—	—

Final Rating: (10 is highest value)   1 2 3 4 5 6 7 8 9 10

Name of Evaluator: _____

_____

SA = Strongly Agree   A = Agree   D = Disagree   SD = Strongly Disagree
N/A = Not Applicable

SUMMARY

In this chapter, ideas for locating educational software for review purposes were presented. Some possible avenues include computer stores, computer clubs, universities, colleges, microcomputer users groups, conferences, and contact with other educators. Procedures for establishing contact with software houses were discussed.

Software directories will expand knowledge of software availability for most subject areas. In addition, location of software review information on specific packages is recommended because repeated favorable reviews usually indicate good educational value. Sources of review information include Microsift, educational computing journals, universities, and some computer center stores.

Free or inexpensive software in the public domain can also help to meet the needs of schools.

Records of software evaluations should be kept for later referral. These forms can be formal or informal in nature, depending upon the extent of planned software purchases. Because software written for one brand of microcomputer generally can not be run on other brands, districts possessing hardware will probably want to limit their search to software for the computers available in their schools. Requirements for memory, color, and special hardware additions should be carefully considered before buying software.

Software review is a subjective process, much like review of books or films. Educators may disagree as to the value of the software under consideration. Not all software can or should be judged under the same set of criteria because the *intent* and applicability of software vary widely. Thus, four different versions of the checklist type of review forms were presented, for the areas of drill and practice, tutorial, simulation, and word processing.

After potential software reviewers have become more aware of the traits that good software possesses, they may prefer to express their opinions in writing rather than by checklist. Software forms for this purpose can be devised, allowing identifying information to be entered quickly and descriptions and evaluations of software to be written. A sample form was provided in this chapter.

Finally, some situations require the use of review forms that can be completed quickly. A short, general checklist form was presented for possible use in workshops, in-services, and classrooms.

SUGGESTED READINGS

Evaluator's Guide for Microcomputer-Based Instructional Packages. Department of Computer and Informational Science, University of Oregon, Eugene, Oregon 97403.

Friend, Jamesine, and James D. Milojkovic, "Successful Student/Microcomputer Interactions." *Apple Journal of Courseware Review,* no. 1. Cupertino, Calif.: Apple Education Foundation, 1982.

Heck, William P., Jerry Johnson, and Robert Kansky. *Guidelines to Evaluating Computerized Instructional Materials.* Reston, Va.: National Council of Teachers of Mathematics, 1981.

Lathrop, Ann, and Bobby Goodson. *Courseware in the Classroom.* Menlo Park, Calif.: Addison Wesley, 1983.

7

Choosing the Right Hardware for Your Classroom

INTRODUCTION

Even a cursory glance at magazines advertising microcomputers and related hardware additions shows the vast array of choices available for purchase. How can educators involved in hardware decisions for their districts begin to sift through all the information and pick out the most relevant facts?

Visits to local computer stores can be helpful, but can sometimes only add to the general confusion. Because most cater to business, and not the educational market, it may be difficult to obtain the information most needed to aid the decision-making process. Specialized computer terminology may float in the air, clouding the picture still further.

The selection process can be lightened considerably if this question is answered first: "What do we want the microcomputer to do?" After all, the computer is just an electronic device, albeit a very sophisticated one, and can only do what it is told to do. For most educational applications this means that *software* availability will determine the value the microcomputer can bring to teachers and students.

Previous chapters in this book introduced you to a variety of possible uses for the microcomputer in schools. Let's review the ideas, and even add a few more.

1. Computer-assisted and computer-managed instruction.

2. Computer literacy classes.

3. Programming classes.

4. Test construction and administration.

5. Administrative duties: gradebooks, attendance, library circulation, IEP reports, schedules and statistics for sports, and so forth.

6. Readability analysis.

7. A classroom demonstration machine.

8. Worksheet and puzzle generation.

9. CLOZE passage generation.

10. Vocabulary placement.

11. Development, maintenance, and reporting of individual records.

12. Word processing, accounting software, VisiCalc,®* and so forth in business education classes.

13. Word processing in English, journalism, and other classes requiring written compositions and reports.

14. Statistical studies and graphing.

15. Using the microcomputer as a laboratory instrument.

16. Music synthesizer systems.

17. As a new art form.

18. Graphics design.

19. Vocational training: driver education, drafting, agriculture, basic electronics, and so forth.

20. Computer programming and math-related subjects.

21. Using microcomputers to access national data banks.

22. Student publications.

23. Guidance information.

24. Aids for the handicapped.

CHOICES BY INDIVIDUALS

Hardware selection may involve just one teacher concerned with his or her classroom use, whether on the elementary level or in a particular subject on the secondary level. For instance, a high school art teacher may wish to explore the field of computer art with students. In this case, the best bet would be to read software directories and advertisements, try to contact some people involved with computer art, and visit computer stores who have knowledgeable salespeople in order to see what art package would be best. Special attention should be paid to how artwork can be *saved*; otherwise students will entertain themselves creating interesting designs, but will not be able to keep any kind of permanent record of their work. Other questions should also be explored. The existence of a compatible, relatively inexpensive printer with the capability to print artwork on paper might be a plus for the selection of a certain art package and microcomputer, although the extra cost may preclude immediate purchase.

If the application desired is *programming, computer mathematics,* or *computer literacy* classes only, selection can be made from a vast array of microcomputers. But keep in mind that if a less well known brand is chosen, then the more complicated programs that students

---

*VisiCalc® is a registered trademark of VisiCorp.

write (perhaps involving sound or graphics) will not be easily transferred and used elsewhere. Still, if flexibility of application warrants little attention, purchase of some very inexpensive microcomputers will serve the purpose. Several computers on the market today cost less than $100, not including the video display.

In elementary schools, interested teachers may wish to use microcomputers for computer-assisted instruction in several subjects. Basic programming skills and word processing may also be desired. Thus, a microcomputer supported by varied educational software and inexpensive, simple-to-use word-processing programs will prove to be of the most value. Programming skills can be learned on any microcomputer, though educational materials for teaching BASIC are more plentiful for the most popular brands of microcomputers. The availability of Logo for a particular brand of microcomputer may also be an attractive feature.

The common theme running through the above description is that educators should decide what *they want the computer to do,* then search out possibilities in both the software and hardware areas.

Another criterion for selection on an individual basis may be the availability of useful software for a teacher's personal use. That way, a teacher who purchases a microcomputer for home applications can take computer-related tasks home at night: for example, entering grades in a grade book program, or looking at compositions or programs students have written. Of course, this plan requires that microcomputers at home and at school be of the same brand.

CHOICE BY COMMITTEE

There is much to be said for an organized plan to implement computer education in a school district. A more widespread and complete search for appropriate software and hardware can be made. Teachers can be asked what applications they hope to provide for their students and for administrative duties. The information collected can be organized, recorded, and can provide some basis for choosing hardware and making plans for where the microcomputers will be located. Districts purchasing microcomputers often will buy only one brand for all schools, reasoning correctly that bids from microcomputer companies will require less expenditure per unit when a greater number of units are involved. Also, maintenance problems can be taken care of more easily; some districts have even gone so far as to train school personnel in microcomputer repair. Hardware peripherals like printers can be shared between users. Senior high programming students from several schools can work closely with teachers to create computer-assisted instruction programs for all educational levels, if the microcomputers located in the district are of the same brand.

Sometimes a middle ground may be taken. Young children have different needs than programming or word-processing students in a high school. At the elementary level location of easily operable, inexpensive, sturdy hardware plus good computer-assisted instruction packages utilizing color, graphics, or sound may take priority. A business education class may best benefit by learning about equipment and accompanying software that they may meet again once they enter the job market.

Every effort should be taken to involve teachers and administrators in the review and selection of software and other computer-related materials. No one person can be an expert in every field; input by a number of individuals should contribute to wiser selection of both software and hardware.

ORGANIZATION AND RECORD KEEPING

Once software availability for desired applications has been determined, one particular microcomputer may come to the forefront of the selection picture. This rather informal method of hardware selection can result in a decision that later proves to be an excellent one.

However, if a more formal method of selection is required by the school board and the public, then a form can be designed for microcomputer comparison and selection. In addition, a choice may seem to be ideal at first, but limiting factors may exist that can create problems later on. If no local dealer support is readily available, for instance, obtaining maintenance and advice when needed will prove to be a problem. Buying more expensive computers may mean giving up some possible applications because less software can be purchased.

One method of record keeping involves the compilation of a list of criteria important to the school district when considering selection of hardware. (Refer to pages 188–191.) Information concerning performance and capabilities must be obtained for each microcomputer. Then each criteria is given a numerical *rating*, usually ranging between 0 and 5. Given the applications desired, a *weight factor* is determined by the selection committee for criteria listed. The weight factor can range from 0 to 5, though this range can be expanded if desired. After all documentation has been completed, the rating is multiplied against the weight factor, and all totals are added to obtain a grand point value for each brand and/or model under consideration.

Some problems arise concerning the *total cost* portion of the following hardware selection form. It is entirely possible that different applications will require different combinations of hardware. Peripheral items like printers can be obtained for almost any microcomputer, and at many levels of expense, so it has been assumed that the cost of these items should not be included when the rating is multiplied by the weight value. Only the cost *for the basic system* will be considered.

When schools plan to purchase in quantity, computer manufacturers may offer considerable savings, well under retail cost. These bids may be based on the keyboard-computer alone, or on the basic system including keyboard-computer, video display, and storage device. It is a good idea to require vendors to prepare bids which also include any small costs for wiring, connectors, and other items which may be required for the running of particular software (Finkel, p. 11).

Although this numerical technique for microcomputer selection has limitations, it does allow much information to be collected, recorded, assimilated, and considered; thus appropriate documentation can be achieved. After the final choice has been made, the extra knowledge gained will be of great benefit. Those working on the selection committee can visit computer stores, contact manufacturers, talk to consultants, and read articles and advertisements in magazines to obtain the necessary data. (When gathering information, make sure that it is correct. Articles in magazines occasionally may be incomplete, misleading, or out of date. Make every attempt to contact vendors who are experts and who can provide accurate facts.)

Ideally, brochures and catalogs referring to desired hardware and peripheral items should accompany the evaluations. If additional connectors or boards are necessary, include the cost and type required when submitting the information.

MICROCOMPUTER SELECTION FORM: DEFINING THE TERMS

The first section of this form allows identifying information to be entered. The brand and model of the microcomputer under consideration will be given. The manufacturer address and the name and number of a contact person from the company can be listed. Another blank can be used to provide the name of a local dealer who sells or services the microcomputer being evaluated.

Criteria for evaluation have been grouped under five headings.

- Hardware Design Features
- Peripherals
- Manufacturer and Dealer Support
- Other Considerations
- Cost

Hardware Design Features

1. Screen Display Size. Microcomputers possess a number of differently sized screen displays. One common size is 40 characters per line, 24 lines. Some inexpensive computers have displays that are only 22 characters across. This may be fine for some purposes, but for word processing or serious programming this can be a limitation. When the computer will be used mostly for word processing, a screen display size allowing 60 or more characters per line is preferable.

2. Graphics capability. How important is graphics capability? Some computers possess limited capabilities in this regard; graphics can only be very crudely drawn. Certain brands of microcomputers have special graphics keys which can be used to create designs, drawn with typewriter keys. Other brands are capable of *low-high-resolution* graphics which may provide clearer, more detailed designs.

3. Color capability. Some microcomputers do not possess color capability. For a course in word processing or BASIC programming, color would not be at all necessary. However, some computer-assisted instruction is improved by the use of color.

4. Portability. If the computer is to be moved from room to room, or from school to school, portability would be an important factor. How easy is it to move the basic computer system?

5. Keyboard design. Most microcomputer keyboards are designed similarly to a typewriter. Others have flat, touch-sensitive surfaces, or calculator type of keys. When a great deal of typing must be done, a typewriter-like keyboard is preferable. For some applications, the other kinds of keyboards will be sufficient. A numeric keypad can be a helpful keyboard inclusion, especially when a lot of numbers must be entered. The 10 digits, 0 through 9, are arranged like the digits on a 10-key adding machine, or on calculators.

6. Editing features. Some microcomputers have especially convenient editing features for correcting programs. Insertions, deletions, and changes can be made easily.

7. Expansion ease. This criterion involves several aspects. First, can the memory of the computer be increased easily? Second, is the computer designed so that extra peripherals, such as printers or modems (see Figure 7-2), can be added later? Third, is the microcomputer supported by numerous vendors who produce hardware for special needs?

8. Hardware reliability. Is the equipment reliable? Have schools owning that brand of microcomputer experienced a lot of equipment breakdown problems? Are there any undue reliability or operating difficulties associated with using the disk drive system, cassette recorder, or video display?

9. Durability. What kind of abuse can the computer take? Is it very delicate, or can it withstand the fingers of curious fifth graders?

Figure 7-1a
Low Resolution Graphics, 40 × 40 Addressable Points
(Moptown by the Learning Company)

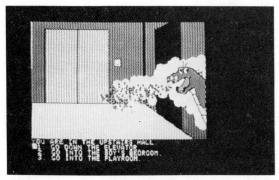

Figure 7-1b
High Resolution Graphics, 280 × 160 Addressable Points
(Dragon's Keep by Sunnyside Soft)

Figure 7-2
Modem
(Courtesy of Commodore Business Machines)

10. *Ease of operation.* Is the operation of the microcomputer easy to learn? Are there any quirks that will frustrate intended users? This will be most important for younger students.

11. *Sound.* Microcomputers vary in the extent that sound and music can be programmed. Many applications do not require sound. Students using computer-assisted instruction may find the inclusion of sound and/or music motivating and entertaining.

12. *Language availability.* Most microcomputers come equipped with a programming language, BASIC. However, the existence of another language to be used with a particular brand of microcomputer may be necessary for programming classes in a high school. Logo or Pilot availability could also increase the desirability of a particular microcomputer.

Peripherals

1. *Compatible printer available.* When applications like word processing, programming, or computer-managed instruction require that a printer be purchased, some attempt should be made to ascertain that one exists that will satisfy printing needs.

2. *Networking available.* Some microcomputers may be tied together in a *network* (see Figure 7-3). A central microcomputer and controller can send software through the wiring to the networked microcomputers. In some cases, computer listings and word-processing jobs can be *uploaded* to the central microcomputer and printed on a centrally located printer. Networking can be desirable for other situations. It allows teachers to download computer-assisted instruction and to keep constant track of what each student is doing. Programming techniques can be demonstrated on the central microcomputer, but all students in the classroom can look at their individual video displays to see what is happening. Students will not be handling diskettes or cassettes because programs can be loaded from the central computer.

However, there are certain limitations. Not all commercially available software can be "downloaded" into networked computers, either because it is copy protected or because something in the program dealing with the hardware does not allow transfer. The person running the host computer must know how to operate the networking system, which involves special commands and requirements. Networks may also involve the use of *hard-disk storage* (see Chapter 1 for a description of hard disks), which also requires more knowledge on the part of the computer room personnel. In addition, commercially available software can not always be stored on hard disk, if it has been copy protected. Special arrangements can sometimes be made with software vendors so that hard disk storage can be used (Fisher, p. 50).

3. *Voice generation available.* If creating or using software accompanied by *synthesized speech* (the computer can talk!), then the availability of speech synthesizers will be of some importance. See Appendix E for a list of some speech synthesizer vendors.

4. *Ability to interface with mainframe computers.* Is the microcomputer supported by hardware and software that allows it to communicate with larger computers? The piece of hardware most needed in the process is the *modem.* To access the larger computer, the user dials a special telephone number, then places the receiver on a device called a modem. The signals will be sent through telephone lines. If access to district computers, national data banks, or informational services is desired, this capability will be necessary. Some microcomputers do not readily interface with large computers; others have been specifically designed for this purpose.

5. *Other.* There may be a peripheral requirement that needs to be added here.

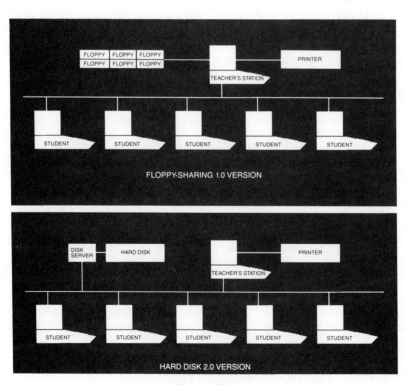

Figure 7-3
Classroom Monitor Networking System
(Courtesy of Software Connections)

Manufacturer and Dealer Support

1. Service contract. Is a service contract offered? How good are the terms?

2. Support of local dealer. Schools often must depend upon local dealers to provide advice and repair equipment quickly. If there is no local dealer, or the computer stores nearby do not wish to work with school hardware repairs, or do not promise quick service, then the district may experience "computer headaches."

3. Teacher training. Do national or local offices of the manufacturer offer teacher training on their equipment? Does the company demonstrate interest in the needs of education? What other kind of help is available?

4. Quality documentation for hardware. Are the manuals and other materials accompanying the hardware clearly written, indexed, and helpful? In general, does the company have the reputation of providing good documentation?

5. Utility programs provided. Sometimes manufacturers or local dealers provide a certain amount of software which can help to run computers more efficiently, allow blank disks to be formatted (that is, prepare disks for use on a particular computer), and so on.

Other Considerations

1. Flexibility. Can this microcomputer be used for a great variety of applications?

2. Compatibility. Is this microcomputer the same as others possessed by the district?

Cost

This page allows prices of considered hardware items to be recorded. The price of the keyboard-microprocessor unit should be entered, as well as the amount of memory desired, for example, 48K. Possible video displays, which are usually televisions or monitors, can be priced, as well as disk drive and cassette recorder cost. Similarly, if other peripherals may be purchased, information about cost and capabilities can be written. Brochures, advertisements, and hardware reviews from magazines can be included.

Final Page, Hardware Selection Form

Because a school or school district may choose to buy computers with and without color video displays, and may choose either cassette recorders or disk drives for storage, the last page allows prices for four different hardware combinations to be recorded and rated.

After all weights and ratings have been determined, each criterion rating is multiplied against the weight value to determine total points for each criterion. These points are summed to determine the Grand Total Point Value for all criteria.

Finally, space is provided to discuss desired peripherals and to mention any other information valuable for hardware decisions.

Microcomputer Selection Form

Brand _____ Model _____

Manufacturer Address _____

Contact Person _____ Telephone No. _____

Local Dealer _____

Hardware Design Features

Criteria	Remarks	Rating	Weight	Total
1. Screen display size				
2. Graphics capability				
3. Color capability				
4. Portability				
5. Keyboard design				
6. Editing features				
7. Expansion ease				
8. Hardware reliability				
9. Durability				
10. Ease of operation				
11. Sound				
12. Language availability BASIC ____ Pascal ____ FORTRAN ____ Assembler ____ COBOL ____ Pilot ____ Logo ____ Other _____				

Peripherals

Criteria	Remarks	Rating	Weight	Total
1. Compatible printer available				
2. Networking available				
3. Voice generation available				
4. Ability to interface with mainframe computers				
5. Other				

Manufacturer and Dealer Support

Criteria	Remarks	Rating	Weight	Total
1. Service contract				
2. Support of local dealer				
3. Teacher training				
4. Quality documentation for hardware				
5. Utility programs provided				

Other Considerations

Criteria	Remarks	Rating	Weight	Total
1. Flexibility				
2. Compatibility				

Cost   (Note: Give prices for single systems.)

Remarks   *Cost*

Keyboard-microprocessor unit, _____ K memory		$_____

Video display		
Color	Brand _____	$_____
Black and white	Brand _____	$_____

Storage		
Disk drive	Brand _____	$_____
Cassette recorder	Brand _____	$_____

Description/Brand   (Include brochures if possible)

Cost

Printer		
Thermal	Brand _____	$_____
Dot matrix	Brand _____	$_____
Daisy wheel	Brand _____	$_____

Voice synthesizer	Brand _____	$_____

Networking system	Brand _____	$_____

Modem and Communication software		
	Brand _____	$_____

Other		$_____

Rating   Weight   Total

		Rating	Weight	Total
Total Price for Basic System (keyboard-microprocessor, video display, storage)	$_____ black and white cassette			
Total Price for Basic System	$_____ black and white disk			
Total Price for Basic System	$_____ color cassette			
Total Price for Basic System	$_____ color disk			

GRAND TOTAL Point Value for All Criteria [   ]

Remarks:
(Include mention of desired peripherals for the various applications under consideration)

ADDITIONAL CONSIDERATIONS

The preceding hardware selection form did not contain information on software availability. Thus, it would be unwise to make microcomputer purchase decisions based solely on the total points earned. A better procedure would involve a thorough comparison of software and hardware benefits for each computer under consideration, according to the specific applications desired within a classroom, school, or district.

Some districts may be interested in creating computer-assisted instruction to be used with their own students. This might indicate that almost any microcomputer could be used because the district would not be dependent on outside software sources. However, several facts should be kept in mind.

First, if the district wishes to share or sell the software created, then it is often better to program the software on the more popular brands of microcomputers. A much larger public will then be interested in buying the software.

Second, when a microcomputer system has been modified in some way, or when certain peripherals are available, programs that take advantage of the modifications can not be run on computers that do not have those exact modifications. For widest appeal, software should be created on hardware which, in its native state, has the features you most care about.

Last—but certainly not least—have realistic expectations. Good software is not written in a day. It takes a great deal of knowledge in the areas of instructional design, subject matter, art, and programming to write a useful, attractive, professional program. Teachers usually do not have the time or the advanced programming knowledge needed to turn out truly high-quality software. If hardware is purchased with the assumption that somehow teachers will program all necessary software quickly, easily, and in a variety of subject areas, then it may happen that computers sit, underused or ignored, for a long period of time.

Authoring languages and systems can help meet some software needs of schools, but still require much effort and time on the part of teachers.

If a school district seriously wishes to create a usable, effective set of software materials for several subject areas, then it must devote financial and human resources to the project for at least a year. Such a project can be organized so that software is written through *team effort*. Teachers who are experts in certain subject areas can help plan the sequences of lesson segments or simulations; that is, the *design* of the program. The team may also include clerical help, computer graphics designers, layout specialists, and of course, talented programmers. If possible, help from students and parents should be organized. When the software is finished, then teachers can write documentation, teacher's guides, and other materials that help integrate the programs into the school's curriculum.

ONE SCHOOL DISTRICT'S APPROACH TO THE SELECTION OF HARDWARE

When the governing board of Glendale, Arizona, Elementary School District No. 40 decided to begin the process of microcomputer selection for their schools, a long discussion resulted in a general statement of their position, including their priority of goals.

1. Teaching computer literacy

2. Computer-assisted instruction

3. Management

Ben Fast, who had worked in the computer field for more than twenty years, attended the discussions. Subsequently he and a co-worker, Merrill Harlan, wrote the "Request for Proposal for Microcomputer Hardware, Software, and Services," which appears on the following pages. We are grateful to Mr. Fast for approving the inclusion of the document in this book, and for the time he spent interviewing with us.

What advice can be given to a district beginning the hardware selection process? First, a project must be designed carefully. It is nearly impossible to overplan, or to pay too much attention to detail. After a reasonable plan has been designed and approved, then the next step will be to write the request for proposals, including the hardware specifications. When defining the hardware requirements, be careful not to eliminate most microcomputer choices by being too specific. In other words, "semi-define" so that the hardware specifications do not point to any particular brand or model of microcomputer. (If the decision has already been made as demonstrated by the specifications, then why go through the process at all?) Keeping an open mind should lead to the best results when selecting hardware.

The district/vendor relationship is vitally important for smooth operation of computer-related programs. This holds true no less for microcomputers than for the larger computer equipment owned by the district. This means that the district has an obligation to the vendor *and* the vendor has an obligation to serve the district. It should be remembered that microcomputer companies are in business for volume and that they are not equipped to provide constant service. Therefore, a district must provide the vendor with information on the exact intentions and expectations of the district. And, of course, the vendor must indicate carefully what services will be provided. After microcomputers are selected and purchased, there should be an open line of communication with the vendor so that questions can be answered, service requested, and additional hardware located as necessary.

The following "Request for Proposal for Microcomputer Hardware, Software, and Services" reflects Glendale's approach to selecting hardware. Note that the bulk of responsibility for providing information fell upon the vendors—including the task of listing available software for specific uses. This approach is in contrast with the "research-your-own" microcomputer selection form presented in the beginning of this chapter. Several comments are in order here. First, Glendale's request for proposals was for the purchase of ninety microcomputer systems and a certain amount of peripheral equipment. Districts purchasing fewer computers may find vendors unwilling to process these forms.

Second, vendors will complete the forms with mixed results. Glendale found the responses to range from poor to acceptable quality. *No* vendors completed the form to the district's complete satisfaction. It is debatable whether the search for and evaluation of software should be left to microcomputer companies. But the response in this regard will at least give the school district some idea of the company's attitude and commitment to educational computing, as well as the range of software available.

Glendale recognized the need for a reasonable amount of pre-packaged software to be available for classroom use. Although teachers were not discouraged from writing their own software for educational uses, neither were they be *expected* to do so.

After all proposals were received, each vendor was invited to make a presentation to the microcomputer selection committee, composed of twelve persons. Money was not to be discussed; the committee had agreed to judge the hardware on performance only.

The selection committee made their final choice after reviewing the proposals, seeing the vendors' presentations, and contacting other districts using the microcomputers in question. Consequently, Glendale Elementary Schools received the microcomputer systems and has now begun the process of microcomputer integration into the schools.

We have included the actual "Request for Proposal for Microcomputer Hardware, Software, and Services" that was sent to microcomputer vendors. The document has been written clearly and specifically, and may add some understanding to how such documents can be written and used to find the best equipment for your school's needs.

Request for Proposal for Microcomputer Hardware, Software, and Services

Requested by
Glendale Elementary School District No. 40
Glendale, Arizona

ADVERTISEMENT FOR PROPOSALS

Note is hereby given that the Glendale Elementary School District No. 40 will receive sealed proposals for computer hardware, software, and related services.

Each proposal must be submitted on the proposal form and in accordance with the specifications on file at the Purchasing Department, 5734 West Glendale Avenue, Glendale, Arizona, 85301.

Sealed proposals will be received until 10:00 A.M. on May 26, 1982, at the Purchasing Department, Glendale Elementary School District No. 40, 5734 West Glendale Avenue, Glendale, Arizona, 85301.

The Glendale School District No. 40 reserves the right to reject any or all proposals or waive any informality in any proposal.

Dated this 14th day of May, 1982.

TABLE OF CONTENTS

1.0 General Statement of Governing Board's Position on Microcomputers

The governing board of the Glendale Elementary School District believes it is important for young people to be exposed to the computer as a basic educational tool. The board further affirms that it is our primary goal to teach our students computer literacy. Our secondary goal is to use computer-assisted instruction in the learning process. Our third priority will be to use the computer as a management instrument.

The governing board intends for microcomputer instruction to be compatible with our overall district curriculum. The opportunity to become involved in this program should eventually be available to every interested student in our district.

Furthermore, the district recognizes that computer hardware alone is not sufficient to fulfill the immediate and future educational needs. For this reason, special consideration will be given to those vendors who demonstrate or identify educational software packages available by their publication divisions or by reputable, established educational publishers from the private sector.

2.0 Preparation of Bid

2.1 Bids shall be time stamped. They shall be accepted up to, and no later than, the time indicated in the notice inviting sealed bids. Those received after this time will be recorded and returned unopened to the bidder. Bidder will assume responsibility for delivery on time at the place specified, whether sent by mail or delivered in person.

2.2 The submission of a bid will indicate the bidder has read the terms and conditions, that the bidder understands the requirements and that he can supply items specified.

2.3 All bids must be submitted on the attached set of forms. All supplied forms must be returned with your bid. Additional information of appendices are welcome.

2.4 All bids must indicate a firm name and be signed by a responsible person or persons as per the certification sheet attached.

2.5 Telephone or telegraphic bids are not accepted.

2.6 Time of delivery is an essential part of the consideration for the contract. If it is impossible to meet the hardware delivery time specified, bidder shall state best delivery time possible.

2.7 Bidders assume all responsibility and file any claims in regard to any lost or damaged merchandise.

3.0 Taxes

The school district is exempt from all federal excise tax and this tax should be deducted from bids or not included in the bid and stated accordingly.

4.0 Prices

All prices are to be firm net prices including all discounts. Please note that we have provided a column for unit price as well as the total price. Please complete both columns and give the brand name.

5.0 Award

The award will be made to the lowest qualified bidder who submits a bid which is considered most advantageous to the district. The Governing Board of the Glendale Elementary School District reserves the right to reject any and/or all bids; to make awards as they may appear to be advantageous to the district; and to waive all formalities in bidding.

6.0 Vendor Statement

The Glendale Elementary School District believes the performance of a vendor is extremely important. Therefore, a written statement of your company's history and its future direction toward the public elementary educational environment must be provided. Include the current priority your company has placed on public elementary education for research and development, both hardware and software, affiliations with educational publishing companies and future expectations for this type environment.

7.0 References

The Glendale Elementary School District requires *three* references from other public elementary educational users of the same hardware and software being bid. It is understood the School District may contact these references directly.

Institution name, address, phone number and person in charge of the educational installation to be contacted:

1.

2.

3.

8.0 Hardware

The initial intent of the Glendale Elementary School District is to purchase 90 basic stand-alone microcomputers. These units must contain all the features and have the capability to execute all software contained in your bid. While the bid requirements are for the basic components of a stand-alone microcomputer, it is equally important that the bids include all additional features and capability for expansion to the basic units. It is the intent of the district to add extra features as the instructional program develops.

Your bid package *must* contain descriptive literature on items bid.

8.1 Microprocessor Unit

- Basic requirements: 16K random access memory, all I/O automatically managed by operating software, floating point BASIC resident in hardware, 110v–120v power

- Additional features: Upgrade to a minimum 48K random access memory; interface capabilities: disk drives—expandable to 650K, cassettes, printers, network (bidirectional load); speech synthesizer; timer; music

8.2 Video Display

- Basic requirements: 1000 minimum character display

- Additional features: Upper- and lower-case letters, graphic format, animation, color monitor

8.3 Keyboard

- Basic requirements: Standard Alpha-numeric ASCII keyboard

- Additional features: Upper- and lower-case letters, cursor control (left, right, up, down), 10 key numeric pad, recess protected key

		Brand Name	Mfg. No.	Unit Price	Total Price	Warranty Period
Basic Requirements:	MICROPROCESSOR: (Indicate all features included) _____ _____ _____ _____ _____ _____					
Additional Features:	Upgrade to a minimum 48K Interface: (explain) Printer Disk Drives Cassettes Network Speech Synthesizer Tuner Music Other **Note:** Include all adapters, monitors, etc., required					

		Brand Name	Mfg. No.	Unit Price	Total Price	Warranty Period
Basic Requirements:	VIDEO DISPLAY (Indicate all features included) _____ _____ _____					
Additional Features:	Upper-Lower Case Letters Graphic Format Animation Color Other _____					
Basic Requirements:	KEYBOARD (Indicate all features included) _____ _____ _____					
Additional Features:	Upper-Lower Case Letters Cursor Control 10 Keypad Recess Protector Key Other _____					

9.0 Software

Complete the forms for education software available for grades K through 8 that can run on your proposed hardware covering each of the four major disciplines: Mathematics, Reading, Language Arts, and Computer Literacy. The availability of elementary instructional software that will operate, without modification, on the bid hardware will be a major consideration in the award of the bid. All software bids must include descriptive literature of the application, title, publisher, grade levels, and cost. This software must cover all of the instructional techniques indicated below:

9.1 Computer Literacy is the first priority of the computer educational program. The Computer Literacy program will encompass grades Kindergarten-Eighth and software packages should include such topics as

9.1.1 What is a computer?

9.1.2 History of the computer

9.1.3 How the computer works

9.1.4 Computer advantages and disadvantages

9.1.5 Computer careers

9.1.6 Computers of the future

9.1.7 Operating the computer

9.1.8 Programming the computer

9.2 CAI (Computer Assisted Instruction)

9.2.1 Drill and practice—Reinforcing basic concepts that need to be learned

9.2.2 Tutorial—Reteaches a child a concept which needs minimal teacher interaction

9.2.3 Simulation—Creates a model of a real-life or imaginary situation and requires the child to make decisions

9.2.4 Games—Reinforces the learning process

9.3 Student Controlled Language—provides the student with the capability of controlling the computer (ex: Logo, etc.)

MATHEMATICS

Title	Description	Instructional Type	Publisher	Grade Level	Cost

This grid should be used as a measure for Reading, Language Arts, and Computer Literacy as well as Mathematics.

10.0 Maintenance/Reliability

10.1 Give the address of nearest service/support center.

10.2 The bidder must provide an extended service plan option that covers labor and parts for a full twelve months. Indicate the kind of service contracts offered:

10.3 State cost of the proposed service contract.

10.4 Indicate the type of service conducted (on-site, delivered, etc.) and if loaners are available while hardware is inoperable.

10.5 What is the reliability of the hardware (average number of times in a school year a piece of hardware must be repaired)?

10.6 What training would you provide for in-house maintenance?

11.0 Training—Operation of the Computer

The successful bidder must provide on-site in-service training sessions.

11.1 What training services will your company provide (minimum of 2–4 hour sessions)?

11.2 Cost of these training sessions?

11.3 What additional support will your company provide beyond the training sessions (hot line, users' groups, etc.)?

11.4 Cost of this additional support?

12.0 Language

Indicate the types of programming languages the hardware supports and cost:

13.0 Delivery

Delivery of all hardware and software must be made by *June 30, 1982*. (If it is impossible to meet the hardware and/or software delivery time specified, vendor shall state best delivery time possible.)

14.0 Demonstration/Evaluation

14.1 Successful bidders will be invited to demonstrate both hardware and software at the Glendale Elementary School District Administrative Center, 5734 West Glendale Avenue, Glendale, Az., 85301.

14.2 Each bidder will be limited to two (2) hours.

14.3 The District will select five (5) programs from the submitted software for demonstration. The five applications will cover the following:

14.3.1 One program from each of the three disciplines: Reading, Language Arts, and Math

14.3.2 Student controlled language

14.3.3 One application from the computer literacy package

14.3.4 Drill and practice, tutorial, simulation, and games should be illustrated in the demonstration.

14.4 The vendor demonstration is scheduled for May 28, 1982, in the District Board Room.

15.0 Certificate of Signature

This is to certify that the person signing and/or submitting the attached bid to the Glendale Elementary School District for

_____

Name

_____   _____

Company's OWNER   OFFICER

Authorized Proposing Agent _____ is fully authorized
to submit such bid on behalf of said.

_____   _____

(Company)   (Date)

_____   _____

(Address)   (Telephone)

_____   _____

(Signature)   (Title)

The above "Certification of Signature" *must* be executed, and *must* be returned with your bid.

SUMMARY

The process of hardware selection should begin with the question, "What do we want the computer to do?" In many cases, software availability should be explored first; then with the range of possibilities narrowed considerably, hardware consideration can begin. A list of possible applications for computers in schools was provided in this chapter.

Occasionally, individual educators make hardware choices on a small-scale basis. A plan of action was described. When hardware decisions will be made in a more formal manner, some way should be devised to record information clearly. A microcomputer selection form was provided, explained, and the criteria listed were defined.

Considerations and limitations concerning the creation of computer-assisted instruction and other software were discussed. School districts need to have realistic expectations in this regard.

Finally, a document entitled "Request for Proposal for Microcomputer Hardware, Software, and Services" was presented, illustrating the process by which one school district chose a microcomputer for its needs.

REFERENCES

Finkel, LeRoy. "Selecting a Microcomputer: It's More than the Hardware." *Classroom Computer News* 1, no. 6 (July-August, 1981): 10–13.

Fisher, Glenn. "Disk Sharing: How to Make One Disk Drive Go 'Round." *Electronic Learning* 1, no. 5 (May-June 1982): 46–51.

SUGGESTED READINGS

Ahl, David. *Creative Computing Buyer's Guide to Personal Computers, Peripherals, and Electronic Games.* Morristown, N.J.: August, 1982. Includes reviews on many microcomputers and information on communications systems, printers, memory expansion, music instrument system, speech synthesis, electronic games, and other peripherals and hardware-related items.

Berger, Ivan. "The TRS-80 Model III." *Popular Computing* 1, no. 3 (January 1982): 16–20.

Billings, Karen, and Stephen Gass. "Adding a Micro to Your School Picture." *Electronic Learning* 1, no. 3 (January-February 1982): 35–41.

Blair, Marjorie. "One Giant Leap for IBM, One Small Step for Micros." *Electronic Education* 1, no. 2 (October 1981): 19–20.

Calkins, Andrew. "State Governments and the New Technologies: A Report on What Each State is Doing." *Electronic Learning* 1, no. 2 (November-December 1981): 56–59, 84.

Datapro Research Corporation. *All About Personal Computers.* New York: McGraw-Hill, 1981.

Erickson, Jonathan. "EL's Guide to Printers: What to Know Before You Invest." *Electronic Learning* 1, no. 4 (March-April 1982): 45–47.

Fastie, Will. "The IBM Personal Computer." *Creative Computing* 7, no. 12 (December 1981): 19–40.

Flint, Glen, and Mark Dahmke. "The ATARI 400." *Popular Computing* 1, no. 7 (May 1982): 74–78.

Kolodziej, Leo and John Holland. "The Vic-20." *Popular Computing* 1, no. 7 (May 1982): 96–102.

Miastkowski, Stan. "Choosing Your Popular Computer." *Popular Computing* 1, no. 1 (November 1981): 15–23.

———. "The Commodore Computers." *Popular Computing* 1, no. 3 (January 1982): 22–23.

———. "The Sinclair ZX81." *Popular Computing* 1, no. 7 (May 1982): 88–94.

Neale, Kathy. "The ATARI 800." *Popular Computing* 1, no. 3 (January 1982): 30–32.

Nelson, Harold. "Another Industry Giant Takes a Micro Step [Xerox]." *Microcomputing* 5, no. 12 (December 1981): 94–98.

Press, Larry. "Getting Started in Personal Computing." *On Computing* 2, no. 4 (Spring 1981): 8–17.

"Putting Printers in Perspective—A Personal Computing Guide Through the Printer Jungle." *Personal Computing* 5, no. 8 (October 1981): 67–110.

Skier, Ken. "Radio Shack's Color Computer." *Popular Computing* 1, no. 7 (May 1982): 80–86.

Staples, Betsy. "IBM Personal Computer: The Big Blue Giant Makes Its Move." *Creative Computing* 7, no. 11 (November 1981): 14–19.

———. "Van Helps Schools Select the Right Computer." *Creative Computing* 7, no. 3 (March 1981): 106–112.

Stewart, George. "The Apple II." *Popular Computing* 1, no. 3 (January 1982): 24–26.

Sturdivant, Patricia. "Raising Money for Technology: Some Do-It-Yourself Ideas." *Electronic Learning* 1, no. 1 (September/October 1981): 22, 24.

———. "Selecting a Microcomputer: It's More Than the Hardware." *Classroom Computer News* 1, no. 6 (July-August 1981): 10–13.

Withrow, Frank B., and Linda G. Roberts. "The Videodisc: Putting Education on a Silver Platter." *Electronic Learning* 1, no. 5 (May-June 1982): 43–45.

Zamora, Ramon. "The Rainbow Machine [Vic-20]." *Recreational Computing* 10, no. 2 (July-August 1981): 14–15.

8

A Computer Literacy Curriculum

Our society is currently in a state of revolution. This revolution is taking place quietly, without soldiers, without weapons, but it promises to change our daily lives within the very near future. Of course, this is a revolution of technology. Daily almost, we read in the papers or hear on a newscast about some technological development that has altered some familiar process or job radically. Reports of larger and more capable computer systems are commonplace.

Opinions about the future of technology may vary from expert to expert, but one thing is certain. We live in an age of more rapid and significant technological advancement than has ever occurred during the history of civilization. What are the implications of this rapid advancement?

First, we must prepare ourselves to live comfortably with, and use the capacities of, computers, which many computer scientists assert will soon be standard appliances in newly constructed homes. We must become computer literate so that we can adjust to tomorrow's computerized society.

Second, we must prepare for the predicted shift in employment emphasis from industrial to technological career fields. The U.S. Bureau of Labor Statistics conservatively estimates that the demand for trained and competent computer professionals will more than double within the next decade. Some estimates are that the number of computer professionals required to keep the computer systems of tomorrow operating will be three times what it is today. In addition, the advent of more sophisticated artificial intelligence and robots will free many workers in manufacturing fields to move into the expanding field of computer science.

All of this revolution and change will require that education be geared toward familiarizing students with the capabilities of computers and computer-related careers. The schools have a responsibility to acknowledge the needs of an increasingly computerized society and prepare students to fulfill those needs as productive citizens. Today, educators wrestle with the questions that arise whenever computer literacy curricula are discussed. What sorts of topics should be introduced to students? At what age should students be introduced to computer fundamentals? How much knowledge about computers must teachers possess before they can be considered competent to teach computer literacy? And, perhaps the most basic of all, what is computer literacy?

A DEFINITION OF COMPUTER LITERACY

Computer literacy may be thought of as consisting of two areas of knowledge: Computer awareness and computer programming. As discussed in Chapter 2, *computer awareness* is basically an ability to recognize computers, their capabilities, and limitations and includes developing an openness in dealing with computers. Computer awareness topics can be introduced to students in a classroom that does not have a computer. It can be taught as a preliminary to actually installing a computer in a classroom.

Although computers are complicated and sophisticated electronic equipment, learning to use them does not require extensive training or experience. Most computer educators feel that no child is too young to be exposed to computers, for the very young child is curious about mechanical devices and has not yet been intimidated by computers.

The average five-year-old kindergartner is probably prepared to begin participating in computer awareness activities. What sorts of information about computers should a five-year-old be given? Kindergartners can be told what a computer is. Of course, this definition will need to be relatively basic, but it provides a foundation for more sophisticated knowledge in subsequent grades. In addition to learning what a computer is, the kindergartner can also be trained to follow directions, a skill that is vital to anyone who works with a computer.

Children of kindergarten age are also able to grasp a number of basic computer terms. Again, these terms must be relatively fundamental and must be explained patiently and clearly. But this knowledge gives small children a way to begin to think of and talk about computer activities.

The first grader is prepared to build upon the foundation of computer awareness received in kindergarten and can now learn what a computer can do. An appreciation of the computer's capabilities will also help the child to see the computer as an extremely useful tool. Typing skills may also be taught to children of this age. In the absence of a computer in the classroom, children can begin typing on a standard typewriter keyboard to develop the manual dexterity they will need to enter commands into the computer terminal later on. If a computer is available, they can begin to learn how to operate it.

Having gained some sense of the value and power of computers in first grade, second graders can go on to learn about the many advantages computers offer society. They can learn about the computer's numerous applications in all segments of daily life. Along with these discussions, it may be appropriate to discuss some of the disadvantages of computers, that they are sometimes used for fraudulent or dangerous purposes, for example. Children can be taught about the ways

computers affect our daily lives by taking field trips to banks where computers are used, or they might be encouraged to compile a list of the many places they find computers in use. This will help them develop an appreciation for the great usefulness of computers in their own lives as well as in business and government. Second graders are also capable of learning about the future of computers so that they can see how rapidly technological advancement occurs and become comfortable in adjusting to the changes in life-style such advancement is likely to bring.

Third graders are prepared to study the history of computers. In addition, they are capable of grasping the rudiments of logic, which will help them to create increasingly complex programs of their own. They can also understand the basics of how a computer works. Again, this material must be presented slowly and basically at a level the children can comprehend. Along with learning how a computer works, they are probably ready also to learn about different parts of the computer. This enhances their vocabulary of computer terms so that as they gain more complex knowledge, they also gain a language with which to talk about their discoveries.

Fourth graders are primed to learn more complex concepts of computer science. They may be exposed to the terms *hardware* and *software,* and they may be shown examples of both. They may also begin to learn the processes of flowcharting and storyboarding, which will improve their programming abilities. Teachers may also choose to present formulas, relations, and binary numbers—mathematical concepts that are crucial to the budding computer scientist!

Fifth graders should be given a thorough understanding of the history of computers, broken down into generations. This will help

them to appreciate the technological advances which have resulted in the invention of today's computers and may encourage them to speculate about the computers they will work with in the future. They can also learn about counters. As they develop the capacity to compose fairly lengthy written texts, they will be eager to learn about word processing. Composition educators are excited about the improvements in student writing that work on word processers seems to foster.

Sixth graders should learn about the different types of computers and how these types vary from each other. They can begin to conceive of the notion of data handling. Another topic of interest to this age group is the numerous computer languages in which programming is done. The teacher may choose to present the basics of looping to students.

Seventh graders are ready to learn about modeling. They will also be fascinated to explore the ever-widening field of robotics. This issue may bring up another important topic for this age group to explore: the social implications of computer usage. These students are mature enough to discuss ethical issues cogently. They may also be exposed to the concept of data bases, which will more than likely be a vital source of information to them when they become adults.

Eighth graders will find the subject of computer crime interesting. This will make them aware of the dangers to be faced in a computerized society and also provides opportunities for teacher and students to talk about ethical issues. They are also prepared to begin to learn about algorithms, another mathematical concept that will prove invaluable to them in subsequent computer experiences.

Ninth graders should be given a solid appreciation for computer capabilities. They are prepared to expand their own horizons as novice programmers, and through this, they can learn about the fabulous power available in systems of all sizes. As they begin to structure their

own high school curriculum with an eye to career choices, they also need to be exposed to the numerous opportunities in computer-related fields. Many of them will work with computers, either directly or in adjunct functions of the careers they choose, and they need to develop an awareness of the options that are open to them.

Tenth graders can be expected to learn to handle data with ease and sophistication. They can be taught to predict, interpret, and generalize data, a skill that will benefit students in all fields they may pursue. They may also be exposed to the growing field of artificial intelligence.

Eleventh graders are prepared to explore the field of computer systems. They may visit various computer installations to learn about the systems that are now in use in different applications. They may also learn about sampling techniques and statistical application of computer capability. This will prepare students for all college majors, including research fields.

Twelfth graders have received fairly sophisticated training in computers. However, there is still material for them to study. They can be taught computer survival skills that will enable them to function competently in any setting where a computer is housed. They should also discuss the social implications of computer usage in terms of invasion of privacy. They may discuss this topic in legal, as well as ethical, terms.

Thus, grade school students acquire a respectable degree of computer awareness throughout their school careers. The topics suggested here may be presented through many techniques. Students may learn best from a combination of lectures, activities directed by the teacher, and class discussions.

Along with this introduction to computer literacy, students should be given the opportunity to develop in the other area of computer skills: computer programming. Of course, this instruction depends on the availability of a computer in the classroom. Again, no child is too young to begin operating a computer. Very small children are capable of writing simple programs.

Papert's computer language designed for educational use with children has been used successfully in nursery schools. Logo is an excellent beginning language for students—especially young students—of programming; it is designed with features that children find attractive and that encourage them to interact with the computer. (See Papert, *Mindstorms,* Basic Books, 1980.)

Papert and other experts in computer education have compared the process of learning to program a computer to the process of learning a foreign language. Young children seem to adapt to foreign languages quite readily, while older students sometimes have difficulty adjusting to new grammar and vocabulary. Indeed, the younger children are when exposed to foreign languages, the more easily and quickly they are likely to learn to speak languages, including computer languages. Very young children bring curiosity, enthusiasm, openness, and confidence to their work with computers. These qualities make the introduction of computer basics to small children simple and fun for both teacher and students.

As students advance, they will naturally want to write programs of increasing complexity and capability. This will motivate them to learn more about the capacity of the systems with which they are working and about the various programming languages available to them. They may also learn to apply their skills with computers to other academic areas. For example, the computer enthusiast may learn a great deal about writing while editing and revising a composition on a word processor.

Both computer awareness and computer-programming themes and activities should be presented at a level that is appropriate to the age and capability of the students. Presenting material tha advanced or too simplified will simply discourage stude ing the field of computers. Also, both areas of compute to be introduced in such a way that they complement other.

Following is a sample suggested computer literacy curriculum offers topics and activities designed for students of various grade levels. The curriculum, by Gary G. Bitter, appeared as a series of articles titled "The Road to Computer Literacy," which was published in *Electronic Learning*.*

THE ROAD TO COMPUTER LITERACY: A SCOPE AND SEQUENCE MODEL

As you read through the Scope and Sequence charts, you'll notice that there are very few indications of when mastery of particular topics should be expected. This is not to say that the topics to be covered in a Computer Literacy curriculum will never be mastered, but rather that at this point, you should not assume previous knowledge of anything on the part of the student. Perhaps five years from now, after a full-blown Computer Literacy curriculum has been in place for a while, it'll make more sense to indicate at what grade levels you should assume mastery of particular topics.

Most likely, given your experiences as educators, you have your own ideas about that now. And, most likely, you have your own ideas about what topics should or should not be included in the chart as well as at what points particular topics should or should not be introduced. Let me reiterate: This Scope and Sequence is just a model. Treat it as a guide, not gospel.

Objectives and Activities for Grades K–3

These topics and their objectives are meant to serve only as guideposts along the road to computer literacy. As you develop your own computer literacy roadmap, you may want to change or modify the scope and sequence outlined here.

The topics for this computer literacy model are divided into two broad areas for each grade level: Computer Awareness and Program-

---

*Gary G. Bitter, "The Road to Computer Literacy: A Scope and Sequence Model," *Electronic Learning* 2, no. 1 (September 1982): 60–63; no. 2 (October 1982): 34–37, 85–86; no. 3 (November/December 1982): 44–48, 90–91; no. 4 (January 1983): 40–42, 46–48; no. 5 (February 1983): 54–56, 60. Reprinted with permission.

Computer Literacy Scope and Sequence
Grades K-3

	Computer Awareness													Programming												
Topics	K	1	2	3	4	5	6	7	8	9	10	11	12	K	1	2	3	4	5	6	7	8	9	10	11	12
K																										
What a Computer Is	IA	C	C	C	C	C	C	C	C	R	R	R	R													
Following Directions	IA	C	C	C																						
Vocabulary	IA	C	C	C	C	C	C	C	C	C	C	C	C													C
Programming Programmable Devices														IA	C	M										
Turtle Graphics (Making Shapes)														IA	C	C										
1ST GRADE																										
What a Computer Can Do		IA	C	C	C	C	C	C	C	R	R	R	R													
Learning to Use a Computer		IA	C	C	C	C	C	C	C	C	C	C	C													
Using the Keyboard		IA	C	C	M																					
Turtle Graphics (Moving Shapes)															IC	C	C									

LEGEND: IA—Introduction with Activities ID—Introductory Discussion C—Expansion of Discussion from Previous Grades R—Review M—Mastery

214

Computer Awareness / Programming Scope Chart

Topics	Computer Awareness													Programming												
	K	1	2	3	4	5	6	7	8	9	10	11	12	K	1	2	3	4	5	6	7	8	9	10	11	12
2ND GRADE																										
Computer Advantages			IA	C	C	C	C	C	C	C	C	C	C													
Computer Disadvantages			IA	C	C	C	C	C	C	C	C	C	C													
Computers in Our Lives			ID	C	C	C	C	C	C	C	C	C	C													
Everyday Applications			ID	C	C	C	C	C	C	C	C	C	C													
Future			ID	C	C	C	C	C	C	C	C	C	C													
Turtle Graphics (Rotations, etc.)																IA	C	C	C	C	C	C	C	C	C	C
Logo (Sprites)									C							IA	C	C	C	C	C	C	C	C	C	C
3RD GRADE																										
History				ID	C	C	C	C	C	C	C	C	C													
Logic				IA	C	C	C	C	C	C	C	C	C				IA	C	C	C	C	C	C	C	C	C
How a Computer Works				IA	C	C	C	C	C	C	C	C	C													
Parts of a Computer				IA	C	C	C	C	C	C	C	C	C													
Logo Programming																	IA	C	C	C	C	C	C	C	C	C
Problem Solving with Logo																	IA	C	C	C	C	C	C	C	C	C

ming. Under each Topic, I've listed Objectives, Introductory Activities and suggested Curriculum Representation Areas for introducing and teaching the topics.

The Objectives: Under each Topic, there is a specific learning objective. These objectives could easily be broken down into smaller, more precise sub-objectives. For example, the topic "Parts of a Computer" could easily be broken into an objective for each part. I've purposely left these objectives somewhat open-ended, however, rather than prescribe a performance-based plan.

Remember that although I've suggested the introduction of these objectives during grades K-3, they are appropriate objectives for any student who has not been exposed to them. The discussion level, of course, is dependent on the audience.

The Curriculum Area: Since I believe that computer literacy should be infused into the total curriculum at each grade level, I've suggested curriculum integration areas for each Topic and its Objective. These, again, are meant to serve only as a suggestion for one way to make the computer a part of every subject area—not simply a tool for mathematics.

The Activities: For each Objective, I've suggested both introductory discussion kinds of activities as well as some "hands-on" activities. While most of the activities under the Computer Awareness topics do not require the actual use of a microcomputer, many of them can be enhanced by the *presence* of a microcomputer. The Programming topics, however, do require access to a machine.

KINDERGARTEN

Computer Awareness

TOPIC: What a Computer Is

Objective: The student can describe the computer as a machine or tool that can help solve problems (with words or numbers) quickly and easily.

Curriculum Area: Reading/Language Arts

Activities: • Look up the word "computer" in a dictionary and an encyclopedia. As you read aloud to students, note key words and concepts. • Gather pictures of a wide range of computers—both large and small—to show to and discuss with the class. Make the pictures into a bulletin board display. • Ask if any student has a microcomputer at home. If so, have that student tell how his or her family uses the computer.

TOPIC: Following Directions

Objective: The student can follow verbal, written, and mimed directions.

Curriculum Area: All

Activities: • Play "Twister." Have students stand with eyes shut. Call out a series of commands to move their bodies in funny positions. Variation: Identify groups (by sex, hair color, first initial, etc.) to make certain moves. When groups are in various positions, have students open their eyes and look around. • Play "May I?" giving directions like "one giant step," or "two baby steps." • Pass out picture-list of objects in classroom, and send students on "scavenger hunt." • Draw picture-map of classroom, and number certain spots. Have a student follow the numbered map around the room.

TOPIC: Vocabulary

Objective: The student will become familiar with common computer words and their meaning.

Curriculum Area: Reading/Language Arts

Activities: • Have a computer word for the day, written on the chalkboard or posted on bulletin board. Define for students, using pictures if possible. • Compare certain words to parallel human activity, e.g., memory. • Later in the year, have students propose computer words for the day—both new and old terms. • Set up a concentration game, having students match words to corresponding pictures.

Programming

TOPIC: Programming Programmable Devices

Objective: The student can program a programmable device to carry out specific directions or activities.

Curriculum Area: Math—counting, logical thinking, and spatial relationships

Activities: • Teach the basic commands and demonstrate the device, e.g. "Big Trak." • Count with students the distance of each "unit"

BIG TRAK by Milton Bradley, Inc.

forward or backward. Find the amount each unit represents in a turn. Determine the number of steps it will accept. • Have the device travel in a square, rectangle, triangle, and circle. Have students operate. • Set up teams. Mark a target point X. Have each team try to program the device to reach Target X. (Make routes to X increasingly difficult over time.)

TOPIC: Turtle Graphics (Making Shapes)

Objective: The student can program a microcomputer to instruct the "turtle" to make geometric shapes.

Curriculum Area: Math—directions

Activities: • Teach the basic commands Forward, Back, Right, Left, Home, Show Turtle. Have students practice giving the turtle single commands. • Explore length and width of the screen with turtle steps. • Have students make squares, rectangles, triangles and circles using turtle graphics commands. • Have student teams plot (on paper) designs which use these basic shapes. Suggestions: Cat, Truck, snowman. Then have them place on screen with turtle graphics.

FIRST GRADE

Computer Awareness

TOPIC: What a Computer Can Do

Objective: The student can describe realistically what a computer can and cannot do for humans.

Curriculum Area: Social Studies

Activities: • Have each student design a fantasy machine which will perform some task for a human being. As students present their "inventions" to the class, discuss whether a computer could be part of that machine. • Have students help compile on the chalkboard two lists: "What a Computer Can Do" and "What a Human Brain Can Do." Compare the two, noting what does what better.

TOPIC: Learning to Use a Computer

Objective: The student can load and run a pre-programmed program on the computer.

Curriculum Area: All

Activities: • Demonstrate the steps involved with loading and running a program. Have students take turns operating the system. • Have students make up chart with directions on how to use the computer. Post at open house to teach parents about computers. • Assign groups to run a pre-programmed team activity, such as a game, drill and practice lesson, or simulation.

TOPIC: Using the Keyboard

Objective: The student can locate and identify the letters, numerals, and special keys for operations and commands on a microcomputer keyboard.

Curriculum Area: Reading/Language Arts—typing, paragraphs, grammar and grammatical requirements

Activities: • Post diagram of keyboard on bulletin board. Compare to diagram of standard typewriter keyboard. Color in the special keys, such as the Enter or Return key, and discuss their purpose. • Show students how to use the keyboard to correct typing errors. • Have students write a sentence with 25 letters or more to type. Let them study the keyboard to locate the letters. Then time them to see how fast they can type their sentence.

Programming

TOPIC: Turtle Graphics (Moving Shapes)

Objective: The student can create various shapes and move them horizontally and vertically.

Curriculum Area: Math—geometry, three-dimensional thinking: Art—shapes, designs

Activities: • Teach the students the commands Penup, Penerase, and Pendown, as well as Hide Turtle and Home. • Have students make a design which requires several movements of turtle with Penup and Pendown commands. (Suggestions: face with eyes, ears, and nose; house with windows, doors, and chimney; automobile with windows and doors.) • Let students "doodle," creating their own designs. (Reward students for good work by giving them blocks of "Doodle Time.")

SECOND GRADE

Computer Awareness

TOPIC: Computer Advantages

Objective: The student will list speed, accuracy, and "repetitious activity" as advantages of a computer.

Curriculum Area: Social Studies

Activities: • Have students do 50 addition problems as fast as they can. Count the errors each makes. Then show students how quickly the computer can do those same problems without error. • Have students print one word 50 times. Then have the computer print that word 50 times. Which was easier and faster?

TOPIC: Computer Disadvantages

Objective: The student will understand the computer as an impersonal, literal machine.

Curriculum Area: Social Studies

Activities: • Ask students to suggest questions a computer could not answer but a human could. (Suggestions: "Do you love me?" "Are you happy?") Note that computers cannot make personal judgments. • Have students misspell their names as they type them into the computer. What happens? • Have students type the command PRINT followed by their name in quotes. What happens? Then have them type the word WRITE followed by their name in quotes. What happens? Relate the results to the computer's language.

TOPIC: Computers in our Lives

Objective: The student can identify several roles the computer plays in our daily lives.

Curriculum Area: Social Studies; Science

Activities: • Ask students to be Computer Detectives. Give points for every example of computer-use students can list in a day or two. Suggest they look for examples in their neighborhoods, ask their parents, or watch for computers on TV. To win a point, they must describe what each computer does. • Invite adults who use computers in their work to come describe their computers to the class. (Suggestions: policemen, bankers, store clerks, travel agents, journalists, librarians, government records clerks.) • Develop with the class a scenario for a science-fiction movie, *The Day the Computers Went on Strike*. What sorts of problems would the computer strike cause? Could we ever get along without computers again?

TOPIC: Everyday Applications

Objective: The student can identify daily applications of computers, such as class attendance, paychecks, telephone bills, "cash machines."

Curriculum Area: Social Studies—everyday living

Activities: • Show students examples of computer-generated reports or bills. • Have students discuss places in the neighborhood where computers are being used, e.g., the grocery store, bank, etc. Take a field trip to local computer facilities.

TOPIC: The Future

Objective: The student can predict new uses for computers in the future.

Curriculum Area: Social Studies

Activities: • Discuss movies they have seen which have robots, two-way TV, spaceships, and other computers in them. Discuss when they think those computerized machines will be part of our lives. • Have students make a list of jobs they would like a computer to handle in the future. How many of those tasks can a computer handle today? • Look at pictures of contemporary family living. (List where computers can be used in the pictures.)

Programming

TOPIC: Turtle Graphics (Rotations, etc.)

Objective: The student can use the commands of turtle graphics to rotate shapes to make designs.

Curriculum Area: Math—geometry: Art—creative design

Activities: • Show students how the Repeat command works. Program a square, circle, triangle, pentagon, etc. to rotate. Before executing, ask students to predict what designs will result. After executing, experiment with effects of single changes in the program. • Develop designs which wrap around the screen to create various designs.

TOPIC: Logo (Sprites)

Objective: The student can give color, directions and speed to sprites as well as create and control them.

Curriculum Area: Science—speed, direction; Math—numerical; Art—shapes

Activities: • Call up and identify all the sprites already in Logo. Give each one speed, color, and direction. (Suggestion: have one sprite be the student's initial.) • Have students create sprites and make up stories to accompany the activities of the sprites.

THIRD GRADE_____

Computer Awareness

TOPIC: History

Objective: The student can describe several historical computing devices.

Curriculum Area: History; Social studies; Math—place value (Abacus); multiplication (Napier Bones)

Activities: • Have class design a large time line of computing inventions. On parallel time line, show other inventions to give historical context. • With class, draw the Computer's Family Tree, showing which machines were predecessors of which other machines. • Demonstrate the multiplication facts using Napier's bones, and place value using the Abacus.

TOPIC: Logic

Objective: The student can apply "and" and "or" to logical thinking events.

Curriculum Area: Math—logical reasoning

Activities: • Form two teams, the Ands and the Ors. Read simple sentences aloud, leaving the conjunctions blank, and have student decide which conjunction fits in the blank. That team gets the point. • Progress to sentence in which either conjunction could fit. Teams compete for the point by being first to describe a situation which would make that sentence need their conjunction. • Get students to describe how "and" and "or" switches in a computer might work. Demonstrate with light switch, turning on for "and" situations and then off for "or" situations. Describe how logic unit in a computer helps the computer to process information, controlling which impulses go along which electronic paths.

TOPIC: How a Computer Works

Objective: The student can describe how a computer works, explaining Input, Memory, the Central Processing Unit, the Arithmetic Unit, and Output.

Curriculum Area: Reading

Activities: • Discuss how human beings do the functions of a computer. Input = hearing, seeing, feeling, smelling, tasting, etc. CPU = brain: memory, reasoning, understanding. Output = speaking, signalling, writing, etc. • Break down problem-solving into a string of simple functions. In one column, show how a human being would add 3 and 7 (hear question, memorize, add, memorize, speak answer). In other column, show how a computer would answer same question (input, store, add, process, store, output).

TOPIC: Parts of a Computer

Objective: The student can name the parts of a computer, including Input, Output, Memory, Arithmetic/logic unit, and central processing unit.

Curriculum Area: Reading

Activities: • Post large, simplified diagram of computer, showing five basic components. List functions of computer on chalkboard, then draw arrows to link each function with appropriate parts of the machine. Trace through the diagram the route of a problem being solved. • On bulletin board, collect pictures of different devices that provide input, output, and memory for a computer. These would include disks, cassettes, punch cards, paper tape, CRTs, line printers, voice (input and output). Group the pictures in the three categories. • Open a microcomputer case, and show students memory, microprocessor, semi-conductors, etc. Look at an enlarged photo of a microcomputer chip. • Have students discuss difference between a general-use computer and a calculator or an arcade game, in terms of which basic parts have been limited.

Programming

TOPIC: Logo Programming

Objective: The student can combine the ideas of turtle geometry and sprites to create animations and sequential graphic displays.

Curriculum Area: Math—geometry

Activities: • Have students write programs, utilizing capabilities of Logo. • Have students generate their own projects, utilizing the capabilities of Logo. • Have the class, or teams, create an animated Fall Scene. Assign to each student one segment (procedure) of the scene (including falling leaves, swaying trees, cars moving, clouds sailing, etc.) Place all the procedures together to show the animated scene.

TOPIC: Problem Solving with Logo

Objective: The student can use Logo to solve problems in various curriculum areas.

Curriculum Area: All

Activities: • Assign problems which require Logo programming to solve. • Set up experiments using Logo and have students estimate the outcomes. (See Bitter and Watson's *Apple Logo Primer,* Reston Publishing Company, 1983, for ideas.)

Objectives and Activities
for Grades 4–6

The computer literacy objectives and activities for Grades K-3 focused primarily in the area of computer awareness. While the objectives for Grades 4-6 also include computer awareness topics, such as hardware, software, computer generations and flowcharting, the thrust of the scope and sequence at this level turns to programming. And the programming language that it centers around is BASIC. Why BASIC? For one thing, it is the most widely used computer language in elementary and secondary schools today; for another, it is available for all microcomputers; and, for a third, until a more conversational computer language comes along, it is, in my opinion, the best language for students.

The programming topics for these grades are introduced sequentially, based on my experience in helping young students become familiar with the computer and the language. Although most BASIC books begin with computing sums, differences, products, etc., I believe it's important for young students (particularly those with "mathphobia") to get an immediate "feeling" for the potential nonmathematical options of the computer. Therefore, I suggest introducing the PRINT and INPUT statements first.

Another consideration in selecting the statements to introduce at these grade levels was to choose those statements that are generic to most computers. Therefore, CATALOG, EDIT, etc., are not included as specific objectives here. Nevertheless, in your expansion of the topic "Learning to Use the Computer" (introduced in First Grade), you should include a discussion of those statements, along with an explanation of your computer's unique characteristics or commands. One word of caution, however: Teaching a particular system's shortcuts may hinder students who have access to other systems at home or at a club. Therefore, I recommend playing down all the "tricks-of-the-trade commands" unless students ask for them or discover them on their own.

Computer Literacy Scope and Sequence
Grades 4-6

4TH GRADE

Topics	Computer Awareness													Programming												
	K	1	2	3	4	5	6	7	8	9	10	11	12	K	1	2	3	4	5	6	7	8	9	10	11	12
Hardware					ID	C	C	C	C	C	C	C	C													
Software					ID	C	C	C	C	C	C	C	C													
Flowcharting					IA	C	C	C	C	R	R	R	R					IA	C	C	C	C	C	C	C	C
Storyboarding					IA	C	C	C	C	R	R	R	R					IA	C	C	C	C	C	C	C	C
BASIC: PRINT & REM																		IA	C	C	R	R	R	R	R	R
BASIC: LET																		IA	C	R	R	R	R	R	R	R
BASIC: INPUT																		IA	C	R	R	R	R	R	R	R
BASIC: GO TO																		IA	C	R	R	R	R	R	R	R
Formulas (Variables & Constants)					IA	C	C	C	C	C	C	C	C					IA	C	C	C	C	C	M		
String Data																		IA	C	C	C	C	C	C	C	R
Relations					IA	C	C	C	M									IA	C	C	C	M				
Binary Numbers					IA	C	C	C	C	C	C	C	C													

LEGEND: IA—Introduction with Activities   ID—Introductory Discussion   C—Expansion of Discussion from Previous Grades   R—Review   M—Mastery

Computer Awareness

Topics	K	1	2	3	4	5	6	7	8	9	10	11	12
5TH GRADE													
Computer Generations					ID		C	C	C				
Counters						IA	C	C	C	M			
BASIC: IF-THEN													
BASIC: ON-GO TO													
BASIC: READ-DATA						IA	C	C	C				
Word Processing													
6TH GRADE													
Computer Types							ID	C	C	R	R	R	R
Data Handling							IA	C	C	C	C	C	C
Computer Languages							IA	C	C	C	C	C	
Looping							IA	C	C	M			
BASIC: FOR-NEXT													
BASIC: Random Number													
Problem Solving with BASIC													
Graphics													

Programming

Topics	K	1	2	3	4	5	6	7	8	9	10	11	12
5TH GRADE													
Computer Generations								C	C	C	C	C	C
Counters						IA	C	R	R	R	R	R	R
BASIC: IF-THEN						IA	C	R	R	R	R	R	R
BASIC: ON-GO TO						IA	C	R	R	R	R	R	R
BASIC: READ-DATA						IA	C	R	R	R	R	R	R
Word Processing						IA	C	C	C	C	C	C	C
6TH GRADE													
Computer Types													
Data Handling													
Computer Languages							IA	C	C	C	C	C	C
Looping							IA	C	C	C	C	C	C
BASIC: FOR-NEXT							IA	C	C	C	C	C	C
BASIC: Random Number							IA	C	C	C	C	C	C
Problem Solving with BASIC							IA	C	C	C	C	C	C
Graphics							IA	C	C	C	C	C	C

In teaching programming, I also recommend the "Guided Discovery" approach. In other words, rather than providing specific instruction, provide guidance with appropriate questions.

FOURTH GRADE

Computer Awareness

TOPIC: Hardware

Objective: The student can describe computer hardware as the physical components or equipment of a computer system, and identify those components.

Curriculum Area: Language Arts; Reading

Activities: • Have students collect computer store ads, catalogs, and flyers, or write to companies for catalogs. Using these, create a class computer file with index cards describing various computer components. • When cards are completed, divide them into categories for INPUT, OUTPUT, CENTRAL PROCESSING UNIT, and MEMORY. • Have students "build" computer systems by putting together sets of cards. (Discuss compatibility of different manufacturers' equipment.) As students "shop" in the file, others may role play as salespersons for computer companies, and try to sell their products by highlighting the best features.

TOPIC: Software

Objective: The student can define software as a set of instructions, called a program, that tells a computer what to do.

Curriculum Area: Language Arts; Reading

Activities: • Explain to students that a computer can't do anything unless it is given a set of instructions or programs called software. (Note the difference between applications software and systems software.) • Discuss different types of applications software or programs, and explain that those programs are written in special languages. • Work with students to invent a special language which could program a robot to vacuum a room.

TOPIC: Binary Numbers

Objective: The student can understand the use of 0 and 1 as the numerals used by computers to represent numbers, letters, and symbols.

Curriculum Area: Math

Activities: • Ask students to show how many different ways they can show the number 5 (Roman numeral V; the number 5; holding up five fingers). Then write "101" on the chalkboard and ask them what number they think that is. Explain that "101" is the number 5 in the binary number system. • If necessary, review with students our decimal system. Then explain that the binary system is based on the number 2 and uses only two numbers, 0 and 1. • Draw a chart like the one below. Have students fill in our number for each binary number. • Explain the "on-off" idea of a light switch, where "on" equals 1 and "off" equals 0. Note that different on-off "switches" in a computer are used to represent numbers and letters.

	Eights	Fours	Twos	Ones	OUR NUMBER
BINARY NUMBER		1	0	1	5
			1	1	
	1	0	0	1	
	1	1	0	0	
		1	1	1	

TOPIC: Flowcharting (also Programming Topic)

Objective: The student can identify common flowchart symbols, write a simple flowchart for a program and convert it to BASIC.

Curriculum Area: All

Activities: • Write a flowchart programming a robot to perform simple classroom tasks. (A full description of this activity can be found in Dr. Bitter's book, *Exploring with Computers,* published by Julian Messner-Simon & Schuster, 1983.) Identify, as you use them, the symbols for START–STOP, INPUT–OUTPUT, DECISION, PROCESS, and CONNECTOR. • Post the chart and have small groups of students write flowcharts programming the robot to perform other tasks. Have groups trade flowcharts and act out the directions. • Write a flowchart for a day in school. Include classes, lunch, special assemblies, and choices of recess or library.

TOPIC: Storyboarding (also Programming Topic)

Objective: The student can develop a short picture program and prepare a storyboard for each display, using graph paper.

Curriculum Area: Language Arts; Art

Activities: Have students design their initials five centimeters high on storyboard graph paper. Convert into a BASIC program. • Design logos for TV networks, movie studios, record labels, or sports teams on graph storyboards, and convert into BASIC programs. • On a series of storyboards, prepare a demonstration of addition, using graphics to represent items being added. Write the programs in BASIC, or use Logo graphics.

Programming

TOPIC: BASIC—PRINT and REM

Objective: The student can write BASIC programs using the PRINT and REMARK statements.

Curriculum Area: Language Arts—spelling, writing; Math

Activities: • Explain the function of the PRINT statement, discussing the use of line numbers, quotation marks, and commas in writing programs. • Let students practice using the PRINT statement. What happens when they use quotation marks around a simple math problem? What happens without the quotation marks? • Explain the REM statement and why it is important in good program writing. • Have students program the computer to print a picture on the monitor, using "X's" or symbols, such as the asterisk. • Work with the class to print their initials eight centimeters high, using the letter "X". • Have students program the computer to print a letter to their parents, telling about their experience with the computer. If a printer is available, get printouts of their letters for them to take home.

TOPIC: BASIC—LET

Objective: The student can use the LET statement in a BASIC program.

Curriculum Area: Reading; Math

Activities: • On the chalkboard, print the following examples of programs using the PRINT and LET statements. Have students predict the computer output:

```
10 LET X = 5
20 LET U = 7
30 LET R = 10
40 PRINT X, X + U, X * R
50 END
```

```
10 LET A$ = "YES"
20 LET B$ = "NO"
30 PRINT A$, B$
40 END
```

• Set up examples of programs which illustrate storage of variables. Before running, ask students to predict the output. Ask what happened to the value of X. • Explain that line 30 replaces line 10 and that there can only be one value of X.

```
10 LET X = 10
20 LET K = 20
30 LET X = 40
40 PRINT X, X + K, K + K, X + X
50 END
```

TOPIC: BASIC—INPUT

Objective: The student can use the INPUT statement in a BASIC computer program.

Curriculum Area: Reading; Math

Activities: • Give the students the following two programs. Have them determine when it's necessary to use the dollar sign with an INPUT statement.

```
10 PRINT "WHAT IS YOUR FAVORITE NUMBER?"
20 INPUT M
30 PRINT "YOUR FAVORITE NUMBER IS"; M
40 END
```

```
10 PRINT "WHAT IS YOUR NAME?"
20 INPUT B$
30 PRINT "YOUR NAME IS"; B$
40 END
```

• Give students programs with "bugs" in them. For example, leave out the dollar sign or the semicolon in the program above. Have the students correct the program (debug it) and run on the computer.

TOPIC: BASIC—GOTO

Objective: The student can use the GOTO statement in a BASIC program.

Curriculum Area: Reading; Math

Activities: • Ask students what they think an "endless loop" is. Then, print the following program on the chalkboard and ask them to predict what will happen when they run the program on the computer:

```
10 PRINT "I LOVE E.T."
20 GOTO 10
30 END
```

• Have students draw a flowchart to illustrate the use of the GOTO statement to repeatedly print their names. Then, have them write and run their programs.

TOPIC: Formulas—Variables and Constants (also Computer Awareness Topic)

Objective: The student can write a formula in BASIC including variables and constants, and can understand the order of operations.

Curriculum Area: Math; Science; Social Studies

Activities: • Have students enter equations with and without parentheses to determine the order of operations. • Have students measure the classroom walls. Divide the group into two teams. Have one team plug length and width into formula A = L × W to find out how much carpet the room needs. Have the other team plug into P = 2L + 2W to see how long a border strip would need to be run around the top of the walls. • Have both groups write BASIC programs using INPUT and PRINT to solve these problems.

TOPIC: String Data

Objective: The student can use words in a BASIC computer program.

Curriculum Area: English; Social Studies

Activities: • Have the students give the output of the BASIC program:

```
10 PRINT "WHAT IS THE WEATHER TODAY?"
20 INPUT A$
30 PRINT "THE WEATHER TODAY IS"; A$
40 END.
```

• Have students distinguish between string data and numbers by asking them to INPUT A and a name and then INPUT A$ and the same name. • Have a student report about keypunch data cards, explaining how holes are placed to represent certain letters. Have students "write" their names by punching out holes in cards. • With class members, list other forms of INPUT and OUTPUT—paper tape, optical scanner, etc. Discuss how these might be coded for different letters. Compare them to other codes such as Morse code or Braille.

TOPIC: Relations (also Computer Awareness Topic)

Objectives: The student can understand the relations "less than" (<), "equal to" (=), and "greater than" (>), and can use them in a computer program.

Curriculum Area: Math; English; Spelling; Social Studies

Activities: • Illustrate the relations "less than" (<) and "greater than" (>) on the chalkboard. Discuss how "equal to" may be combined to expand the relations. Use numbers to practice the relations on paper. • Write a BASIC program using IF/THEN statements to illustrate the three relations. • Demonstrate the relation for "equal to" using letters: IF X$ = "YES" THEN 80.

FIFTH GRADE

Computer Awareness

TOPIC: Computer Generations

Objective: The student can explain the impact of the vacuum tube, transistor, and integrated circuits upon the computer revolution.

Curriculum Area: Math—graphing; Social Studies; History

Activities: • Assign small groups to report on the vacuum tube, the transistor, the integrated circuit, and the chip. How did each advance computer technology? Look especially at improved speed, cost advantages, and changes in size. • Draw a family tree for computers, or prepare a bulletin board time line, showing the generations of computers.

TOPIC: Counters (also Programming Topic)

Objective: The student can explain the counter statement X = X + 1, and variations of it.

Curriculum Area: Math

Activities: • One student, playing X, writes a numerical value on the board. As other students call out "X = X + 1", the student has to keep changing the value. Act out X = X + 2 and Y = Y − 1. Ask students to figure out a formula to count by fives. Write these programs in BASIC and run them. • Have students explain this program:

```
10 PRINT "WHAT IS YOUR NAME?"
20 INPUT B$
30 LET A = A + 1
40 PRINT A, B$
50 GO TO 10
60 END.
```

• Have students create other programs using the counters.

Programming

TOPIC: BASIC—IF-THEN

Objective: The student can write a program using the IF-THEN statement for branching.

Curriculum Area: Math; Reading; Social Studies

Activities: • Write a flowchart to ask for a number, print the number, and designate whether it is even or odd. Convert this to a BASIC program. • Program a multiple-choice question. Have the computer indicate whether the chosen answer is right or wrong. • Using IF-THEN statements and a counter, write 10 multiple-choice multiplication questions. Show at the end how many were answered right or wrong. • Have students write social studies and science quiz questions for each other.

TOPIC: BASIC—ON-GOTO

Objective: The student can make use of the ON-GOTO statement in a BASIC computer program.

Curriculum Area: Math; Social Studies; Reading

Activities: • Write a flowchart which illustrates the ON-GOTO statement. • Have students write short trivia quizzes, and program them in BASIC using the ON-GOTO STATEMENT. • Help students to write a program to simulate the tossing of a die 50 times. Use an ON-GOTO statement and a counter to accumulate the results.

TOPIC: BASIC—READ-DATA

Objective: The student can use the READ-DATA statement to enter data into the computer.

Curriculum Area: Math

Activities: • Have students use the READ-DATA statement to add the numbers 10, 15, 20, and 30. Have them write the same program using the INPUT statement. Discuss which method works better in different situations. • Program:

```
10 READ A, B, C, D
20 PRINT A, A + B, C - A, D
30 DATA 10, 20, 30, 40
40 END.
```

• Have students predict the program output before running.

TOPIC: Word Processing (also Computer Awareness Topic)

Objective: The student can explain the applications of word processing, and write a letter using a word processing program on a microcomputer.

Curriculum Area: Writing; Language Arts

Activities: • Use an overhead projector to look at a form letter, a legal document (affidavit, lease, etc.), page of a technical manual, and a newspaper article. Discuss how a word processor might be useful in writing any of these. • Give students copies of a badly written story to correct by hand. Demonstrate how the story might be edited on a word processor. • As a class, write an announcement about a class activity, using the word processor program.

SIXTH GRADE

Computer Awareness

TOPIC: Computer Types

Objective: The student can distinguish between a mainframe, a mini, and a microcomputer.

Curriculum Area: Reading

Activities: • Divide the class into groups representing the mainframes, the minis, and the micros. Have each group comb through computer ads and catalogs for models fitting their category. Each group should prepare a catalog showing various models, noting speed, memory, cost, and applications. • Have groups trade their catalogs and discuss the pros and cons of each type. • Have a student report on the difference between digital and analog computers.

TOPIC: Data Handling

Objective: The student can understand the uses of a computer to process data.

Curriculum Area: Reading; Social Studies

Activities: • Discuss the term "data bank" with your students. Have them suggest different kinds of data banks that might be useful to them in school (e.g., important dates in history) • Invite the business manager of the school district to speak to the class, explaining what kind of data is handled by the school computer. • Have small groups of students create a data bank about someone in each group, listing such things as "color of hair," "favorite sport," and "height." Then have each group leader read the data in the data bank while other groups try to guess whom the data bank is about. • Have students research various existing data banks in the country and report on the purpose of each.

TOPIC: Computer Languages

Objective: The student can identify the common computer languages and their applications.

Curriculum Area: English; Reading; Math

Activities: • Assign teams to research various computer languages (BASIC, Logo, COBOL, FORTRAN, Pascal, etc.), and have the teams report on their languages, including what the names stand for, year developed and their primary application areas. • Have students "sell" a particular language to other students who assume roles of a small business owner, corporate executive, school principal, scientist, engineer, or student.

TOPIC: Looping (also Programming Topic)

Objective: The student can explain looping and its advantages in computer programming.

Curriculum Area: Math

Activities: Have students draw a flowchart to add five 100 times. Convert to a BASIC program. Relate to multiplication. Write a looped subtraction problem to illustrate divison. • Discuss looping situations in everyday life, such as in alphabetizing a list of names. • Write a

BASIC program to divide 1,750 by five continually until there is no remainder. Use a counter to count the number of times 1,750 can be divided by five. Print the result. • Discuss "nested loops," where one loop is completed between steps of another loop.

Programming

TOPIC: BASIC—FOR-NEXT

Objective: The student can utilize the FOR-NEXT statement in a BASIC computer program.

Curriculum Area: Math

Activities: • Have the students write a short program using the GOTO statement. Write the same program with the FOR-NEXT statement. • List some uses of the FOR-NEXT statement in a BASIC computer program. • Have students INPUT values (including negative numbers) for N in the following program. Ask them to predict the OUTPUT before running.

```
10 PRINT "GIVE VALUE OF N."
20 INPUT N
30 FOR I = 1 TO 15 STEP N
40 PRINT I
50 NEXT I
60 END
```

• Write a program to illustrate a "nested loop."

TOPIC: BASIC—RANDOM NUMBER

Objective: The student can use the RANDOM statement to write BASIC program simulations.

Curriculum Area: Social Studies; Science; Math—probability and statistics

Activities: • Demonstrate use of the RANDOM statement to program the tossing of a die. • Have the class write a program to simulate crossing a river. Random conditions may include success, drowning, partial success, and return to try again. • Discuss how the random number generator can be used in video game simulations. Study a video game and list the random conditions which seem to be part of the program. • Discuss how a flight simulator, randomly giving flight conditions, may be used to train pilots.

TOPIC: Problem Solving with BASIC

Objective: The student can solve problems by writing a BASIC program.

Curriculum Area: All

Activities: • Convert a graph of social studies data to a BASIC computer program. • Run a classroom opinion poll and graph the results using BASIC. • Write a BASIC program to simulate a science experiment. • Write a BASIC program to solve math problems, formulas, and equations.

TOPIC: Graphics

Objective: The student can use a microcomputer to create graphics.

Curriculum Area: Math; Art

Activities: • Use the graphics mode to print your name on the screen. Have students do the same with their names. • Have students create art matrices, preparing a storyboard first, then programming the graphics. • List different graphics features of the class computer system. Have students choose one feature (such as color or low- or high-resolution) and draw a graphic which uses it in an interesting way.

Objectives and Activities
for Grades 7–9

We concentrated previously on building a foundation of computer literacy skills during grades K-3 and 4-6—skills essential in understanding what a computer is and how it works, including such topics as binary numbers, computer vocabulary and using the keyboard. We also introduced students to the rudiments of programming in BASIC with topics like storyboarding, flowcharting and BASIC commands.

Having had this introduction to BASIC programming skills, students in grades 7-9 no longer program for programming's sake. Instead, they write programs to solve algorithms, simulate an event or produce graphics and sound. By starting with a specific objective, like tossing a coin, drawing a picture or composing a song, these junior high schoolers learn the necessary problem-solving skills to meet that objective with a computer program. Hopefully, students will be able to bring

Computer Literacy Scope and Sequence
Grades 7-9

Computer Awareness

Topics		K	1	2	3	4	5	6	7	8	9	10	11	12
7TH GRADE	Modeling								IA	C	C	C	C	C
	Robotics								ID	C	C	C	C	C
	Social Issues								ID	C	C	C	C	C
	Data Bases								IA	C	C	C	C	C
	BASIC: Arrays (One-Dimensional)													
	BASIC: Functions													
8TH GRADE	Computer Crime									ID	C	C	C	C
	Algorithms									IA	C	C	C	C
	BASIC: Arrays (Two-Dimensional)													
	Graphics (Sound and Color)													

Programming

Topics		K	1	2	3	4	5	6	7	8	9	10	11	12
7TH GRADE	Modeling													
	Robotics													
	Social Issues													
	Data Bases													
	BASIC: Arrays (One-Dimensional)								IA	C	C	C	C	C
	BASIC: Functions								IA	C	C	C	C	C
8TH GRADE	Computer Crime													
	Algorithms									IA	C	C	C	C
	BASIC: Arrays (Two-Dimensional)									IA	C	C	C	C
	Graphics (Sound and Color)									IA	C	C	C	C

9TH GRADE

Computer Awareness

Topics	K	1	2	3	4	5	6	7	8	9	10	11	12
Computer Capabilities										ID	C	C	C
Computer-Related Fields										ID	C	C	C
BASIC: Simulation Programming													
BASIC: Matrices													
BASIC: Files													
Pilot: Introductory Language Commands													

Programming

Topics	K	1	2	3	4	5	6	7	8	9	10	11	12
Computer Capabilities													
Computer-Related Fields													
BASIC: Simulation Programming										IA	C	C	C
BASIC: Matrices										IA	C	C	C
BASIC: Files										IA	C	C	C
Pilot: Introductory Language Commands										IA	C	C	C

LEGEND: IA—Introduction with Activities   ID—Introductory Discussion   C—Expansion of Discussion from Previous Grades   R—Review   M—Mastery

241

all their skills under one roof by writing a simulation program which includes graphics, sound and color (if available) as a final term project.

As their skills are put to more practical use, students begin to acquire a better understanding of the advantages—and limitations—of computers. They recognize computers as a powerful problem-solving tool for performing tasks that require vast amounts of paperwork, machine-like accuracy or multiple solutions. But they also understand that certain problems are more easily solved on paper or with other tools, and that many tasks—those which require thinking or creativity—are better left to humans.

When considering the following activities for classroom use, I suggest you keep this paradoxical nature of computers in mind. Try not to limit your awareness discussions to the impersonal and dehumanizing side of computers, and try not to assign problems that only computers solve well. To do so is to deprive students of a full understanding of the computer revolution.

The activities in this installment are designed to introduce students to some broader concepts about computers, but they are just that—an introduction. These first steps are, as before, open to changes to better suit your curriculum. I suggest that you use them only as a guideline.

Note: Because of the variations in BASIC, certain modifications of the programming activities may be necessary. Check your user's manual for modifications before assigning the programs listed in the activities.

SEVENTH GRADE

Computer Awareness

TOPIC: Modeling

Objective: The student can develop a specific plan to solve general problems.

Curriculum Area: Math; Social Studies; Reading; Science

Activities: • Create various-sized rectangles on the chalkboard. Have students record lengths, widths and perimeters of each. Identify a model (in this case a formula) to find the perimeter of a rectangle. Develop other models (formulas) to compute the area of any region enclosed by lines. • Have students collect data on the school population for the past ten years. Using this information, develop a model to predict the enrollment for the next ten years.

TOPIC: Robotics

Objective: The student can discuss robotics and give example of applications.

Curriculum Area: Science; Social Studies

Activities: • Look up the word "robotics" in various resources. Have students collect fiction and non-fiction articles on robotics and bring them into class for discussion. Discussion topics should include robot intelligence; the credibility of science fiction robots presented on TV, in movies and in books; advantages and disadvantages of robots; future impact of robots on jobs and people; and the Japanese plan to find new jobs for people displaced by robots. Point out that there will be many new jobs to manufacture, maintain and market the robots. • Determine if there are any robot applications in nearby factories or businesses. If so, plan a field trip to the site so that students can see robots in action. • Assign a short essay or story to each student on the topic of robotics. Topics could include robotics in factories; a report on the development of robotics in the last ten years; or a story on what robots might be doing in the year 2100.

TOPIC: Social Issues

Objective: The student can discuss the impact of computers on our lives.

Curriculum Area: All

Activities: • Have students prepare a debate on the positive and negative aspects of computers. Encourage them to bring in examples from articles, real-life situations and other sources to back up their arguments. • Have each student write an essay on a computer-related social issue. Topics could include dehumanization; technological culture shock; the "computer generation"; minority disadvantages in a computerized society; the computer revolution; privacy; "instant democracy" (computerized voting and poll-taking); automation; and advantages for the handicapped. • Have student groups interview psychologists, ACLU members, sociologists, computer programmers, businesspersons, and teachers in the community to determine their views and concerns about computers in society. • Organize student skits to dramatize both positive and negative computer-related social issues.

TOPIC: Data Bases

Objective: The student can explain the purpose of a data base and list several examples.

Curriculum Area: All

Activities: • Have the students list as many data bases as possible (airlines, medical records, banks, school files, government offices, etc.). List possible categories of information for each. • Contact various government agencies (IRS, Health Dept., etc.) to determine the number of computers they use and the number of people listed in their data base files. If a school printout is available, use it to show how information is printed and categorized. • Develop a detailed bulletin board display of the airline data base and how it generally works.

Programming

TOPIC: BASIC: Arrays (One-Dimensional)

Objective: The student can utilize one-dimensional arrays in BASIC programs.

Cinriculum Area: All

Activities: • Have students write a BASIC program using a one-dimensional array to read and print 10 test scores. Have them modify the program to find the average score. • Ask students to explain what this program does:

```
10 DIM A(20)
15 FOR I = 1 to 20
20 INPUT A(I)
30 NEXT I
40 FOR J = 1 to 20
50 LET B = B + A(J)
60 NEXT J
70 FOR R = 1 to 20
80 PRINT A(R); A(R) * A(R)
90 NEXT R
100 PRINT "THE SUM ="; B
110 END
```

• Describe situations where the one-dimensional array is very useful.

TOPIC: BASIC: Functions

Objective: The student can use BASIC statements to define functions.

Curriculum Area: All

Activities: • Have students use the DEF statement to define a function for use in a computer program. Write a BASIC program to graph a function. For example:

```
10 For I = 1 to 40
20 PRINT TAB (I);
30 PRINT "*"
40 NEXT I
50 END
```

• Have students graph $Y = X + 1$ first on paper and then using a computer. Make sure they draw the X/Y axes on the computer. Select another function, such as $Y = 2X + 4$ and have students take turns plotting the points on a chalkboard. Then plot the graph on a computer. • Discuss the value of functions. Include how functions are used to describe application data.

EIGHTH GRADE_____

Computer Awareness

TOPIC: Computer Crime

Objective: The student can describe several criminal uses of computers.

Curriculum Area: Social Studies

Activities: • Research data to compare the average amount of money lost in physical robberies and computer robberies. Also collect information on the number of detected computer crimes which are prosecuted successfully. • Have students write a report on a major computer crime (such as the "round down" fraud of 1968) and present it to the class. • Create a bulletin board display of the types of computer crimes and examples of present-day safeguards to deter this type of crime. Include electronic funds transfer frauds and embezzlements, computer whizzes who create havoc on computer systems and vandalism of computers.

TOPIC: Algorithms (also Programming Topic)

Objective: The student can give an example of an algorithm and its application.

Curriculum Area: Math; Science; Social Studies

Activities: • Have the students list all the algorithms they know. • As a class, write an algorithm for assigning a letter grade to a class test, for changing Celsius to Fahrenheit, for averaging grades, and for dividing one fraction by another. • Discuss the advantages of using algorithms in computer programs.

Programming

TOPIC: BASIC: Arrays (Two-Dimensional)

Objective: The student can write a BASIC program utilizing a two-dimensional array.

Curriculum Area: All

Activities: • Discuss uses of the two-dimensional arrays in programming, listing reasons why computers are ideal for array analogies. • Set up a two-dimensional array of your class to include name, address, city, state, zip code, telephone number, sex, age, etc. Have each item be one column of the array. • Discuss why an array is convenient to use and how large an array is needed for your class and school district. • Explain the following BASIC program:

```
5 DIM K$(10, 10)
10 FOR I = 1 to 5
20 FOR R = 1 to 3
30 PRINT "TYPE A FIRST NAME"
40 INPUT K$ (I,R)
50 NEXT R
60 NEXT I
70 FOR B = 1 to 5
80 FOR C = 1 to 3
90 PRINT K$ (B,C)
100 NEXT C
110 NEXT B
120 END
```

TOPIC: Graphics (Sound and Color)

Objective: The student can utilize sound and color in a computer program.

Curriculum Area: Art; Music; Graphic Applications to All

Activities: • Discuss how your microcomputer can be made to produce music and sound. Hold a contest with two categories for the best computerized song and the best graphics. Display the entries at open house. • Illustrate examples of both graphics and music in a program and advantages/disadvantages of using either or both. Include discussion of business, education and home applications. Demonstrate the difference between low- and high-resolution graphics. • Have students write a program to flash all the colors on the screen. As a class, write a program to produce different colored squares on the screen.

NINTH GRADE

Computer Awareness

TOPIC: Computer Capabilities

Objective: Students can discuss general computer capabilities.

Curriculum Area: All

Activities: • Have the student list all the things they think computers—from micros to mainframes—can do and why. Give examples of tasks a computer can do, but which are more advantageous for humans to do. Then list activities which a computer cannot do and why. • Have student teams choose a field such as science, education, government, medicine, etc., and study the difference between "human" tasks and "computer" tasks in that field. Discuss each group's findings and draw general conclusions about those findings.

TOPIC: Computer-Related Careers

Objective: The student can name the most common computer-related careers and the general responsibilites of each.

Curriculum Area: Career Education

Activities: • Collect data from employment agencies, colleges and universities on the most in-demand computer-related jobs, the responsibilities and education required, the average salary, and courses or degrees available. Assemble the data on a bulletin board, along with advertisements, articles, want ads, or other related resources. Include information on computer specialists (programmers, system analysts, software developers, etc.) and non-specialists (engineers, teachers, secretaries, etc.). • Find examples of programmer aptitude tests (Computer Learning Center, Washington, D.C.) and vocational education tests that measure computer skills. Discuss other skills and talents—logical thinking, attention to detail, knowledge of mathematics, typing, etc.—that are required for computer-related jobs. • Have students interview career counselors, computer specialists, math/computer teachers and others to determine their outlook on computer-related fields.

Programming

TOPIC: BASIC: Simulation Programming

Objective: The student can write a BASIC program to simulate some event or activity.

Curriculum Area: All

Activities: • List the purposes of simulation programs. Have students explain the following program for simulating the toss of a coin:

```
10 DIM X(2)
20 LET X(1) = 0
30 LET X(2) = 0
40 FOR X = 1 to 100
50 LET N = INT (RND(X) + 1.5)
60 LET X(N) = X(N) + 1
70 NEXT X
80 PRINT "HEADS ="; X(1)
90 PRINT "TAILS ="; X(2)
100 END
```

Have students change line 40 to read FOR X = 1 to 1000. Explain that the answer is not always 50/50 because of the laws of probability. • As a class, write a computer simulation of a historic event. Draw a flowchart of the event. Assign groups to program each part. • As a term project, assign students to write a computer simulation program using graphics, sound and color, if available. The projects could be in arcade-format or could include group exploration simulations.

TOPIC: BASIC: Matrices

Objective: The student can use the BASIC matrix command and apply it to problems.

Curriculum Area: Math—application to the real world

Activities: • Discuss matrices and their application in the real world. • Get access to several matrix problems with solutions and write a program using the BASIC MAT statements to solve them. Compare answers. • Find a book which shows the actual BASIC programs for the MAT commands. Discuss the advantages of having the computer store programs.

TOPIC: BASIC: Files

Objective: The student can build a file to be accessed by a BASIC program.

Curriculum Area: All

Activities: • Discuss the application of files and determine the format required for your computer. • Write a BASIC program using a file. • Find several large programs which use files and determine their value in programming.

TOPIC: Pilot: Introductory Language Commands

Objective: The student is familiar with the introductory Pilot commands.

Curriculum Area: All

Activities: • Discuss the use of Pilot and its advantages. • Discuss the difference between BASIC and Pilot. Write a multiple choice response activity in both languages. • Write a multiple choice social studies exam using Pilot.

Objectives and Activities
for Grades 10–12

Since many elementary and junior high schools still do not offer separate computer literacy courses, the activities and objectives presented previously were integrated into all curriculum areas.

Upon reaching high school, these same students are more likely to have the opportunity to choose a computer literacy, computer science, programming or data processing course as an elective. That does not mean, however, that English, foreign language, social studies, business and other non-computer teachers should abandon computer literacy as an objective in their own subject areas.

The reason is simple: Computers are not only becoming commonplace in all curriculum areas (a survey by Market Data Retrieval has revealed that nearly 60 percent of all high schools have at least one micro), but they are also becoming widespread tools in many professional fields. As a result, the need to prepare all students—not just advanced math and science students—for a future with computers becomes all the more urgent. See *Computers in Today's World* (John Wiley and Sons, 1983), a computer literacy text.

In short, I suggest that teachers of all disciplines consider integrating some of the following activities into their lesson plans, especially since this may be the last exposure to formal education in computer literacy for many students.

TENTH GRADE

Computer Awareness

TOPIC: Prediction, Interpretation and Generalization of Data

Objective: The student can write programs to collect and organize data and interpret, predict or generalize the output.

Curriculum Area: All

Activities: • As a class, write a program to survey students on what radio stations they listen to, their favorite musician/author/color, or their favorite subject in school. Have students take turns entering their opinions. Include a graph of the results as final output. • Discuss how national elections are predicted by polls such as

Computer Literacy Scope and Sequence
Grades 10-12

Computer Awareness

Grade	Topics	K	1	2	3	4	5	6	7	8	9	10	11	12
10TH GRADE	Prediction, Interpretation, Generalization of Data											IA	C	C
	Artificial Intelligence											IA	C	C
	Pascal: Introduction													
11TH GRADE	Computer Systems												ID	C
	Sampling Techniques												IA	C
	Statistical Application												IA	C
	Pilot: Programming													
12TH GRADE	Computer Survival													ID
	Invasion of Privacy													ID
	Pascal: Advanced													
	Data Bases: Advanced													

Programming

Grade	Topics	K	1	2	3	4	5	6	7	8	9	10	11	12
10TH GRADE	Prediction, Interpretation, Generalization of Data													
	Artificial Intelligence													
	Pascal: Introduction											IA	C	C
11TH GRADE	Computer Systems													
	Sampling Techniques												IA	C
	Statistical Application												IA	C
	Pilot: Programming												IA	C
12TH GRADE	Computer Survival													
	Invasion of Privacy													
	Pascal: Advanced													IA
	Data Bases: Advanced													IA

LEGEND: IA—Introduction with Activities   ID—Introductory Discussion   C—Expansion of Discussion from Previous Grades   R—Review   M—Mastery

Gallup and Harris. How accurate are these polls? Have groups of students conduct computer polls to predict the outcome of the class election, a school board election or a millage vote. Compare each group's results and determine the range of accuracy after the election. • Write a computer program to graph the population in your city, school and state for the last 50 years. (Census information should be available at the city, county or state office of statistics.) From this graph, generalize about the population next year, ten years from now and 50 years from now.

TOPIC: Artificial Intelligence

Objective: The student can define artificial intelligence and discuss its impact on the future.

Curriculum Area: Social Studies; Science; Literature

Activities: • Review literature on the history of artificial intelligence. (Articles have recently appeared in *Business Week, Science Digest, Creative Computing,* and *Scientific American.*) Discuss implications for the 80s, 90s and the next century. • Assign a book about artificial intelligence. (Suggested titles: *Introduction to Artificial Intelligence: Can Computers Think?,* Boyd and Fraser 1978; *Micro Millennium,* Viking Press 1980; *The Third Wave,* Morrow 1982) • Have students research Japanese projections that the fifth generation of computers will have artificial intelligence. (Articles on this topic have appeared recently in *Business Week, Info World, Computer World, Time* and *Newsweek.*) • Discuss improvements in computer chess programs in the last 20 years. Compare the capabilities of current chess programs and programs made in the 1970s. Explain that the new programs examine more alternatives to making chess moves and are much more extensive. • Have students prepare an essay on artificial intelligence. Suggested topics include the difference between artificial intelligence and cybernetics, if machines think, and how machines become intelligent.

Programming

TOPIC: Pascal: Introduction

Objective: The student can write simple Pascal programs.

Curriculum Area: Programming; Computer Science; Reading; Literature

Activities: • Discuss the general applications of Pascal and why it illed a structured language. • Have students work with a Pascal computer simulation program like *Karel the Robot* (Cybertronics International, Morristown, NJ, (415) 566-4566) to get familiar with Pascal. • Have students convert some of their BASIC programs into Pascal. Discuss the differences of each language.

ELEVENTH GRADE

Computer Awareness

TOPIC: Computer Systems

Objective: The student is familiar with brands and types of computer systems.

Curriculum Areas: Computer Science; Data Processing

Activities: • Have students collect brochures from major computer companies and make a comparative listing of the systems. Include type of computer (micro, mini, mainframe, pre-programmed learning aids etc.), cost, purpose, speed, peripherals, memory and other functions. Summarize the advantage and disadvantages of each. Discuss the components that make up a computer system. • Have a computer sales representative give a speech on a computer system. • Have students create a model of a system and label all the parts. Have them draw a system of the future and write a paper on how it works, added features, what it's used for, how much it costs, etc.

TOPIC: Sampling Techniques (also Programming)

Objective: The student can set up a sampling technique for making decisions or predictions.

Curriculum Areas: Math; Science; Social Studies; Statistics

Activities: • If possible, have a representative from a poll service or a statistician lead a discussion panel with your class on sampling techniques. Discussion topics could include ways of gathering data, where polls are conducted and why, factors to consider when compiling data. • Have small groups gather information and write a report on the factors involved in picking samples to predict election outcomes. Include party affiliation, regional influence, occupation, sex, ethnic background, and past voting history. Relate these to writing a computer program which analyzes this data. • List the professions which depend heavily on sampling: insurance, sales, television, politics, etc. Discuss what influence survey results have on each of these.

TOPIC: Statistical Application (also Programming)

Objective: The student can use the computer to do statistical computations.

Curriculum Areas: All

Activities: • Have students use a commercial statistical package to compute mean, standard deviation and related statistics of several class tests. Have students write a program to compute the mean and standard deviation of their own tests. • Have a sales representative demonstrate statistical software to show its many capabilities. Discuss advantages of mainframes, minis and microcomputers for doing statistical computations.

Programming

TOPIC: Pilot Programming

Objective: The student can develop programs using Pilot.

Curriculum Areas: Computer Science; Programming

Activities: • Have students write a detailed multiple choice test for a subject of their choice using Pilot. Include a posttest and a printout of final score, percentage of correct answers, and mean score of several tests. • Have small groups write a Pilot program with graphics. Have them share the programs with other classes. • Discuss the features of Pilot and compare it to BASIC and Pascal. • As a final project, have students prepare a multiple choice testing program in Pilot for another teacher to use in class. Require that the program use graphics (charts or diagrams), compute scores, and compile statistical information about the class results.

TWELFTH GRADE

Computer Awareness

TOPIC: Computer Survival

Objective: The student is aware of the future impact of computers on society.

Curriculum Areas: All

Activities: • Have students review studies indicating the future role of computers on our society. Have them write a report on their findings. Issues to look for include the social impact, impact on trade unions, employment, and government predictions on jobs. • Have students read at least one futuristic novel about technology. Suggested titles are *Brave New World* (Huxley), *Future Shock* and *The Third Wave* (Toffler), *1984* (Orwell), and Ray Bradbury fiction. Discuss the similarities and differences between fictional accounts of computers and scientific fact. Hold a debate on this topic. • Discuss preparations for making people computer literate (teaching the role of computers, what computers can do and cannot do, computer applications, and communications). • Compare the role of computers in various professions both now and in the future. Make a table listing education, politics,

business, and other professions on one side, and "past," "present" and "future" across the top. Have the class fill in the table. • Have each student write a paper on their future plans for living with computers.

TOPIC: Invasion of Privacy

Objective: The student can explain what kind of information computer files contain and what laws protect that information.

Curriculum Areas: Social Sciences; Computer Science; Computer Literacy

Activities: • Have students list all the data banks that store information about themselves. Discuss security measures for keeping this information private. • Visit a credit bureau and have someone explain what information is on the bureau's computer, its purpose, methods of security, changes to be made if there are errors, and how individuals can access their file. • List all the government data banks you can think of and the purpose of each. Refer to a directory of federal institutions for more listings. Include lists of the types of information on each.

Programming

TOPIC: Pascal: Advanced

Objective: The student can write a Pascal program to solve problems.

Curriculum Areas: Computer Science; Programming; Application to all

Activities: • Have students list all the Pascal statements and compare them to BASIC statements • Write an advanced program for math, physics, chemistry, geology, social studies, or other classes in each language. Discuss advantages and disadvantages of each. • Have students read a self-study Pascal text such as *Apple Pascal* (McGraw-Hill, 1981), *Speaking Pascal* (Hayden, 1981), and *Computers in Today's World Pascal Handbook* (Wiley, 1984).

TOPIC: Programming Data Bases: Advanced

Objective: The student can outline the procedure to prepare, access, and update a data base.

Curriculum Areas: All

ties: • Have a travel agent, businessperson or bank teller s with data bases talk to the class on requirements of a data ude preparation, security, access, updating, etc. • Have the are a data base of information on each student: name, social security number, sex, age, class schedule, etc. • Have the class design a security system for the data base they developed for the class.

DISCUSSION

Students in grades ten to twelve get exposure to computer literacy in computer literacy, computer science, programming, or data-processing classes. The context of these classes usually varies depending on the instructor.

Some school districts have carefully defined courses for students to enroll in, but few have a sequence of classes. Sometimes instruction is included as part of the mathematics curriculum, usually in the form of a computer-programming class. Other options include applications in business, calculus, algebra, physics, home economics, chemistry, social sciences, and so forth. The involvement of any curriculum area is mainly dependent upon the instructor's interest in computers. Statistics reveal that most secondary schools have access to some type of computer, that is, terminals, mini or micros. Also, secondary schools have been involved with computers since the late 1960s, with terminals in computer rooms. But indications are that the advanced students were the only ones to receive exposure. Of course this is changing with the microcomputer, and it is now apparent that secondary schools need to consolidate their efforts and integrate computing into the curriculum. In most cases "hands-on" programming is a must and students graduating from secondary school will benefit with computer exposure.

Remedial high school courses use computers for drill and practice, but the strength of the microcomputer is its ability to manipulate data which would make many topics and subjects in the secondary school much more meaningful to the students. For example, see *Microcomputer Applications for Calculus* (Bitter, PWS Publishers, 1983). Simulations are invaluable for topics in business, science, and the social sciences. Statistical computations on a computer also have meaning for these areas. Data banks are the basis of many social issues of the future, and programming a computer is an invaluable skill. These topics comprise the scope and sequence chart for computer literacy for grades ten through twelve. Knowledge of programming in a structural language such as Pascal will prepare students for future computer applications in most fields. More than likely students will acquire this experience in a programming course during their secondary education. In the future, a computer-related class will be required for high school graduation. Obviously, the content of that class would be the Kindergarten through twelfth grade scope and sequence presented here. The sophistication of this course will advance each year as knowledge is gained at each grade level. A computer literacy class to insure that all students receive exposure to computer awareness and "hands-on" computer access (preferably a microcomputer) is highly recommended.

Teachers conducting this class will need a computer science background in the years ahead. Therefore, interested secondary school teachers should be prepared to teach this computer literacy class as its levels of sophistication increase.

Secondary students are involved in some of the issues of artificial intelligence, survival, and privacy, and they will be affected by them upon graduation and going on their own. Keep in mind that all the topics require discussion or introduction if they are not part of the students' previous education. This is the last formal education for some students so an exposure to computer literacy is a must. Therefore, secondary schools should provide a formal experience on computer literacy for all students in the future.

This concludes this series on computer literacy which deserves more than just the casual discussion it has been given in the past. Computer literacy is a common discussion topic, but few educators were developing a curriculum for education because of the different definitions applied to the subject. Many schools and school districts have used this series as a starting point for development. This was the intent. Refer to *Computers in Today's World* (Wiley, 1984) for a detailed discussion of all the Scope and Sequence topics.

CONSIDERATIONS FOR THE TEACHER

After you have designed your computer literacy curriculum, you are nearly ready to power up the computer and begin forming the next generation of computer professionals. Before you do, however, there are a number of considerations you should keep in mind. First, do you know why the computer curriculum you will be teaching has been implemented? It is essential to the experience of both teaching and learning about computers that you understand the need for and support such a program. If you are unsure about your role, or if you do not feel a commitment to teach computer literacy, your attitude will certainly affect the performance of your students.

Second, have you considered broadly what computer education should entail? Do you feel confident that your students can handle the material that you intend to present? It is unwise to frustrate students by either introducing them to material that they cannot grasp or by boring them with material that is too simple to challenge them. To avoid these problems, you should establish a hierarchy of objectives and work toward those objectives that your students are capable of accomplishing with relative ease.

Third, if you will be teaching a programming language, have you carefully chosen an appropriate language to teach? There are numerous computer languages available to you, and your particular objectives should determine which language is most appropriate for your curriculum. Very young children work well with Logo while older students are prepared to begin programming in BASIC. More computer literate students may want exposure to more sophisticated languages such as Forth, COBOL, FORTRAN and Pascal. You should know the different capabilities of these languages, so that your choice is a well-advised one.

Fourth, have you structured your curriculum in such a manner that discussions and activities geared toward computer awareness complement those geared toward computer programming? Can you establish a relationship among the areas you intend to cover to assure your students that they are receiving a balanced and cohesive education in computers? You may also consider the possibility of designing activities in other academic areas so that they complement computer-related activities. Can you use computer programming to reinforce mathematical skills, for example? It is good to demonstrate to your students that computers can help in many areas of their studies as well as in their lives.

Finally, have you considered at what pace you will present the material that you intend to cover? Remember that some children will demonstrate a natural ability to work easily with computers while others may be slower to catch on. Slower students may grow frustrated easily and demand individual attention from the teacher. Of course, one major advantage of computers is that they allow the user—in this case, your student—to work at his or her own pace. Computers are infinitely patient, a feature that makes them especially effective as instructional tools. Allow your students to determine their own rate of learning whenever possible as frustrating them may cause them to be intimidated by computers.

PRACTICAL HINTS FOR THE TEACHER

As you begin actual computer instruction, you may find some of the following hints helpful. There are a number of ways that you can ensure that your experience and your students' experience will be positive and conducive to learning. First, because computers lend themselves well to group work, encourage your students to work together whenever this is practicable. They will learn from each other's mistakes and develop the skill of discussing abstract concepts and, at the same time, will sharpen social skills.

Second, do not assume that simply because there is a microcomputer in the corner of your classroom that your students will automatically be motivated to work with it. They will undoubtedly monitor and register your response to the computer and take their cue from your attitude. Enthusiastically, encourage your students to explore the infinite possibilities of computer capabilities.

Third, you may feel insecure about your own level of knowledge about computers, but this is unnecessary. After several class sessions, some of your students may know as much as you do about your computer system. Some may even know more than you do. Do not allow this to intimidate you. Instead, remain open to the experience of sharing in your students' discoveries. For seeing you learning and exploring with them just may spark your students' enthusiasm. You may also seek outside resources to which you may direct students who show exceptional skill and interest. Your community probably offers a number of such resources, whether books and journals in the public library, computer professionals eager to share their expertise with young people, or computer hobbyist groups that provide an opportunity for computer enthusiasts to compare notes and learn from each other.

Fourth, you may find that it is sometimes difficult to gauge the pace at which your students can absorb the material that you are presenting. Again, students will learn at very different rates. For this reason, it is a good idea to make sure that you have extra activities and exercises on hand to occupy students who have finished their work while their classmates catch up. This avoids frustrating students who have a natural facility with the computer.

Last, if you are teaching a special computer class that is scheduled to meet during other than regular school hours, do not attempt to teach students until they have had a chance to have a snack or meal. Hungry students have difficulty concentrating on the material at hand, and this will prove frustrating to you and your students. Also, tempers are more likely to flare, and students may be less tolerant of their own and others' errors, which are really the key to learning about working with computers.

TEACHING THE TEACHER

You should be warned that computers are addictive! Although you may walk softly past that shiny microcomputer in the corner of the classroom, once you begin to use it you are likely to develop a long and meaningful relationship with it. Should you find yourself wanting to know more about the field of computer science, there are a number of resources available to you.

One such resource is the local university, community college, or technical school. Many courses in computer science are offered by institutions of higher learning, providing you with a structured environment in which to study and an instructor who is an expert in this field. Some school systems offer tuition assistance, and many reward teachers who take extra coursework with salary credit. Many universities offer courses that are designed specifically for teachers who work with computers and computer education.

Those persons curious about computers should also consult computer-oriented books and journals. Perhaps your school library subscribes to computer periodicals, or would do so at your suggestion. This would make the materials available to your students as well as to you. Most public libraries contain collections of these materials, but if not, you can browse through a number of such publications at any computer retail store. You may even choose to purchase subscriptions to journals that you find particularly enlightening.

Practically every large city also has several computer hobbyist groups. You can find out about them either at the library or through computer retail stores. At a meeting of such a group, you are likely to meet other teachers who share your concerns. At least you will meet a number of people who share your newfound curiosity about computers.

Curiosity is contagious, and when your students see that you are genuinely interested in that computer in the corner of the room, they will develop more interest in it. Perhaps the best thing that you can accomplish is to inspire this interest in your students so that they will go on to learn more about computers on their own.

SUMMARY

Our society is becoming increasingly oriented toward technology in general and computers in particular. The need to become computer literate is now as basic as the need to read, write, and solve mathematical problems. Accordingly, it is imperative that schools implement computer literacy curricula. There is a good deal of debate about how precisely to implement such programs and what the computer literacy curriculum should include, but the need for such a program is a given.

A fundamental question about computer education is at what age children are capable of understanding the basics of computers. Experts tell us that the earlier children are exposed to computers, the more comfortably they will adapt to them. Certainly a child old enough to attend school is ready to explore the fascinating world of computers. Very young children are at ease in a computer environment because they are enthusiastic, curious, and open to new experiences. The teacher should take advantage of this attitude because it is conducive to laying a foundation for subsequent and increasingly complex computer knowledge.

Children should be trained in two areas: computer awareness and computer programming. Computer awareness instruction should cover such topics as what computers are, what they do, how they operate, computer history, social implications of computer usage, and computer-related career fields. Computer programming should develop the child's ability to work with the computer and to instruct it to perform specific functions.

Both computer awareness and computer programming should be taught within a curriculum that begins with simple and basic concepts and then builds gradually toward more complex ideas. They should be taught in conjunction with each other; that is, computer awareness discussions should complement the learning that occurs during computer-programming activities.

Before implementing a computer literacy curriculum, the teacher needs to consider the following issues:

- Why has this curriculum been implemented? Does the teacher feel dedicated to teaching this material? Can the teacher convey to the students the need for learning about computers?

- What should computer education entail? Can the students handle the material that will be covered? Is it too complicated? Too basic?

- What programming language will be taught? Which language is most appropriate to this curriculum? Small children function well with a simple language such as Logo while older students may want to learn a language such as BASIC or COBOL.

- Is the curriculum structured in such a way that all of its components complement each other and, together, make up a complete and cohesive body of information?

- At what pace will the material be presented? Is this a realistic pace for students of a given age and level of capabilities?

When questions like these are resolved, the curriculum is ready to be implemented. The teacher may benefit from several practical hints that will make the computer education experience more pleasant for teacher and student alike.

- Encourage students to work with each other on computer activities. This allows them to learn from each other's mistakes and successes.

- Display an enthusiastic and positive attitude toward the computer experience in order to encourage your students.

- Do not feel intimidated by students who soon know as much about the computer as you do. Remember that you can learn from each other.

- Always keep extra exercises on hand for students who are able to finish more quickly than others.

It is also a good idea for a teacher to develop a list of computer-related resources. These resources may include libraries, journals, and books in the field; computer professionals who are willing to give time to schools; computer retail stores; hobbyist groups; and universities, community colleges, and technical schools.

9

The Microcomputer Classroom

INTRODUCTION

Recent data (Melmed 1982) reveal that thousands of microcomputer terminals are now in use in schools. Public school districts in Florida were surveyed to determine whether or not computers were used for instruction. Of fifty-five respondents, thirty-three (60 percent) reported using computers for instructional purposes (Dickerson and Pritchard 1981). Even though school budgets are notoriously limited, computers are becoming increasingly popular classroom tools now that computer literacy is a current issue in education.

The latest developments in semiconductor technology have made the compact, relatively inexpensive microcomputer of the 1980s more powerful than a roomful of computers in use during the 1950s. With only a little care and forethought on the teacher's part, the microcomputer can stimulate students to learn new facts to "beat the computer." Microcomputers also display inexhaustible patience in administering repetitious drills, challenging precocious students with programming tasks, and performing some clerical tasks—at a cost of eighteen cents an hour. Microcomputers require only relatively simple care. They supplement teachers, who are still necessary to provide sensitivity, knowledgeable overview, and classroom management skills.

THE SELF-CONTAINED CLASSROOM

When a computer is introduced into your self-contained classroom, you will need to secure a table. A cabinet with wheels is convenient because it enables you to move the computer to different places, but this is certainly not essential. You will need to plug the computer into a standard 110-volt outlet, three-prong plug. You should also consider using lightning surge protectors to protect the computer from damage if it is operated during an electrical storm.

If you have only one computer, it is best to place the table near your desk so that you can easily demonstrate and supervise its use. If you have several computers, you have a number of options for arranging them. You may cluster the computers into a computer learning center where students work individually. Sign-up sheets and computer materials may be kept in this location. In some schools, computers are contained in a centralized computer room, media center, or even in a corner of the library. Again, they are usually clustered. Teachers are often asked to check out individual floppy diskettes or cassettes from the media center to guard against vandalism.

Teachers may also use computers to instruct a number of students simultaneously. In this case, students should be grouped so that the teacher can stand before them. Again, the computers should be in a room of their own or in a portion of the room so that the teacher may demonstrate before them. These approaches can be combined into the "computer corner," where students may be taught in a group.

Two types of computer systems are popular in the classroom: *terminal systems* and *stand-alone systems*. A *terminal system* is a screen and keyboard that communicates with a central computer housed in another location, either in the school building or in another location altogether. One advantage of this time-sharing system is centralization of responsibility for computer maintenance. Also a community of users is available to you for courseware generation, training, and consultation—or simply for answering questions when you are baffled. However, you are dependent on a single mainframe (central computer) so that when the system malfunctions, all users are without service. Also the system can be vandalized by individual users, disturbing programs in the central computer. Another disadvantage of this type of system is its prohibitive initial cost (Dickerson and Pritchard 1981).

The most commonly used system now is the *stand-alone microcomputer,* although terminals are particularly prevalent in larger schools. This type of system is very reliable. It is also much less expensive to install, and software is readily available from the system's manufac-

turer and various software firms. Several disadvantages of the smaller system are its slower speed, its restriction to fewer users, and its support of less powerful languages with limited capabilities. However, microcomputer user groups are forming to share information and expertise.

The typical computer comes with a CRT (video screen), a keyboard to communicate with the computer, and an audio cassette player-recorder or a disk drive for program storage. Many microcomputers in schools use cassette storage because it is less costly than floppy disk drives. However, cassette storage is much slower than disk storage, and you may find it useful to add floppy disk drives even though their initial expense is greater. Floppy disk drives are available in sizes of eight inches, five and one-quarter inches, and the new three-inch size that is bound to become more popular.

If you are not operating under strict budgetary limitations, you may consider several higher-priced hardware options that are useful though not essential to your microcomputer system. For example, you may select a printer that will print your program in a hard copy or, more elaborately, in colorgraphics. Printers are cost-effective only where large program development is done (requiring a printed program listing to preserve the programmer's sanity), when word processing is desired, or where a good deal of record keeping and written reports are necessary (see Doerr 1979).

Another hardware addition you might consider is a voice module—a board that can be added to the computer to make it capable of speech synthesis. This device especially appeals to children. Some modules allow children to respond orally. Music modules teach children to discriminate between musical tones and encourage them to create music of their own. Light pens allow children to mark answers directly on the video screen.

In many school systems, computers are used as part of gifted programs or enrichment programs. Eligible students are removed periodically from their regular classes. During the first session, a teacher orients a group of students to the computer. The teacher typically covers programming skills (BASIC), math skills, and computer games that stress numerical concepts. In subsequent sessions, students are encouraged to work independently. This allows exceptional students to determine their own rates of progress. It is also often useful to schedule free time on the computer so that "computer buffs" may have extra opportunities to work with the computer system. However, no student should be allowed to monopolize that free time.

As your students gain experience with the microcomputer, you may find some of them surprisingly adept at programming and operating the computer. Do not allow yourself to feel threatened by students who surpass you, the teacher. Working with the computer often becomes a group activity in which it is difficult to determine who is teaching and who is learning. Above all, be open to learning from your students as well as teaching them.

Because computer programming is such a trial-and-error endeavor, you will learn a great deal about the computer by observing your students' interaction with it. Teachers and students can work together to solve problems and correct errors.

You may want to compile a list of resources to recommend to students who are eager to learn more about computers than you are prepared to teach. These resources might include books available in libraries, names of microcomputer hobbyist groups, computer-related journals, and other computer resources available in your community.

Actual classroom experience has shown that teachers use the computer most often to handle special problems of the slow and the accelerated student. The computer is very well suited to meeting special needs.

THE MICROCOMPUTER AS LEARNING CENTER

The Elementary School

Teachers today face a bewildering amount of preparatory and management tasks, particularly when their philosophy is to teach in a student-centered fashion, where individual and small-group activities are emphasized over whole-class instruction. The computer is a chameleon, changing its function according to the software used and the programming tasks performed. Thus, with the computer a teacher can be freed from designing as many learning-center environments as would otherwise be necessary.

Duties involved with keeping track of student progress can be alleviated by using software that records student performance and offers class summaries, which are helpful in planning small-group instruction and the selection and/or development of additional learning centers. Some microcomputer time can be designated for this purpose.

If the microcomputer is to be used efficiently and fairly in the classroom, then the teacher must plan lessons in such a way that the microcomputer is used during most school hours. This tends to preclude a primarily whole-class teaching approach, although, of course, there will be times when this approach is both necessary and productive. If whole-class instruction is the primary instructional pattern in the classroom, then it is likely that only gifted students and slower learners will be able to use the microcomputer for any significant amount of time. What about the average learner?

Programming activities, word processing, and some CAI packages do lend themselves to small-group and paired-student activities, as do traditional learning centers in the classroom. When microcomputers are limited, some computer activities should be planned so that more than one student takes part at a time, ensuring that students have extra time on the computer and that an atmosphere of collaboration can be established. A schedule and/or sign-up sheet should be designed; user time and assignments can be recorded.

Some children may use the computer more often than others, according to their special needs. Schedules should allow each child to have some "alone" time on the computer if at all possible.

The children must learn to operate the computer competently and with little adult supervision. For software that requires operational training, it is effective to select a group of students to learn the software operation thoroughly. Then these students can train the other children in the classroom and answer their questions, thereby freeing the teacher.

The Secondary School

The school organization of seventh through twelfth grades is generally quite different from the self-contained elementary classroom. Classes are departmentalized, and the teacher meets with a new group of students every hour. The placement of microcomputers, then, can be a more substantial problem. There is, of course, a definite need for microcomputers placed in a laboratory for computer programming instruction and training in word-processing and business-related software. But what about the mathematics, science, social studies, industrial education, or English classes? How can effective plans to utilize microcomputers be made? There are no easy answers to this question, and what may be perfect for one subject area may not be perfect for another.

Three distinct plans are discussed, with the understanding that more than one plan can be implemented within a school.

PLAN A. Computer lab time for subject area teachers and students, other than programming and business education: Instructors sign up for lab hours and bring the entire class. The instructor conducts the class, but volunteer student or adult aides can oversee details of the room's operation. The lab preferably should be located near the media center so that software can be signed out in an organized fashion. Networking the microcomputers makes sense in such a computer lab, since programs can then be loaded more quickly, and since there would be no need to constantly check out software from the library.

PLAN B. One or two microcomputers in individual classrooms: Major uses include demonstrations, computer activities involving small groups, and for the instructor's word-processing needs and administrative tasks. A wide-screen monitor will increase flexibility.

Three or more microcomputers in individual classrooms: A more complicated plan of computers for instructional tasks can be used when there are three or more microcomputers in a classroom. The whole class, in small groups, could be involved with computer activities at one time. Tutorial and drill and practice kinds of activities on an individualized basis will be harder to plan and manage.

PLAN C. A computer center housed in or near the media center with an aide, librarian, or teacher overseeing its use: Students receive passes from teachers which include information on projects to be done or software to be utilized. Plan C requires that careful scheduling arrangements be made, and that computer-center personnel are familiar with software operation and programming techniques.

CARE OF EQUIPMENT

If your computer is to operate efficiently, it must be properly maintained. Computer equipment requires some special care, and your students must know several rules that apply to equipment maintenance.

The computer should not be turned off between periods of use unless there is a large time lapse between usage times. An antistatic mat should be installed in the area of the computer so that accidental discharge of electrostatic electricity does not damage the machine or the floppy disk. These mats are available locally at reasonable prices in discount or department stores.

The computer should be dusted every day and the screen cleaned with a glass cleaner and a soft cloth. Use a dust cover if your area is unusually dusty. The disk drive should be cleaned with a disk drive kit every six months. These kits are available at local computer stores. Cassette recorders should be cleaned periodically with a head cleaner available at music and stereo equipment stores. The ribbons on printers wear out just as typewriter ribbons do. Computer stores sell replacement ribbons. Occasionally the printer head breaks and must be repaired.

Students should not touch exposed sections of the floppy disk, roughly equivalent to the center area of a 45 RPM record. Floppy diskettes should not be bent; diskettes must always be inserted right side up. Only felt-tip pens should be used for marking disks—not ballpoint pens or pencils. Floppy disks should be removed from the machine before it is turned off; they should not be placed on electrical or magnetic devices. Excess heat or cold can destroy diskettes.

Computer stores sell inexpensive plastic cases for storing floppy diskettes. Cases are also available for cassettes. They should be stored vertically.

MAXIMIZING YOUR COMPUTER EXPERIENCE

You will want to make optimal use of the computer in your classroom by using its three functions: as tool, tutor, and to program. Older students can use the computer to solve problems in any subject area. First they must break the problem down to its component parts—a good exercise in logic—and arrange a solution by logical steps: the algorithmic approach. Virtually any subject matter can be approached in this way. The computer performs the calculations and solves problems that are unwieldy for the student to solve manually: for example, advanced mathematics, historical and sociological statistics, chemistry and physics data, or stock market vacillations.

Some of the most innovative software being produced is in the area of computer simulation and games, sparking enthusiasm in students of all ability levels. Students acquire skills while doing, rather than thinking about, the process. For example, in one such program a wagon train leaves Kansas headed for Oregon. The student is an imaginary wagon owner. Will he/she survive the trip? He/she must make decisions and choices along the way. Will he/she run out of provisions? Will he/she survive an Indian attack? He/she learns about history, planning, and decision making along the way. Winning, or surviving in this case, requires him/her to polish valuable learning skills.

The computer as tutor makes use of drill and practice programs—Computer-Assisted Instruction. These programs are individualized to various levels and can usually be varied in speed. The computer performs this repetitive task, freeing the teacher for other activity and enhancing performance. The underachiever is not forced to compete against other students, but against him/herself or the machine. He/she receives immediate feedback. Efficient CAI programs keep track of the student's level and performance. The teacher serves in a supportive capacity—supplying encouragement, not assignments.

CAI drills have been used mainly with underachieving students with good results both in attendance and in raising the grade level of skills. (See Doerr 1979, p. 121.)

Some drawbacks of CAI are the scarcity of programs for average and gifted children, the lack of human interaction, costly programs that are difficult to finance, and software that lacks development. (See Doerr 1979, p. 136.)

CAI can be useful also as makeup lessons for absentees. Math, spelling, and foreign language are particularly adaptable to this approach.

Finally, the computer is used to learn programming skills. Microcomputers are usually programmed in BASIC, but time-sharing systems often support more powerful programming languages. With the help of how-to manuals, students can learn to program through hands-on experience. They then possess a powerful tool for problem solving and for writing their own programs.

If you are comfortable with programming, you can use the computer to assume some of your clerical tasks: maintaining performance records, recording student proficiency levels, even managing milk money!

SUMMARY

As educators of today begin to learn about and experiment with the microcomputer as a unique kind of learning device, we will begin to see a number of philosophies developing concerning its most appropriate use. Some will picture the microcomputer as a testing, tutorial, and drill device, allowing an individualized approach to learning and limited teacher control or intervention. Others will see the most effective role to be related to full control of the computer, i.e., programming and user-controlled computer environments. Still others will emphasize the computer as a tool to enhance other kinds of learning experiences. These approaches are not mutually exclusive; they can be melded together to create a productive classroom environment sensitive to the varying learning styles of students.

When the number of computers is limited, there will necessarily be competition between these different visions of the computer's role in the classroom. In the future, purchase of more microcomputers to be placed in the classroom as an integral part of the educational environment will allow teachers to use the computer more effectively in ways that emphasize communication, problem solving, *and* nonjudgmental opportunities for practice based upon student needs and the management needs of their teachers.

On the other hand, this vision of the future does not belittle the importance of all the other paths of learning and understanding possible in the social environment of the classroom.

With several other teachers, take a set of district curriculum objectives for your grade level, in a specific area, and you will find that some objectives could be met very well by using the computer. However, others are best or more efficiently met by using tape recorders, filmstrip viewers, calculators, and other devices; or by lecture, discussion, role-playing, experiments, art, and so on. If certain objectives are better served by other means, then do not waste valuable computer time on them.

In addition, we suggest that any school considering the expansion of computer usage seriously examine and reconstruct the present curriculum, deleting or de-emphasizing skills not so necessary in a technological society, and adding objectives which will enhance students' abilities to think, solve problems, and to initiate their own learning activities.

Microcomputers in the classroom provide infinite opportunities for enjoyable and valuable learning experiences. Increasing numbers of school systems are instituting computer-related curricula in the awareness that students may use computers to master traditional academic areas and, at the same time, to gain the computer literacy they will need to live comfortably in the computerized society of tomorrow.

REFERENCES

Bitter, Gary G. *Microcomputer Applications for Calculus.* Boston: Prindle, Weber, and Schmidt, 1983.

Dickerson, Laurel, and William H. Pritchard, Jr. "Microcomputers and Education: Planning for the Coming Revolution." *Educational Technology* 21, no. 1 (January 1981).

Doerr, Christine. *Microcomputers and the Three R's: A Guide for Teachers.* Rochelle Park, N.J.: Hayden Book Co., 1979.

Melmed, Arthur S. "Information Technology for U.S. Schools." *Phi Delta Kappan* 30, no. 5 (January 1982): 308–313.

Papert, Seymour. *Mindstorms: Children, Computers, and Powerful Ideas.* New York: Basic Books, 1980.

SUGGESTED READINGS

Bitter, Gary G. *Computers in Today's World.* New York: John Wiley and Sons, 1984.

Bork, Alfred. "Stand-Alone Computer Systems: Our Educational Future." *Journal of Educational Technology Systems* 7, no. 3 (1978–79): 201–220.

Braun, L. "Some Bases for Choosing a Computer System: Suggestions for Educators." *Journal of Educational Technology Systems* 7, no. 3 (1978–79).

Carlstron, G. "Operating a Microcomputer Convinced Me and My Second Graders to Use It Again and Again." *Teacher* (February 1980).

Doerr, Christine. *Microcomputers and the Three R's: A Guide for Teachers.* Rochelle Park, N. J.: Hayden Book Co., 1979.

Dugdale, Sharon. "What's the Student Doing? A Crucial Aspect of Instructional Design." *Educational Leadership* 39, no. 5 (February 1982): 384–385.

Greene, Maxine. "Literacy for What?" *Phi Delta Kappan* 63, no. 5 (January 1982): 326–329.

Grimes, Lynn. "Computers are for Kids: Designing Software Programs to Avoid Problems of Learning." *Teaching Exceptional Chidren* 14, no. 2 (November 1981): 48–53.

Miller, Benjamin S. "Bringing the Microcomputer into the Junior High: A Success Story from Florida." *Phi Delta Kappan* 63, no. 5 (January 1982): 320.

Roecks, Alan L. "How Many Ways Can the Computer Be Used in Education? A Baker's Dozen." *Educational Technology* 63, no. 5 (January 1982): 303–307.

Shane, Harold G. "The Silicon Age and Education." *Phi Delta Kappan* (January 1982).

10 The Future of Technology

We live in an age of snowballing technological advancement. With the advent of computers in science and industry, technological developments occur almost daily. The present and the future are sometimes hard to distinguish: what was science fiction ten years ago is reality today and will be obsolete in ten years. Engineering and computer science students are often told that their education will most likely be outdated by the time they graduate and enter their professional fields. The lightning speed of technological advancements in our age makes predictions of the future tentative and difficult. However, some technological trends have emerged over the past several years that permit us to speculate about how technology will revolutionize our society and our daily lives in the future.

One fact is certain: computers are here to stay! The work of our complex society could not be accomplished without the speed and accuracy that computers allow. Also, the multifaceted work of computers in research and development, coupled with the research of scientists and engineers, will produce the next generation of computers, more capable than those in use today. Their work is oriented toward several areas: continued miniaturization, greater memory capacity, speech synthesis and recognition, and enhanced graphic displays.

One of the most noticeable characteristics of computers during the past ten years especially has been their decreasing physical size. Many of the powerful computers of the 1960s were room-sized; in the 1980s, a home computerist can own and operate an equally powerful personal computer that can be set up in the corner of a study or family room! What accounts for this decrease in size of computer hardware? The integrated circuit.

The first generation of computers (1944–58) relied on vacuum tube technology which was cumbersome and required huge amounts of energy. The second generation of computers (1959–64) introduced transistor technology, an improvement over vacuum tubes. Still the distance between transistors kept computers relatively large and, more importantly, relatively slow. Consequently, the third generation of computers introduced the integrated circuit, a wafer of silicon on which thousands of transistors have been connected with tiny wires.

Integrated circuitry technology improved so much that even more transistors could be integrated on a chip through the process of Large-Scale Integration. As this occurred, computers became physically smaller, but retained their power, becoming even faster data processors. This trend continues with Very Large-Scale Integration. As integrated circuitry becomes more sophisticated, computer power can be housed in smaller and smaller pieces of equipment. And as the size of computer hardware decreases, so does the purchase price of such equipment. That means that a greater number of people than ever before can afford to have computer power at their fingertips.

An important result of integrated circuit technology has been a wide range of microprocessors that perform many types of functions. A microprocessor is a small computer that has been programmed to carry out a set of specific tasks. For example, microprocessors now control fuel intake of automobiles, monitor cooking in microwave ovens, and perform calculations for owners of pocket calculators. Many traditional household appliances will depend on computer power in the homes of tomorrow, as we shall explore later.

The amount of power that a computer has is directly related to the amount of data and instructions it can store in its memory. The greater a computer's memory, the more powerful the computer. Computer scientists are now in the process of researching alternate memory systems, such as bubble memory, to store a maximal amount of information in a minimum of space.

Another important area of technological development is speech synthesis and recognition. Speech recognition refers to the computer's ability to recognize and interpret human speech. This would have a number of advantages. For example, speech recognition just may make house keys obsolete and, at the same time, cut down on home burglaries. Imagine a computerized "lock" that opens doors only to those people whose voices it recognizes as members or guests of a household. Speech synthesis, on the other hand, refers to the computer's ability to duplicate sounds similar to the human voice. The speech synthesizers of today are crude and often difficult to understand, but researchers are constantly improving their quality. This technology has the potential for great impact on the lives of people who are voice-impaired, and experiments are now being conducted with computers that speak for those who have no voice.

Yet another area of technological advancement is graphics. With the phenomenal popularity of videogames, both at home and in game parlors, computer graphics is becoming a popular art form. Researchers are working to make computer graphics more sophisticated. Graphics will display a wider range of colors and more realistic effects. This will also have a great impact on classroom computers; spectacular graphics displays attract children to the computer and hold their attention through series of drills and practices.

The computers of the future, then, will most likely be physically smaller and less expensive, have greater memory capacity, be able to recognize and synthesize speech, and generate more sophisticated graphics displays. As the price of computers declines, more and more people will take advantage of the seemingly infinite benefits of computer technology. But specifically how will tomorrow's computers be used?

APPLICATIONS OF TOMORROW'S TECHNOLOGY

We can see the roots of tomorrow's technology in the computers we use today. For example, some cities now use computers to monitor and control the flow of rush hour traffic. This system cuts down on accidents and helps alleviate the frustration of bumper-to-bumper traffic in congested areas. Such systems are likely to be more widespread in the future. Many experts predict that within ten years the use of autopilots in automobiles will be commonplace. Drivers will program their automobiles to deliver them safely to predetermined destinations. This will certainly decrease the number of deaths and injuries caused by traffic accidents in which human error is the culprit.

Similarly, airplane pilots will be assisted by computer-controlled devices that regulate takeoffs and landings. Because most serious airplane accidents occur during either takeoff or landing, we can expect that these computer-controlled devices will save a substantial number of lives.

Health care is another area that will be greatly aided by computer power. Already some hospitals use sophisticated computerized devices to monitor patients' vital signs. This allows health care professionals to be aware of unusual conditions that jeopardize human lives and to circumvent the devastating effects of such conditions. Research in this area will result in increasingly precise monitoring devices. Along with this, computers are being used to assist doctors in diagnosing illness. Given a set of symptoms and conditions, the computer draws from its memory of diseases an accurate diagnosis, prognosis, and treatment.

Law enforcement agencies will find it easier to locate and keep track of offenders. Complex monitoring devices will help police officers to detect violations of motor vehicle laws. Monitoring devices note speed limit violations, for example. In addition, centralized computers will keep track of records of law violations, and this will help law enforcement agencies to coordinate efforts in apprehending offenders who move from state to state to avoid prosecution.

Other government agencies will also rely on new and better computers. Major employers will use computer terminals to record the earnings of their employees, and this information will automatically be reported to various tax authorities. This system will make tax evasion more difficult and tax reporting much easier.

COMPUTERS IN THE SCHOOLS

One of the most exciting and promising areas of technological advancements is in Computer-Aided Instruction. As costs of computers decrease and the social demand for computer-literate adults increases, school systems will install large numbers of microcomputers in traditional classrooms. Even very young children will learn to use computers not only for the purpose of becoming computer literate, but also to study conventional academic areas such as mathematics, history, composition, science, and foreign languages. Indeed every subject that is taught in schools today can be adapted to computer learning.

Widespread use of CAI will have a radical effect on education. Perhaps most importantly, it will make education available to virtually everyone. Handicapped students who cannot attend regular classes, for example, will be able to "attend" class via the microcomputer. Students will be able to take courses offered at schools five miles or five thousand miles from their homes without ever having to travel to the sites where these classes are taught. Imagine being able to study physics with a professor from the Massachusetts Institute of Technology and philosophy with a professor from the University of California at Berkeley in the same semester. This will be commonplace in the near future.

Programming activities, CAI, and functional software, such as text editing, will allow for more individualized instruction. Instead of gearing most of the class's activities toward the average student, teachers

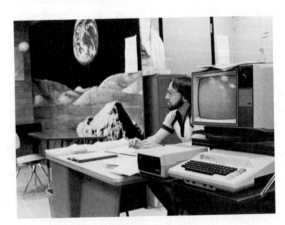

Figure 10-1
Future Technology

can challenge gifted students and provide remediation for students who require it. The computer is a patient teacher that allows students to determine their own pace for learning, thus freeing the teacher to work with students on a one-to-one basis. The computer serves as a kind of "instant learning center," suitable for a myriad of purposes. And, freed from the necessity of conducting routine drills and performing many management duties, the teacher has more time to be the vital human link between student and knowledge. The computer does not supplant teachers; it supplements them.

One of the problems with CAI today is that CAI software is still in its infant stages. Teachers often find it difficult to find and purchase programs that meet their particular needs. Software development is certainly an important area for the future. Writing software is a time-consuming and expensive process, and the limited market for the finished product makes software development a risky business. However, as a greater number of school systems implement CAI programs and the market for such software increases, better and more affordable software will become available.

Although the classroom of tomorrow will most likely have a few microcomputers in the corner, it will probably not have a traditional library down the hall. The storage capacity of computers will make traditional libraries obsolete in the years ahead. Tomorrow's libraries will include fewer shelves of books and periodicals; instead there will be a number of computer terminals through which students can access the very latest information on whatever topics they are researching. This process of data storage and retrieval, or data *bases,* will become vital links between information and the people who require that information to function.

DATA BASES IN THE FUTURE

A natural consequence of the trend toward buying and using personal computers will make data bases important in the future. Many data bases exist today, serving the medical profession, the legal profession, and many other groups. These data bases provide access through a computer terminal to vast amounts of information that would be too expensive and too bulky for most people to purchase and store. They have the additional benefit of being updated constantly so that the information they contain is the latest and best available. Consider, for example, how vital this is to a doctor who must treat an illness that is obscure or that is currently being researched. The doctor can access up-to-the-minute information about such an illness, and this information may mean the difference between life and death.

There are also a number of general information data bases in existence today. The SOURCE is a much publicized data base that offers its subscribers access to information on a wide range of subjects. For a monthly fee, subscribers can tap into the latest information on hobbies, health concerns, financial information, and an impressive number of other topics. All that the subscriber needs is a computer terminal through which to receive this information.

As we have already mentioned, it is likely that libraries as we know them today will someday become obsolete. Rather than having to drive to a library, search through the stacks for the volumes we want, and then find that we may have to wait until those volumes are returned by another borrower, we will simply sit down at our home computer terminal, punch in a particular code, and then request the text we want to read. Should we desire to purchase a copy of that text for our home library, we will use our printer to generate a hard copy.

Data bases for special interests will develop rapidly in the future. Information of all kinds will be available at the touch of a finger. As society becomes more complex and more facets of our life are affected by technology, it will become essential that we have immediate access to accurate and constantly updated information. Data bases will help us to stay finely tuned to the world around us.

DATA COMMUNICATIONS

Another area destined for rapid and significant development in the future is data communications, or the transfer and reception of data by electronic means. Many large computer users already rely on data communications via telephone lines. This allows large corporate offices to keep in constant communication with branch offices. It allows for centralized record keeping and enables a corporation to coordinate the efforts of all its branches to best meet the needs of its customers. It is an effective means of keeping business healthy. This trend toward communicating over data networks will continue to grow, becoming faster and more accurate than it is today.

Government will certainly work toward developing more effective means of data communication. It is important for governmental agencies to keep in contact with each other, for remote military bases to maintain communication, and even for nations to monitor each other's activities. More sophisticated means of data communications, such as fiber optics, will make communication fast and effective in the future.

ARTIFICIAL INTELLIGENCE

Along with data bases and data communications, the field of artificial intelligence (AI) will undergo rapid changes and development. Artificial intelligence refers to devices capable of imitating human cognitive processes: thinking, remembering, learning, inferring, and so forth. For the past twenty-five years, researchers have been working to develop a "teachable" computer. Although today's computers process numerical data, the AI computers of the fifth generation are expected to process nonnumerical data with technology that is being developed all over the world, particularly in Japan.

In addition, fifth-generation computers with artificial intelligence are expected to be able to decode instructions given them in ordinary human language. They may be able to compile their own instructions to perform virtually any task they are asked (literally!) to perform. Researchers say that these fifth-generation computers will be available by 1990.

The primary reason that so much attention is being devoted to developing artificial intelligence is the phenomenal impact such technology will have on industry. By the early 1990s, experts say, there will be a 50 percent shift of the labor force now involved in manufacturing and other major industries. Most probably, they will move into other technical fields, where the jobs of the future lie.

Much of the work that is done by humans today will be performed by robots in the future. The term *robot* calls to most minds an image of a metal humanoid similar to the Tin Man in *The Wizard of Oz*. Yet robots are highly sophisticated machines capable of performing many tasks. They are particularly well-suited to jobs that are repetitious, dangerous, or difficult for humans to perform. Robots can be exposed to situations that might injure the health of human workers. In addition, they are capable of working twenty-four hours a day, seven days a week, with very little need for work stoppage. Although the initial purchase price of robots today is prohibitive to most companies, robots are extremely cost-effective workers.

The advent of computerized robots in manufacturing raises an important issue. Many people fear computers because they believe that these technological wonders will make human workers obsolete. What will happen to the 50 percent of the labor force whose jobs are eventually automated? Actually there will be plenty of employment opportunities available in the future, but the nature of those jobs will be different than the jobs today.

According to the U.S. Bureau of Labor Statistics, the need for qualified people to work in computer-related careers will double in the next decade. Many experts say that that estimate is too moderate and predict that the demand for such workers will easily triple in the 1990s. It is logical to assume, then, that those workers who find themselves displaced by automatons on the job will be retrained to assume computer-related positions. The robots cannot exist, after all, without human workers to design, manufacture, operate, and maintain them.

But robots in industry are merely one facet of the fascinating field of artificial intelligence. The impact of AI on computers in the schools will be momentous. Very young children will be able to operate computers without the need for typing skills or knowledge of programming languages. They will be able to "teach" the computer to carry out the activities they want done. Since AI computers function as intelligent aids to their users rather than as merely programmable machines, computers will become more effective teachers, listening to students, responding according to information stored in memory, and then storing information away for later use. They will no longer rely on rigidly defined software.

COMPUTERS IN THE HOMES OF TOMORROW

Some of the most significant changes that we in the computer age will witness will take place in our own homes. During the past several years, there has been a significant increase in the number of microcomputers being purchased for home use. No longer is computer power an advantage enjoyed by a few very large corporations. Indeed, the decreasing size and price of powerful microcomputers will result in microcomputers becoming common household appliances by the dawn of the twenty-first century. How will this affect our daily lives?

Microcomputers are capable of performing any number of routine tasks now done by humans. Many microcomputer users now monitor budgets and bank accounts with their computer systems. Their computers are faster and more accurate than the users are. Tomorrow's homeowner will not need to keep account books, budgets, and voluminous files of papers to maintain a close watch on household matters; the microcomputer will assume these tasks.

When it is not busy balancing the checkbook, the home computer will keep an electronic "eye" on other household appliances. It will regulate the climatic conditions inside and outside the house in order to maintain a comfortable environment with the least amount of fuel. It may be used as a recipe file to store family favorites. The microcomputer may serve to turn lights on, the microwave oven off when dinner is fully cooked, and keep inventory of food items on the cupboard shelves, adding items to a grocery list as they are used.

Because much of our shopping will be done via computer, the microcomputer will report its grocery list to a computer at the grocery store. The necessary items will be ordered automatically. Microcomputers may even perform comparative shopping for users, compiling lists of prices from various stores and determining which store is most economical for the items needed.

After dinner is finished, children will use the microcomputer to do their homework. They will be able to use CAI software at home as well as in their classrooms. They can learn from mathematics tutorials, practice spelling, and even compose essays on their home computers. Schools and parents will communicate with each other to a greater extent than before. Teachers will recommend software to be purchased, borrowed, or rented that will meet the individual needs of children and substitute for some of the more traditional kinds of homework assignments. Since computers will be part of your color television set, most, if not all, children will have home access to computers.

When the children are finished with their homework, parents and older sisters and brothers can take college courses on a correspondence basis via the microcomputer. Even graduate and postgraduate courses will be available to microcomputer users. Best of all, students of any age can set their own pace for learning. The computer is both patient and challenging.

Because the computer will save its user many hours spent in dull household chores, microcomputer owners will have more leisure time. Some of this time they may choose to spend enjoying the many fascinating and challenging games available for use with microcomputer systems. There will be many sorts of games to enjoy: educational, chance, strategy. Again, the computer can be challenged by all ages and levels of ability. It can play "Go Fish" with a very small child and chess with an adult.

If the user is not in the mood for games, then he or she may use the microcomputer to create art of many types. For example, a visual artist can use the graphics capability to create stunning displays. A writer can use the word-processing capability to compose the Great American Novel or to write a sonnet. Musicians can compose complex pieces of music and then hear their compositions immediately performed by computerized music synthesizers.

All of these functions are available for use with microcomputer systems today. As more and more people purchase home computers and experiment with their capabilities, more applications of computers in the home will become apparent. Homelife as we know it is destined to change in the future as computers relieve us from routine, often boring chores that we now perform. More than likely, we will find the microcomputer no more intimidating than an oven or a refrigerator.

COMPUTERS AND THE HANDICAPPED

One of the most promising areas of technological advancement to watch in the future is the research and development of devices to aid the handicapped population. Many such devices are under study today and will become more accessible as computer technology develops smaller and less expensive computers.

CAI has proven extremely effective in special education environments. Slow learners are comfortable using computers to learn academic subjects that have proven difficult for them in the past. Also, students who are paralyzed or suffer muscle impairment that prevents them from holding a pen are capable of writing essays and solving mathematical problems with a computer. Severely handicapped students can use CAI to learn in their homes if they are unable to attend classes.

Computers also help the handicapped in other ways. Voice synthesizers allow the speech-impaired to communicate their thoughts, perhaps for the first time. Still other devices help the vision-impaired to read and generate written texts. Because artificial intelligence research promises to make computers more capable of imitating human activities, computer aids for the handicapped are sure to be developed in the future. This gives hope to many today.

Clearly we are on the brink of a technological revolution. As we look around us daily, we often wonder whether we have accidentally stepped into a time machine that has carried us into the future. The phenomenal advancements in technology that we have witnessed during the past twenty years is only the tip of the iceberg. What technological achievements lie in our future is anyone's guess!

SUMMARY

In the future we may expect to see rapid technological advancements in computers. Research and development is geared toward four areas in particular: continued miniaturization, greater memory capacity, speech synthesis and recognition, and enhanced graphics displays. Greater amounts of computer power will be built into physically smaller units that will be more affordable and, hence, more accessible to the average person. These smaller computers will be made more powerful by new systems of memory that allow for greater storage. Speech synthesis and recognition will make computers easier to use because they will be able to communicate directly with humans. Finally, improved graphics capabilities will make computers more attractive to those who wish to generate visual displays.

The computers of tomorrow will be used in a great number of applications—social and personal. They will help regulate traffic flow, control airplane landings and takeoffs, and monitor the vital signs of hospital patients. They will serve to diagnose illnesses and prescribe treatment. In addition, they will play a more important role in the educational system as greater numbers of schools implement curricula which employ CAI, programming activities, and functional software, such as text editors and data bases.

We can also expect to see widespread use of data bases by the general public. Data bases give computer users access to up-to-the-minute information on a wide range of subjects. Not only are data bases extremely useful to professionals such as doctors, lawyers, and law enforcement officers, but they also provide special-interest information on hobbies, first aid, and current events. Tomorrow's complex society will make fast access to updated information a necessity.

Data communications, or the transfer and retrieval of data via electronic means, will develop to become an important way for large corporations to keep in constant contact with their branch offices. It will also be used more widely by government agencies and others who must maintain close contact with a remote location.

Yet another promising area of technological advancement is artificial intelligence. The fifth generation of computers will be capable of imitating human cognitive activities such as thinking, remembering, and inferring. They will be able to compile their own instructions based on commands given them in ordinary human language, allowing more people to "program" computers without extensive knowledge of computer programming languages. Also, AI robots will be used widely in industry, causing a significant shift of the labor force from industrial work to technically oriented jobs.

Home computers will expedite the work of homeowners by keeping records, maintaining budgets, and regulating household inventories. They will also serve as important learning tools to either supplement education received in traditional classrooms or to serve as a medium for taking classes from distant schools on a correspondence basis. They will be able to provide entertainment in the form of games. Many people will use their microcomputers to work at home without the need for traveling to a remote work site.

Handicapped persons will enjoy numerous new computerized devices that will improve the quality of their lives. Speech synthesizers, for example, will allow the speech-impaired to communicate orally.

The future holds great promise of technological advancements that will change our lives for the better.

Software Directories and Review Publications

Please write or call for current ordering information.

Software Directories

The Addison-Wesley Book of Apple
  Computer Software, 1983
The Book Company
16720 Hawthorne Blvd.
Lawndale, CA 90260
(213) 417-8031
(Directory also rates quality of
  software described)

The Apple Software Directory
Vol. 3, Education
WIDL Video
5245 W. Diversey
Chicago, IL 60639
(312) 622-9606

Atari Program Exchange
Atari, Inc.
P.O. Box 427
155 Moffett Park Dr.
Sunnyvale, CA 94086

Atari Special Additions
Listing of Software Vendors
Sally Bowman, Editor
Atari, Inc.
60 E. Plumeria
P.O. Box 50047
San Jose, CA 95150
(408) 942-6500
(Includes third-party software and
  hardware descriptions)

Commodore Software Encyclopedia
Commodore Business Machines
Software Group
681 Moore Rd.
300 Valley Forge Square
King of Prussia, PA 19406

Educational Software Directory
  (for Apple II)
Sterling Swift Publishing
  Company
P.O. Box 188
Manchaca, TX 78652

Educator's Handbook and Software
  Directory (for Apple II)
Vital Information, Inc.
350 Union Station
Kansas City, MO 64108

Radio Shack TRS-80 Educational
  Resource Series
Educational Software Sourcebook
Cat. No. 26-2756
Radio Shack, Education Division
400 Atrium, One Tandy Center
Fort Worth, TX 76102-2805
(817) 390-3832

School Microware (for Apple, PET,
  TRS-80)
Dresden Associates
P.O. Box 246
Dresden, ME 04342

Texas Instruments Program
  Directory
Texas Instruments
P.O. Box 53
Lubbock, TX 79408
(800) 858-4565

TRS-80 Software Directory
Vital Information, Inc.
350 Union Station
Kansas City, MO 64108

TRS-80 Software Source
COMPUTERMAT
P.O. Box 1664
Lake Havasu City, AZ 86403

Software Review Information

Apple Computer Clearinghouse for
  the Handicapped
Prentke Romich Co.
R.D. 2, P.O. Box 191
Shreve, OH 44676
(216) 767-2906

Apple Education Foundation
20605 Lazerno Ave.
Cupertino, CA 95014

The Apple Journal of Courseware
  Review
30863 Stevens Creek Blvd.
Building B-2, Suite A-1
Cupertino, CA 95014

Booklist
50 E. Huron St.
Chicago, IL 60611

The Book Report
Box 14466
Columbus, OH 43214

Courseware Report Card
150 West Carob St.
Compton, CA 90220
(213) 637-2131

Creative Computing's 1982
  Software Buyers Guide
P.O. Box 640
Holmes, PA 19043

Curriculum Product Review
530 University Ave.
Palo Alto, CA 94301
(415) 321-1770

Curriculum Review
517 South Jefferson
Chicago, IL 60607
(New computer section, includes
  software reviews, ideas for
  integration)

Dataspan
University of Michigan
109 E. Madison St.
Ann Arbor, MI 48104
(313) 763-4410

Digest of Software Reviews:
  Education
1341 Bulldog Lane
Suite C
Fresno, CA 93710

Educational Software Library
262 Park Lane
King of Prussia, PA 19406

Educational Software Preview
  Guide—1983
Educational Software Evaluation
  Consortium
California TEC Center Software
  Library and Clearinghouse
SMERC Library
San Mateo Co. Office of Education
333 Main St.
Redwood City, CA 94063

Educator's Micro Digest and
  Software Exchange
Educorp 21 LTD
P.O. Box 1692
Madison, WI 53791
(Software reviews and other
  information)

Electronic Data Systems Group
14580 Midway Rd.
Dallas, TX 75234

Elementary and Secondary School
  Subcommittee of the ACM
Dept. of Computer and Information
  Science
University of Oregon
Eugene, OR 97403

EPIE Institute
P.O. Box 620
Stony Brook, NY 11790
(516) 246-8664

Florida Cooperative Extension
  Service
Survey of Availability of Micro and
  Mini Computer Software
G113 McCarty Hall
University of Florida
Gainesville, FL 32611

MACUL Journal
Wayne County ISD
P.O. Box 807
Wayne, MI 48184
(Winter 1981 issue included 143
  software reviews of several
  brands of microcomputers)

Materials Review and Evaluation
  Services
Division of Educational Media
State Dept. of Public Instruction
2905 Reedy Creek Park Rd.
Raleigh, NC 27611

Microcomputer Education
  Applications Network
1030 15th St., NW
Suite 800
Washington, DC 20005

Microcomputer Research Clinic
College of Education
Arizona State University
Tempe, AZ 85287

Microcomputer Resource Center
Teachers College
Columbia University
525 W. 121st St.
New York, NY 10027

Microsift Reviews
Northwest Regional Educational
  Laboratory
300 SW Sixth Ave.
Portland, OR 97204
(503) 248-6800

Peelings II
P.O. Box 188
Las Cruces, NM 88004
(A magazine evaluating software
  and hardware that includes
  some educational software
  evaluations)

Pipeline
Conduit
University of Iowa
Box 388
Iowa City, IA
(319) 355-5789

Project Local
200 Nahatan St.
Westwood, MA 02080

Purser's Atari Magazine
Box 466
El Dorado, CA 95623

Purser's Magazine
Box 466
El Dorado, CA 95623

School Microware Review (for
  Apple, Atari, Pet, TRS-80)
Dresden Associates
P.O. Box 246
Dresden, ME 04342
(207) 737-4466
(Fifty reviews each issue; index to
  reviews in other publications)

80 Software Critique
RWC Microcomputing Services
P.O. Box 134
El Dorado, CA 95623

TABS Project
Ayss Hall 202-A
1945 N. High St.
Columbus, OH 43210

TALMIS
115 North Oak Park Ave.
Oak Park, IL 60301

Technical Education Research
  Centers
8 Eliot St.
Cambridge, MA 02138

In addition, many educational and
popular computing magazines contain software review information.
See Appendix F for addresses.

Software Resources

Initial Contacts, Inexpensive or Free Software

Alameda County Office of
  Education
224 West Winton Ave.
Hayward, CA 94544
Attn: Glenn Fisher, School
  Computer Specialist
(415) 881-6201

The Apple Avocation Alliance
721 Pike St.
Cheyenne, WY 82001

Apple Portland Program Library
  Exchange
1915 NE Couch
Portland, OR 97232
(503) 233-5711

Cassette Net (public domain
  software, PET)
San Ramone Valley U.S.D.
699 Old Orchard Dr.
Danville, CA 94526
(415) 837-1511

Georgia Micro Swap
Dept. of Mathematics Education
University of Georgia
Athens, GA 30602

Earl Keyser
22 Clover Lane
Mason City, TX
(Pilot Exchange/Apple Exchange)

Microcomputers in Education
Robbinsdale Area Schools
Independent School District 281
4148 Winnetka Ave. North
Minneapolis, MN 55427
(612) 533-2781

Orange County TRS-80 Users
  Group
2531 E. Commonwealth Ave.
Fullerton, CA 92631

Puget Sound Program Library
  Exchange
2110 Salty Dr. NW
Olympia, WA 98502

San Mateo County Office of
  Education
c/o Ann Lathrop
SOFTSWAP
SERC Library
333 Main St.
Redwood City, CA 94063

Tri-County Computer Consortium
  Project
Attn: Tom Schmeltzer
Oakland Schools
2100 Pontiac Lake
Pontiac, MI 48054
(313) 858-1895

YPLA Software Exchange (Logo)
1208 Hillsdale Dr.
Richardson, TX 75081

Educational Publishing Companies with Electronic Publishing Divisions, and Software Distributors

Note: Consult software directories and advertisements to locate addresses and to contact companies producing software in your own areas of interest. We do not suggest a full-scale mailing to all software companies, since many of these companies will not have software applicable to your situation. Use directories, advertisements, and advice to narrow your field of research.

Addison-Wesley Publishing
  Company
2725 Sand Hill Rd.
Menlo Park, CA 94025
(415) 854-0300

Borg-Warner Educational Systems
600 West University Dr.
Arlington Heights, IL 60004

Developmental Learning Materials
One DLM Park, P.O. Box 4000
Allen, TX 75002

Encyclopaedia Britannica
  Educational Corp.
425 N. Michigan Ave.
Chicago, IL 60611
(800) 554-9862
(CAI information)

Gamco
P.O. Box 1911
Big Spring, TX 79720-0211

Eston Corporation
P.O. Box 5176
Louisville, KN 40205

Hayden Book Co.
50 Essex St.
Rochelle Park, NJ 07662
(201) 843-0550

Holt, Rinehart & Winston School
  Dept.
383 Madison Ave.
New York, NY 10017

Houghton Mifflin Company
One Beacon Street
Boston, MA 02107
(617) 725-5000

K-12 Micro Media
P.O. Box 17
Valley Cotage, NY 10989

Marck
280 Linden Avenue
Branford, CT 06405
(203) 481-3271

McGraw-Hill Book Co.
Webster Division
1221 Avenue of the Americas
New York, NY 10020
(212) 997-1221

Milliken Publishing Company
1100 Research Blvd.
St. Louis, MO 63132
(314) 991-4220

Milton-Bradley Company
443 Shaker Rd.
East Longmeadow, MA 01028
(413) 525-6411

Opportunities for Learning, Inc.
8950 Lurline Ave., Dept. 390
Chatsworth, CA 91311
(213) 341-2535

The Psychological Corp. and the
Learning Achievement
Corporation
757 Third Ave.
New York, NY 10017

Queue, Inc.
5 Chapel Hill Dr.
Fairfield, CT 06432
(203) 372-6761

Random House
201 East 50th St.
New York, NY 10022
(212) 751-2600

Reader's Digest Services
Educational Division
Pleasantville, NY 10570
(914) 769-7000

Scholastic Software
Scholastic, Inc.
904 Sylvan Ave.
Englewood Cliffs, NJ 07632

Science Research Associates
155 North Wacker Dr.
Chicago, IL 60606
(312) 984-2000

Scott, Foresman and Company
1900 East Lake Ave.
Glenview, IL 60025
(312) 729-3000

Society For Visual Education
Division of the Singer Company
1345 Diversey Pkwy.
Chicago, IL 60614

Sterling Swift Publishing Co.
P.O. Box 188
Manchaca, TX 78652
(512) 444-7570

Sunburst Communications
39 Washington Ave.
Room T161
Pleasantville, NY 10570
(800) 431-1934

John Wiley and Sons, Inc.
Dept. 2-0464
605 Third Ave.
New York, NY 10158

Authoring Languages and Authoring Systems

"Codes" (TRS-80, Apple, PET, others)
Academic Computing Associates
P.O. Box 27561
Phoenix, AZ 85061

"The Tutor Drill and Practice System" (Apple and others)
Active Systems, Inc.
Hanover, NH

"Apple Pilot," "Apple Super Pilot," "Shell Games" (mini-authoring* for Apple II)
Apple Computer, Inc.
10260 Bandley Dr.
Cupertino, CA 94017
(408) 996-1010

"Atari Pilot"
Atari, Inc.
1272 Borregas Ave.
Sunnyvale, CA 94086
(408) 745-5069

"Zenith Education System" (Apple)
Avant Garde Creations
P.O. Box 30160
Eugene, OR 97403

---

*Entire game format is in place; user inserts spelling, vocabulary, definitions to be learned.

"GENIS," "MARK PILOT," "Courseware Development System I" (Bell & Howell, Apple II)
Bell & Howell
Audio-Visual Division
Dept. 8876
7100 McCormick Rd.
Chicago, IL 60645

"Microteach"
Compumax, Inc.
P.O. Box 7239
Menlo Park, CA 94025
(415) 854-6700

"The Game Show" and "Tic Tac Show" (Apple)
Computer-Advanced Ideas, Inc.
1442A Walnut St.
Suite 341
Berkeley, CA 94709
(CAI with mini-authoring capability)

"C-Bits, Computer-Based Individualized Testing System" (Apple)
Educational Software Midwest
414 Rosemere Lane
Maguoketa, IA 52060
(319) 652-2334

Educational Software
    Professionals, Ltd.
38437 Grand River
Farmington Hills, MI 48018
(313) 477-4470
(Test-writing programs, Apple)

"Super-CAI Authoring System"
    (TRS-80)
"Eclips CAI/CMI Authoring
    System"
"CAIWARE-2D CAI Authoring
    System"
Fireside Computing Inc.
Don Coyne
5843 Montgomery Rd.
Elkridge, MD 21227
(301) 796-4165

"Medalist Create" (Apple) and
    other "Create" programs
Hartley Courseware, Inc.
P.O. Box 431
Demodale, MI 48821
(Mini-authoring and authoring
    systems)

"Spelling Bee" (Apple II)
Instant Software
Peterborough, NH 03458
(603) 924-7296
(CAI with mini-authoring
    capability)

"AIDS" (Assisted Instructional
    Development System for Apple
    II)
Instructional Development
    Systems
2927 Virginia Beach Blvd.
Virginia Beach, VA 23452

"CATS 80," "VCATS 80," and
    "GRAFICAT" (ISC
    microcomputer)
ISC
Educational Services Program
Intercolor Dr.
225 Technology Park
Atlanta, GA 30092

"Create a Lesson" (Apple)
Msss D, Inc.
3412 Binkley
Dallas, TX 75205
(214) 522-8051

CAIWARE 3D (TRS-80)
MicroGnome
5843 Montgomery Rd.
Elkridge, MD 21227

"The Learning Lab" (Apple II)
Micro Lab
2310 Skokie Valley Rd.
Highland Park, IL 60035

"Appilot II Edu-Disk" (Apple)
MUSE Software
330 N. Charles St.
Baltimore, MD 21201
(301) 659-7212

"The Adaptable Skeleton" (Apple)
Micro Power & Light Co.
12820 Hillcrest Rd.
Suite 224
Dallas, TX 75230
(214) 239-6620

"PILOT and FIVE PILOT" (PET)
Peninsula School Computer Project
Peninsula School, Peninsula Way
Menlo Park, CA 94025
(415) 325-1584

"PET/CBM Study Made Easy"
    (PET)
Creating drills or tests
Robert Purser
Box 466
El Dorado, CA 95623

Pilot language and authoring
    systems (TRS-80)
Radio Shack Education Division
1600 One Tandy Center
Fort Worth, TX 76102
(817) 390-3832

"Blocks Authoring System" (Apple)
San Juan Unified School District
3738 Walnut Ave.
Carmichael, CA 95608
(916) 484-2011

"Aristotle's Apple" (Apple)
Stoneware
1930 Fourth St.
San Rafel, CA 94901
(415) 454-6400

"Automated Instruction, Drill, and
  Evaluation (AIDE)"
Science Research Associates
155 N. Wacker Dr.
Chicago, IL 60606
(800) 621-0664

"T.E.S.T." (TRS-80)
TYC
40 Stuyvesant Manor
Geneseo, NY 14454

Microcomputer Manufacturers

(Note: Many manufacturers offer software for sale as well as hardware.)

Apple Computer, Inc.
10260 Bandley Dr.
Cupertino, CA 95014

Atari, Inc.
1265 Borregas Ave.
Dept. C
Sunnyvale, CA 94086

Bell & Howell
Audio-Visual Products Division
7100 N. McCormick Rd.
Chicago, IL 60645

Commodore
950 Rittenhouse Rd.
Norristown, PA 19401

Compucolor
Compucolor II Renaissance
    Machine
P.O. Box 569
Norcross, GA 30091

Cromemco, Inc.
280 Bernardo Avenue
Mountain View, CA 94043

Digital Equipment Corp.
146 Main St.
Maynard, MA 01754

Heath Company
Heathkit
Benton Harbor, MI 49022

Hewlett-Packard Company
HP-85 Inquiries Manager
1507 Page Mill Rd.
Palo Alto, CA 94304

IBM Personal Computer Division
P.O. Box 1328
Boca Raton, FL 83432

Intelligent Systems Corp.
(See Compucolor)
Intecolor Dr.
25 Technology Park
Atlanta-Norcross, GA 30092

Monroe Systems for Business
The American Rd.
Morris Plains, NJ 07950

North Star
Horizon II
1440-4th St.
Berkeley, CA 94710

Ohio Scientific
Challenger Series
1333 S. Chillocothe
Aurora, OH 44202

Osborne Computer Corp.
26500 Corporate Ave.
Hayward, CA 94545

Radio Shack
TRS-80
1300 One Tandy Center
Fort Worth, TX 76192

Rockwell
Sinclair Research Corp.
Sinclair Microcomputer ZX80 and
    Spectrum
50 Staniford St.
Suite 800
Boston, MA 02114

Texas Instruments
12501 N. Central Expressway
Dallas, TX 75222

Xerox Corp.
Retail Marketing Division
Stamford, CT 06904

Appendix E

Speech Synthesis and Voice Recognition Hardware Vendors

VOICEBOX Speech Synthesizer
(Atari and Apple)
The Alien Group
27 W. 23rd St.
Dept. CU-2
New York, NY 10010

Lisa Voice Synthesizer (RS-232C)
Centrigram Corp.
155A Moffett Park Dr.
Sunnyvale, CA 94086

CBM 4010 Voice Synthesizer
Commodore Computer Systems
Division
681 Moore Rd.
King of Prussia, PA 19406
(215) 337-7100

S.A.M.
Don't Ask Computer Software
2265 Westwood Blvd.
Suite B-150
Los Angeles, CA 90064
(213) 397-8811
(Software for Apple and Atari
which allows speech to be
accessed from BASIC language.
No special hardware necessary.)

General Instruments
600 W. John St.
Hicksville, NY 11802
(516) 733-3000

Heuristics
1285 Hammerwood Ave.
Sunnyvale, CA 94088
(408) 734-8532

Micromouth and Sweet Talker
Micromint Inc.
917 Midway
Woodmere, NY 11598
(800) 646-3479

Supertalker SD200 (Apple)
Mountain Computer
3800 Harvey West Blvd.
Santa Cruz, CA 95060
(408) 438-6650

The Voice
Muse Software
330 N. Charles St.
Baltimore, MD 21201
(301) 659-7212
(Software speech synthesizer)

National Semiconductor
2900 Semiconductor Dr.
Santa Clara, CA 95050
(408) 737-5000

Panasonic
One Panasonic Way
Secaucus, NJ 07094
(201) 348-5270

Percom Data Co.
211 N. Kirby
Garland, TX 75042
(214) 272-3421

Programma International, Inc.
2908 N. Naomi St.
Burbank, CA 91504
(213) 954-0240

Echo II (Apple)
Street Electronics
3152 E. LaPalma Ave.
Anaheim, CA 92806
(714) 632-9950

PC-Mate Speech Master (IBM)
Tecmar, Inc.
23600 Mercantile Rd.
Cleveland, OH 44122
(216) 464-7410

Several types
Telesensory Speech Systems
3408 Hillview Ave.
P.O. Box 10099
Palo Alto, CA 94304
(415) 856-8255

Texas Instruments
12501 N. Central Expressway
Dallas, TX 75222

Type 'N Talk (RS-232C)
Votrax
500 Stephenson Hwy.
Troy, MI 48084
(800) 521-1350

V-100 Interactive Voice
    Synthesizer (Apple and IBM)
Vynet Corp.
2405 Qume Dr.
San Jose, CA 95131
(408) 942-1037

Voicetek
P.O. Box 388
Goleta, CA 93116
(Voice input and output for Apple
    and PET)

F

Resource Guides, Educational Computing Magazines, and Brand Name Microcomputer Magazines

Resource Guides

Classroom Computer News
Directory of Educational Computer
  Resources
Intentional Educations, Inc.
341 Mt. Auburn St.
Watertown, MA 02172

Computer Graphics Directory
730 Boston Post Rd.
P.O. Box 392
Sudbury, MA 01776
(617) 443-4671

Instructor's Computer Directory for
  Schools
P.O. Box 6099
Duluth, MN 55806

The Microcomputer Index
2464 El Camino Real
Suite 247
Santa Clara, CA 95051
(408) 984-1097
(Subject and abstract guide to
  microcomputer articles from 32
  periodical sources. Also on-line
  through DIALOG Information
  Retrieval Service.)

Encyclopedia for the TRS-80
Microcomputing
Book Dept.
80 Pine St.
Peterborough, NH 03458
(Ten-volume reference series
  contains programs and articles.
  Companion software can be
  purchased to load programs,
  rather than having to keyboard
  programs in yourself.)

Educational Computing Magazines

*Access: Microcomputers in
  Libraries*
P.O. Box 764
Oakridge, OR 97463
(Published quarterly)

Classroom Computer Learning
19 Davis Dr.
Belmont, CA 94002
(Published bimonthly)

*Computer-Using Educators
  Newsletter*
Computer-Using Educators
Independence High School
1776 Education Park Dr.
San Jose, CA 95133
(Published bimonthly)

The Computing Teacher
Dept. of Computer and Information
  Science
University of Oregon
Eugene, OR 97850
(Published nine times per year)

Courseware Magazine
4919 N. Millbrook, #222
Fresno, CA 93726
(Published five times per year.
  Includes software on disk or
  tape for Apple, TRS-80, and
  PET.)

Educational Computer
P.O. Box 535
Cupertino, CA 95015
(Published monthly)

Educational Technology
140 Sylvan Ave.
Englewood Cliffs, NJ 07632
(Published bimonthly)

Electronic Education
Electronic Communications, Inc.
Suite 220
1311 Executive Center Dr.
Tallahassee, FL 32301
(Published ten times per year)

Electronic Learning
902 Sylvan Ave.
Englewood, NJ 07632
(Published nine times per year)

The Journal of Computers in
Mathematics and Science
Teaching
P.O. Box 4455
Austin, TX 78765
(Published quarterly)

The Journal of Computers,
Reading and Language Arts
(CRLA)
NAVA
3150 Spring St.
Fairfax, VA 22031
or Gerald H. Block, CRLA
P.O. Box 13039
Oakland, CA 94661

Teaching and Computers
Scholastic Inc.
902 Sylvan Ave.
Box 2001
Englewood Cliffs, NJ 07632

The Logo and Educational
Computing Journal
Suite 219
1320 Stony Brook Road
Stony Brook, NY 11790

T.H.E. JOURNAL
Information Synergy, Inc.
P.O. Box 992
Acton, MA 01720
(Published six times per year)

Brand Name Microcomputer Magazines

Apple-Related
Apple
Apple Computer Co.
10260 Bandley Dr.
Cupertino, CA 95014

Apple Barrel
c/o Ed Seeger, Editor
Houston Area Apple Users Group
3609 Glenmeadow Dr.
Rosenberg, TX 77471

Apple for the Teacher
5848 Riddio St.
Citrus Hts., CA 95610

The Apple Orchard
International Apple Core
P.O. Box 2227
Seattle, WA 98111

Appletree
Programmer's Institute, A Division
of Futurehouse
P.O. Box 3191
Dept. AA
Chapel Hill, NC 27514
(Magazine on diskette)

Call A.P.P.L.E.
304 Main Ave. S.
Suite 300
Renton, WA 98055

InCider Magazine
Subscription Dept.
P.O. Box 911
Farmingdale, NY 11737

Nibble
The Reference for Apple
  Computing
Box 325
Lincoln, MA 01773
(617) 259-9710

Peelings II
POB 188, Dept. CC
Las Cruces, NM 88004
(505) 526-8364
(Apple software and hardware
  review)

Window
469 Pleasant St.
Watertown, MA 02172
(617) 923-9147
(A magazine on floppy disk)

Atari-Related
A.N.A.L.O.G. (Newsletter)
P.O. Box 23
Worcester, MA 01603

Antic: The Atari Resource
297 Missouri St.
San Francisco, CA 94107
(Published bimonthly)

Magatar
Programmer's Institute
A division of Futurehouse
P.O. Box 3191, Dept. AA
Chapel Hill, NC 27514
(919) 489-2198
(Magazine on cassette or diskette)

IBM-Related
PC Magazine
P.O. Box 2443
Boulder, CO 80321

PC World
P.O. Box 6700
Bergenfield, NJ 07621

Personal Computer Age (IBM)
P.O. Box 70725
Dept. K1
Pasadena, CA 91107
(800) 227-2634 ext. 936
(800) 772-2666, ext. 936, in
  California

PET/Commodore-Related
Commodore Magazine
Computer Systems Division
Commodore Business Machines
681 Moore Rd.
King of Prussia, PA 19406

Home and Educational Computing
P.O. Box 5406
Greensboro, NC 27403
(VIC-20)

The Paper
P.O. Box 460
Livingston Manor, NY 12758

PET Newsletter
Computer Project
Lawrence Hall of Science
University of California
Berkeley, CA 94270

Radio Shack-Related
Chromasette Magazine
P.O. Box 1087
Santa Barbara, CA 93102
(805) 963-1066
(Cassette-tape magazine for
  extended BASIC color computer)

Cload Magazine
P.O. Box 1448
Santa Barbara, CA 93102
(805) 962-6271
(Cassette-tape magazine)

Color Computer News
P.O. Box 1192
Muskegon, MI 49443

Computeronics
Box 149
New York, NY 10956
(914) 425-1535
(Monthly magazine)

80 Micro
80 Pine St.
Peterborough, NH 03458
(Published monthly)

80-Microcomputing
P.O. Box 981
Farmingdale, NY 11737

80-U.S. Journal
3838 South Warner St.
Tacoma, WA 98409

HOT CoCo
Subscription Services
P.O. Box 975
Farmingdale, NY 11737

TRC
Programmer's Institute
A division of Futurehouse
P.O. Box 3191
Dept. AA
Chapel Hill, NC 27514
(Magazine on cassette or diskette
    for Radio Shack Color
    Computer, extended BASIC)

TRS-80 Users Journal
P.O. Box 7112
Tacoma, WA 98407
(206) 759-9642

Texas Instruments-Related
99'er Magazine
P.O. Box 5537
Eugene, OR 97405
(503) 485-8796

TI Logo Source and *TI Source*
Microcomputers Corp.
P.O. Box 191
Rye, NY 10580
(914) 967-8370

Timex/Sinclair-Related
SYNC
39 E. Hanover Ave.
Morris Plains, NJ 07950

**Personal Computing
Magazines**
Byte
70 Main St.
Peterborough, NH 03458

Compute!
The Journal for Progressive
    Computing
Circulation Dept.
515 Abbott Drive
Broomal, PA 19008
(Twelve times each year)

Creative Computing
P.O. Box 789-M
Morristown, NJ 07960

Infoworld
Circulation Dept.
530 Lytton Ave.
Palo Alto, CA 94031
(Weekly news)

Microcomputing
80 Pine St.
Peterborough, NH 03458

Nibble
Box 325
Lincoln, MA 01773

Personal Computing
50 Essex St.
Rochelle Park, NJ 07662

Popular Computing
70 Main St.
Peterborough, NH 03458

Softalk
Softalk Publishing, Inc.
10432 Burbank Blvd.
North Hollywood, CA 91601

Softside
6 South St.
Milford, NH 03055

Computer-Related Films

Classroom Applications of
  Microcomputers
Using a Computer in the
  Elementary School
Educational Software
Teaching Computer Literacy and
  Programming
Alameda County Superintendent of
  Schools
Learning Resource Services
Public Sales
685 A St.
Hayward, CA 94541
(Presentation on videotape, given
  by Glenn Fisher; each 40
  minutes long)

Computers: The Inside Story
Computers: Tools for People
Churchill Films
662 N. Robertson Blvd.
Los Angeles, CA 90069

The Computer Programme
Films Incorporated
733 Green Bay Rd.
Wilmette, IL 60091
(800) 323-4222
(A series of ten 25-minute
  computer literacy video
  programs, produced by the BBC)

The Personal Touch
Hardware and Software
Speaking and Language
Data Processing, Control, Design
For Better or Worse
Extending Your Reach
Audio Visual Center
Indiana University
Bloomington, IN 47405
(Films, 15 minutes each, 1981)

Future Shock
Don't Bother Me, I'm Learning
McGraw Hill Films
1221 Avenue of the Americas
New York, NY 10020

Computer Technology: The Endless
  Revolution 1979, 24 minutes
Introduction to Digital Computers,
  24 minutes, 1969
Among Us, 20 minutes, 1973
At the Forefront, 23 minutes, 1976
The Catalyst, 13 minutes, 1970
Sperry Univac
Worldwide Communications
Blue Ball, PA 19425

A Company of the Future, 31
  minutes, 1978
West Glen Films

Resources: Learning Materials for BASIC Programming and Computer Literacy

ARCsoft Publishers
P.O. Box 132N
Woodsboro, MD 21798
(301) 663-4444
(Program worksheets; printed forms for planning BASIC programs; Radio Shack Color Computer, Apple, Pocket, IBM, Universal coding forms)

Camelot Publishing
P.O. Box 1357
Armond Beach, FL 32074
(Visual masters and other materials for teaching BASIC programming)

Classroom Consortia Media
28 Bay St.
Staten Island, NY 10301
Computer Awareness and Literacy
(Tutorials on diskettes)

Computer Tutor
by Sandra Markle
Learning Works, Inc., 1981
(48 reproducible pages—Computer literacy activities)

The Continental Press, Inc.
Elizabethtown, PA 17022
Computer Literacy: An Introductory Course
(7th grade to adult, fifteen 45-minute lessons; teachers' guide, lesson plans, student activity and support materials)

Cow Bay Computing
Box 515
Manhasset, NY 11030
(Computer literacy and programming materials)

Creative Publications
Computer Products Catalog
3977 E. Bayshore Rd.
P.O. Box 10328
Palo Alto, CA 94303
(415) 968-3977
(Books, filmstrips, audio tutorials, etc.; Basic Discoveries: A Problem Solving Approach to Beginning Programming, by Linda Malone and Jerry Johnson, 1981, 80 reproducible pages, grades 5 and above)

Computeronics
2757 W. Pensacola St.
Tallahassee, FL 32304
(904) 487-1520
(Teaching materials for computer programming, computer literacy, 5th-12th grades—workbooks, activity packets, teacher guides)

Cybertronics Internations, Inc.
999 Mount Kemble Ave.
Morristown, NJ 07960
(212) 532-3089
Karel the Robot
Cyberlogo
(Book, diskette, simulator—teaches Pascal and Logo languages)

Educational Activities, Inc.
Filmstrip Division
P.O. Box 392
Freeport, NY 11520
(800) 645-3739
(*Computer Programming—BASIC for Elementary Grades* and *Computer Careers,* two filmstrip series)

Electronic Data Systems Corp.
Dallas, TX
(Apple BASIC Teaching Kit— series of 20-30 videocassettes and corresponding course books)

Gregg/McGraw-Hill
29th Floor
1221 Avenue of the Americas
New York, NY 10020
(COMPUTER POWER—Computer Literacy program, utilizing PASCAL, student textbook, teacher's manual, courseware)

J.L. Hammett Company
Hammett Place
Box 545
Braintree, MA 02184
(800) 225-5467
(800) 972-5056, Mass. only
(Topics in computer literacy and basic programming)

Harbor Software
Box 267
Cold Spring
Harbor, NY 11724
(516) 271-4462
(Computer Literacy Unit on diskette or tape; input, CPU, output, languages, review game; teaching materials included for Apple, ATARI, PET, TRS-80 and individualized programming books)

Innovative Programming
   Associates
One Airport Place
Suite EL-9
Princeton, NJ 08540
(609) 924-7272
(Computer Literacy educational software modules; introduction, printer, graphics, applications, statistics, etc.)

K-12 Micro Media
172 Broadway
Woodcliff Lake, NJ 07675
(201) 391-7555
(*Getting Down to Basic,* introductory programming workbook, grades 6-12)

Krell Software
21 Milbrook Dr.
Stonybrook, NY 11790
(Logo for the Apple)

Meka Publishing Company
9120 Galaxie Dr.
Indianapolis, IN 46227
(1 Computer/30 Kids— programming, includes activities that do not involve computer use)

National Business Institute
407 Galloway St.
Eau Claire, WI 54702
(*Elementary Computer Literacy Programs* includes Curriculum guide, implementation manual, filmstrip/audiotape, student activity handbook)

Prismatron Productions
The Audio Visual Library of
   Computer Education
155 Buena Vista Ave.
Mill Valley, CA 94941
(415) 383-0449
(Presentations in videocassette, sound/slide, filmstrip formats)

Program Design Inc.
11 Idar Court
Greenwich, CT 06830
(203) 661-8799
(*The New Step by Step* teachers
programming by CAI: Computer
graphics, animation, sound
effects, and voice track)

Radio Shack
1800 One Tandy Center
Forth Worth, TX 76102
(Radio Shack Computer
Demonstrator—inexpensive
cardboard training aid, teaches
basic computer functions)

Reston Publishing Co.
11480 Sunset Hills Rd.
Reston, VA 22090
(703) 437-8900
(Books on computer literacy,
programming languages, games
on diskettes with accompanying
books, etc.)

RMI Media Productions Inc.
120 W. 72nd St.
Kansas City, MO 64114
(800) 821-5480
(*Computer Operational Series,
Computer Concepts Series,* and
Computer Literacy;
presentations available on
filmstrip, slide set, or video
tape; TRS-80 Model III, Apple,
ATARI, PET, Bell & Howell)

Scholastic Inc.
904 Sylvan Ave.
Englewood Cliffs, NJ 07632
(Multimedia package to aid
teacher and administrator in-
service)

Science and Mankind, Inc.
Communications Park
Box 2000
Mount Kisco, NY 10549
(*At Home with the Computer: What
Can it Do for You?; Basic: An
Introduction to Computer
Programming; Computers: From
Pebbles to Programs; Careers in
Computer Science and Service;
Computer Hardware: What It Is
and How it Works; Computer
Software: What It Is and How it
Works;* Most in three formats:
video, sound-slide, filmstrip)

SRA
155 North Wacker Dr.
Chicago, IL 60606
(Computer Literacy Program—
workbook, diskettes, instructor's
guide)

Sterling Swift Publishing Co.
1600 Fortview Rd.
Austin, TX 78704
(512) 444-7570
(Computer books and other
materials; Computer tutorials
on BASIC programming;
Computer Literacy Show and
Tell Kit; Simulation:
Programming in BASIC, plus
accompanying "Care Package")

Terrapin Inc.
678 Massachusetts Ave.
Cambridge, MA 02139
(617) 492-8816
(Terrapin Turtle—robot for young
children)

Vital Information Inc.
7899 Mastin Dr.
Overland Park, KS 66204
(800) 255-5119
("Cardboard Computer Kit" to
teach computer parts)

Apple Computer Clearinghouse for the Handicapped
Neil Russell, Computer Manager
Prentke Romich Co.
Box 191, R.D. 2
Shreve, OH 44676

Closing the Gap
Route 2, Box 39
Hendersen, MN 56044
(612) 665-6573
(Handicapped and special education articles and information)

Computeronics
Gifted Child Project
925A Miccosukee Rd.
Tallahassee, FL 32303
(904) 487-1520

Disabled Programmers, Inc.
One West Campbell Ave.
Suite 35
Campbell, CA 95008
(Company to educate physically handicapped for careers in computer programming, and to locate projects for programmers)

Eastern Pennsylvania Regional Resources Center for Special Education
PA Resources and Information Center
1013 W. Ninth Ave.
King of Prussia, PA 19406
(215) 265-7321

The Handicapped Education Exchange (HEX)
Richard Barth
11523 Charlton Drive
Silver Spring, MD 20902
(301) 681-7372 (voice)
(301) 593-7033 (computer)
(Computerized bulletin board, idea & information exchange)

Learning Disabled Students and Computers: A Teacher's Guide Book and
Computer Technology for the Handicapped in Special Education and Rehabilitation: A Resource Guide
International Council for Computers in Education
135 Education
University of Oregon
Eugene, OR 97403
(Indexed abstracts for articles, books, and other materials relevant for special education applications)

National Conference: Use of Microcomputers in Special Education
Council for Exceptional Children
Dept. of Field Services
1920 Association Dr.
Reston, VA 22091
(703) 620-3660

National Paraplegia Foundation
3400 Hulen
Fort Worth, TX 76107
(817) 737-6661

*Proceedings: Special Education
  Microcomputer Faire*
Joanne Doell
17710 DeWitt Ave.
Morgan Hill, CA 95037

The Use of Apple Computers with
  Handicapped Preschoolers
Laura F. Meyers, Project Director
UCLA Intervention Program
1000 Veteran Ave.
Los Angeles, CA 90401
(213) 825-2404

Apple Backpack: Humanized Programming in BASIC
by Scott Kamins and Mitchell Waite
Byte Books/McGraw Hill, 1982
Peterborough, NH 03458

Apple Logo Primer
by Gary G. Bitter and Nancy Watson
Reston Publishing Company, 1983, 206 pp.
11480 Sunset Hills Rd.
Reston, VA 22090

BASIC for Beginners
by Gary G. Bitter
McGraw-Hill
1221 Avenue of the Americas
New York, NY 10020

The BASIC Handbook: An Encyclopedia for the BASIC Computer Language
by David A. Lien
Compusoft Publishing, 1978, 360 pp.
San Diego, CA 92119
(Helps convert programs written for one computer to another brand of computer)

BASICally Speaking: A Young Person's Guide to Computing
by Frances Lieberman Cohen
Reston Publishing Company, 1983, 129 pp.
11480 Sunset Hills Rd.
Reston, VA 22090
(Children's introduction to computers and programming)

Be a Computer Literate
by Marion J. Ball and Sylvia Charp
Creative Computing Press, 1977, 61 pp.
Morristown, NJ 07960
(Introduces computer literacy terms and topics briefly)

Computer Readiness
by Eloise C. Babcock
Think Ink Publications, 1981, 102 pp.
Phoenix, AZ 85018
(Activities for children)

COMPUTE's! First book of . . . series
PET/CBM, VIC, ATARI
515 Abbott Dr.
Broomal, PA 19008
(High school to adult; introduces readers to specific computers)

Computers for Everybody
by Jerry Willis and Merl Miller
Dilithium Press, 1981, 172 pp.
Beaverton, OR 97075
(Introduction to personal computing)

Computers for Kids
by Sally Greenwood Larsen
(Paperback books for specific computers; very easy to use and understand versions for Apple, TRS-80, ATARI, and Sinclair)

Computers and Mathematics
by James Poirot and David Groves
Sterling Swift Publishing
    Company, 1979
P.O. Box 188
Manchaca, TX 78652
(Includes computer literacy topics,
    flowcharting, programming in
    BASIC, logic and boolean
    algebra, careers, calculators,
    microcomputer information;
    accompanying student
    workbook)

Computers in Mathematics; A
    Sourcebook of Ideas
Creative Computing
Dept. C028
39 E. Hanover Ave.
Morris Plains, NJ 07950
(800) 631-8112
(Ideas for using computers to build
    mathematics concepts and
    skills)

Computer Literacy: Problem-
    Solving with Computers
by Carin E. Horn and James L.
    Poirot
Sterling Swift Publishing Co.,
    1981, 304 pp.
Austin, TX
(Computer literacy text)

Computers in Today's World
by Gary G. Bitter
John Wiley and Sons, 1984
New York, NY 10158
(Computer literacy text; includes
    study guide, teacher's manual,
    tests, visuals, BASIC and Pascal
    programming workbooks)

Courseware in the Classroom:
    Selecting, Organizing, and
    Using Educational Software
by Ann Lathrop and Bobby
    Goodson
Addison-Wesley, 1983, 187 pp.
Menlo Park, CA
(Appendix includes information on
    software that has been
    favorably reviewed in
    magazines and journals)

Every Kids' First Book of Robots
    and Computers
by David Thornburg
Compute! Books
P.O. Box 5406
Greensboro, NC 27403
(Library book for children)

Exploring with Computers
by Gary G. Bitter
Julian Messner, 1981, 64 pp.
New York, NY 10020
(Children's book on computer
    literacy topics)

Learning with Computers
by Alfred Bork
Digital Equipment Corp., 1981
Bedford, MA
(Collection of articles concerning
    the design of computer-assisted
    instruction and other related
    topics)

Mindstorms: Children, Computers,
    and Powerful Ideas
by Seymour Papert
Basic Books, Inc.
10 E. 53rd St.
New York, NY 10022
(Philosophical background for
    invention of Logo)

*The Mind Tool: Computers and
    Their Impact on Society*
by Neill Graham
West Publishing Co., 1980, 398 pp.
P.O. Box 3526
St. Paul, MN 55102
(Computer literacy text)

*My Students Use Computers:
    Learning Activities for Computer
    Literacy*
by Beverly Hunter
Reston Publishing Company, 1983,
    341 pp.
11480 Sunset Hills Rd.
Reston, VA 22090
(Ninety computer-related activities
    for the K-8 curricula)

Run: Computers in Education
by Dennis O. Harper and James H.
    Stewart
Brooks/Cole Series in Computer
    Education
Wadsworth Publishing Co., 1983
Belmont, CA 94002

The Turtle's Sourcebook
by Donna Berden, Kathleen
    Martin, and Jim Muller
Reston Publishing Company, 1983,
    226 pp.
11480 Sunset Hills Rd.
Reston, VA 22090
(Practical guide to learning and
    teaching Logo)

Teaching BASIC Programming*
By Marilyn Sue Ford

Before attempting to teach BASIC programming, especially to young children, it is necessary to prepare students adequately for their work with the computer. To develop a sufficient degree of computer readiness, consider discussing the following topics with your students before they are actually introduced to the computer:

- The history of computers
- Applications of computers today and in the future
- Computer capabilities and limitations
- How a computer works
- How to operate a computer
- Computer terminology
- Flowcharting
- Software types and evaluations
- Values and feelings about computers

Of course, the level of these discussions will be determined by the age and experience of your students. Be prepared to explain the reasons that programming is being taught, and keep in mind that your attitude will influence the attitude and performance of your students.

Along with a certain degree of computer awareness, your students must have acquired some basic competence at typing in order to enter their instructions into the computer. You may find it useful to provide very young children with an opportunity to familiarize themselves with a keyboard before attempting to teach programming.

BASIC Commands of Operation

As noted earlier, BASIC is comprised of approximately twenty simply worded commands that instruct the computer to perform specific functions. Among the most fundamental and useful to introduce to your students immediately are the commands NEW, SAVE, and RUN.

---

*Marilyn Sue Ford, "Teaching BASIC Programming," *Microcomputers in Education: Uses for the '80s,* Conference Proceedings, Dept. of Elementary Education, Tempe, Arizona, 1982.

The command NEW allows you to delete old programs and establish a new one each time you return to the computer. Type:

NEW

Then press the RETURN or ENTER key. This command instructs the computer to establish a new program under the name that you have assigned to the program that you are writing.

To replace a program that already exists in the computer's memory, type:

NEW   (replace)

Then press the RETURN or ENTER key. This command instructs the computer to delete material already stored in the computer's memory and to store your new program in place of the material you have deleted.

The command SAVE is a vital one. It prevents the loss of your newly written program when you are ready to sign off the computer. When you have finished writing your program, type:

SAVE

Then press the RETURN or ENTER key. This command instructs the computer to save your new program so that it will not be lost when power to the system is discontinued. Be sure to consult the manual that comes with your microcomputer because commands vary slightly with different systems.

The command RUN instructs the computer to execute the commands that you have written into your program. Once you are satisfied that your program is complete, type:

RUN

Then press the RETURN or ENTER key. The computer will read your instructions, translate them into machine-readable code, and then carry them out. After the computer has executed your instructions, it will return to the *cursor* or *ready* position.

Other BASIC Commands

In a BASIC program, each line of instructions is preceded by a line number that maintains the order of the instructions. One of the attractive features of BASIC is that lines may be inserted between existing lines in any stage of the programming process merely by assigning the new lines numbers that fall between numbers of lines already written into the program.

Another useful BASIC command is the PRINT STATEMENT. Simply type in PRINT and whatever you wish the computer to print enclosed in quotation marks. If your print statement extends over more than one line, the computer will automatically return the carriage for subsequent lines. You do not need to assign new line numbers to these lines.

The DELETE STATEMENT allows you to remove unwanted lines from your program. When you have determined the line numbers of the lines you no longer wish to include in your program, type:

DEL line number(s)

Then press the RETURN or ENTER key. This instructs the computer to remove the designated lines from your program. The deleted line numbers are now ready to be used again.

When you wish to read your program, use the LIST statement. Type:

LIST

Then press the RETURN or ENTER key. This instructs the computer to display a listing of all the instructions contained in your program. This will enable you to review the statements you have already written and determine what instructions still need to be written.

These are a few of the most frequently used commands in BASIC. You will want to consult your manual in case the system you are using calls for slight variations of these commands. After some practice, you will find these commands simple to remember and use.

BASIC in Ten Easy Steps*

By Marilyn Sue Ford

Step I—PRINT

The PRINT statement tells the computer to display information for the user.

- Printing strings (words)

```
10 PRINT "COMPUTERS ARE FUN."
```
(return†)

RUN
  COMPUTERS ARE FUN.

- Printing problem solutions

```
20 PRINT 20/5
30 PRINT 3*46
```

LIST
10 PRINT "COMPUTERS ARE FUN."
20 PRINT 20/5
30 PRINT 3*46
RUN
  COMPUTERS ARE FUN.
  4
  138

- Printing number sentences

```
40 PRINT "12 − 7"
```

LIST
10 PRINT "COMPUTERS ARE FUN."
20 PRINT 20/5
30 PRINT 3*46

---

*Marilyn Sue Ford, "BASIC in Ten Easy Steps," *Microcomputers in Education: Uses for the '80s,* Conference Proceedings, Dept. of Elementary Education, Tempe, Arizona, 1982.
†Press the RETURN or ENTER key after typing a line or command.

```
40 PRINT "12 - 7"
RUN
  COMPUTERS ARE FUN.
  4
 138
 12 - 7
```

* Printing blank lines

```
┌─────────────────┐
│ 25 PRINT        │
└─────────────────┘
```

```
LIST
10 PRINT "COMPUTERS ARE FUN."
20 PRINT 20/5
25 PRINT
30 PRINT 3*46
40 PRINT "12 - 7"
RUN
  COMPUTERS ARE FUN.
  4

 138
 12 - 7
```

Step II—PRINT

Given a program with the PRINT statement determine the output. Then type the program into the computer and RUN it to check yourself.

Here's the program.

```
NEW
10 REM PRINT STATEMENT
20 PRINT "BIG"
30 PRINT
40 PRINT "YELLOW"
50 PRINT 5*7
60 PRINT "6 - 3"
70 END
```

Show the output.

```
┌─────────────────┐
│ RUN             │
│   BIG           │
│                 │
│   YELLOW        │
│   35            │
│   6 - 3         │
│                 │
└─────────────────┘
```

Step III—LET

The LET statement refers to the content of a memory location in the computer.

- Storing numeric data

```
10 LET N = 25
20 LET E = 2*N
30 PRINT N;"ƀ";E
```

RUN
  25 50

- Storing alphanumeric data

```
30 LET C$ = "I LIKE COMPUTERS."
40 PRINT N;"ƀ";E,C$
```

LIST
10 LET N = 25
20 LET E = 2*N
30 LET C$ = "I LIKE COMPUTERS."
40 PRINT N;"ƀ";E,C$
RUN
  25 50   I LIKE COMPUTERS.

Step IV—LET

Given a program with the LET statement, determine the output. Then type the program into the computer and RUN it to check yourself.

Here's the program.

```
NEW
10 REM LET STATEMENT
20 LET Q$ = "I'M SPEEDY"
30 LET D = 36
40 LET P = 22
50 LET F = D*P
60 PRINT Q$
70 PRINT D; " × " ;P; " = " ;F
80 END
```

Show the output.

```
RUN
  I'M SPEEDY
  36 × 22 = 792
```

Step V—INPUT

The INPUT statement accepts new data typed in by the user each time the program is RUN.

• Storing one value

```
10 PRINT "ENTER A NUMBER."
20 INPUT N
```

RUN
  ENTER A NUMBER.
  ? 16

• Storing more than one value

```
30 PRINT "ENTER 3 NUMBERS SEPARATED WITH COMMAS."
40 INPUT X,Y,Z
```

LIST
10 PRINT "ENTER A NUMBER."
20 INPUT N
30 PRINT "ENTER 3 NUMBERS SEPARATED WITH COMMAS."
40 INPUT X,Y,Z
RUN
  ENTER A NUMBER
  ? 31
  ENTER 3 NUMBERS SEPARATED WITH COMMAS.
  ? 22, 34, 41

• Storing words and phrases

```
50 PRINT "ENTER YOUR NAME."
60 INPUT N$
```

LIST
10 PRINT "ENTER A NUMBER."
20 INPUT N
30 PRINT "ENTER 3 NUMBERS SEPARATED WITH COMMAS."
40 INPUT X,Y,Z
50 PRINT "ENTER YOUR NAME."
60 INPUT N$
RUN
  ENTER A NUMBER.
  ? 41

ENTER 3 NUMBERS SEPARATED WITH COMMAS.
? 910, 17, 78
ENTER YOUR NAME.
? MARILYN

Step VI—INPUT

Given a program with the INPUT statement determine the output. Then type the program into the computer and RUN it to check yourself.

Here's the program.

```
NEW
10 REM INPUT STATEMENT
20 PRINT "NAME A ROOM IN YOUR HOUSE."
30 INPUT R$
40 PRINT "ENTER THE LENGTH AND WIDTH SEPARATED WITH COMMAS."
50 INPUT L,W
60 PRINT "AREA OF ";R$
70 PRINT "IS ";L*W
80 END
```

Show the output.

```
RUN
   NAME A ROOM IN YOUR HOUSE.
   ? LIVING ROOM
   ENTER THE LENGTH AND WIDTH SEPARATED WITH COMMAS.
   ? 20, 14
   AREA OF LIVING ROOM
   IS 280
```

Step VII—READ/DATA

The READ and DATA statements allow the programmer to store information the program will use.

• Storing one value

```
10 READ A
20 DATA 12
30 PRINT A
```

```
RUN
   12
```

- Storing more than one value

```
40 READ C,D
50 DATA 15, 17.5
60 PRINT C,D
```

LIST
10 READ A
20 DATA 12
30 PRINT A
40 READ C,D
50 DATA 15, 17.5
60 PRINT C,D
RUN
  12
  15   17.5

- Storing words or phrases

```
70 READ Y$,Z$
80 DATA MARILYN, "LOVES COMPUTERS."
90 PRINT Y$;"b";Z$
```

LIST
10 READ A
20 DATA 12
30 PRINT A
40 READ C,D
50 DATA 15, 17.5
60 PRINT C,D
70 READ Y$,Z$
80 DATA MARILYN, "LOVES COMPUTERS."
90 PRINT Y$;"b";Z$
RUN
  12
  15   17.5
  MARILYN LOVES COMPUTERS.

Step VIII—READ/DATA

Given a program with the READ and DATA statements, determine the output. Then type the program into the computer and RUN it to check yourself.

Here's the program.

NEW
10 REM READ/DATA STATEMENTS
20 READ L$,L,W$,W

```
30 DATA LENGTH, 14, WIDTH, 12
40 PRINT "AREA OF ROOM ";L;" BY ";W
50 PRINT "IS ";L*W
60 END
```

Show the output.

```
RUN
    AREA OF ROOM 14 BY 12
    IS 168
```

Step IX—PROBLEM

A bicycle wheel is 16 inches in diameter. How far will the bike travel during one revolution of the wheel?

Hint: Apply the circumference of a circle formula, $C = \pi D$.

Using only the PRINT statement, write a computer program to solve this problem.

Sample program:

```
10 PRINT 3.14 * 16
20 END

RUN
    50.24
```

Step X—BICYCLE PROGRAM

Using the LET statement, write a computer program to solve the bicycle problem.

Sample program:

```
10 LET P = 3.14
20 LET D = 16
30 PRINT P*D
40 END

RUN
    50.24
```

Using the INPUT statement, write a computer program to solve the bicycle problem.

Sample program:

```
10 PRINT "WHEEL DIAMETER"
20 INPUT D
30 LET P = 3.14
40 PRINT P*D
50 END

RUN
   WHEEL DIAMETER
   ? 16
   50.24
```

Using the READ/DATA statements, write a computer program to solve the bicycle problem.
Sample program:

```
10 READ P,D
20 DATA 3.14, 16
30 PRINT P*D
40 END

RUN
   50.24
```

Sidenotes: Start each program with the command NEW. This clears the computer's memory.

Each microcomputer has a command to clear the screen. For example, on the TRS-80 type CLS to clear the screen.

Approximately 80 percent of the preceding programming outline was presented at a hands-on microcomputer workshop. Two to three participants crowded around eight TRS-80 Model IIIs, and the remainder of the audience discussed the computer input and output for each of the BASIC programming steps. In the hour and a half workshop, the novice programming participants covered all but steps 7 and 8. At the conclusion of the workshop, several participants claimed excitement over their acquisition of some BASIC programming skills—enough knowledge to comfortably read and understand a beginning programming textbook or microcomputer programming manual.

Unfortunately, the outline omits much of the narrative explanation followed by the participant's questions with answers. Even so, any novice programmer with access to a microcomputer should be able to work through the programming steps. Just find the "on" switch and begin typing.

Index

Access to computers, 75, 265–266, 269–270
Administrative applications, 81–83
Aikin, Howard, 30
AIM, 96
Algorithms, 93, 102–103, 246
ALU. *See* Arithmetic Logic Unit
Analog computers, 2
Analog to digital conversion, 96–97
Analytic Engine, 28
Animation, 24, 100, 103, 115
Apple, 6, 96
"Apple Pilot," 113–116
Applications, in schools, 177–178, 207–264. *See also* Tool, Computer as a
Applications software, 3
Arithmetic Logic Unit (ALU), 4, 5
Arrays (in BASIC)
  one-dimensional, 245
  two-dimensional, 246–247
Artificial intelligence, 253, 280–282
Arts, computer applications
  art, 24, 76, 100–102
  films, 24
  music, 24, 98
The Association for Computers in Math and Science Teaching, 103
Atanasoff, John, 30
ATARI, 6
Attendance software, 82–83
Attribute puzzles, 62–64
Authoring capabilities, educational software, 136
Authoring languages, 113–116. *See also* Pilot
Authoring systems, 118

Babbage, Charles, 28
Back-up policies, software, 126–127
"Bagels," 59
"Bank Street Writer," 90–91
Bardeen, John, 32
BASIC, 16–17, 27, 225. *See also* BASIC statements and activities
BASIC statements and activities
  arrays, one-dimensional, 245
  arrays, two-dimensional, 246–247
  counters, 234
  delete, 323
  files, 250
  flowcharting, 230, 235

BASIC statements (*Cont'd.*)
  FOR–NEXT, 238
  functions, 245–246
  GOTO, 232
  IF–THEN, 234–235
  INPUT, 225, 231–232, 328–329
  LET, 231, 327
  LIST, 323
  LOAD, 78
  NEW, 321–322
  PRINT, 225, 230–231, 322, 325–326
  RANDOM NUMBER, 238
  READ–DATA, 235, 329–331
  relations, 233
  RUN, 322
  SAVE, 78, 322
  storyboarding, 230
  string data, 233, 327
  variables, 232–233
Bell Laboratories, 32
"Big Trak," 217–218
Binary numbers, 8, 28, 32, 229
Bit (binary digit), 8
Boards, 7
Bubble memory, 36, 276
Bugs, 131–132
Bulk eraser, 9
Business education, applications, 49, 84
Bytes, 8, 96

CAD. *See* Computer-aided design
Calculator, electronic, 35
California, University of, Educational Technology Center, 73–75
Cambridge University, England, 32
Canned programs, 39
Card reader. *See* Optical card reader
Cards, computer, 28, 29, 83, 233
Cassette tape, 10, 40
Cassette tape player, 11, 40
Cathode ray tube (CRT), 4, 12
Census, 28
Central processing unit (CPU), 3, 4, 5, 224
Character sets, 115
Characters per line, 181–182
Chips, 11, 32–37, 96. *See also* Integrated circuits
Circuit board, 7
Classroom management concerning computers, 265–272
Cloze passage generation, 80

333

LIST command (BASIC), 323
Literacy. *See* Computer literacy
LOAD command (BASIC), 78
Loading instructions, 131
Loading software, 138, 219
"Log to any Base," 60
Logo, 27, 103, 111–113, 219–220, 222, 224–225
Looping (in programming), 237–238
Low-resolution graphics, 182

Magnetic disk, 9
Magnetic tape, 10–11
Maintenance, microcomputers, 203, 270–271
Management in classroom, 265–272
Management systems, educational software, 137
Mathematics education
  Association for Computers in Mathematics and Science Teaching, 103
  attribute puzzles, 62–64
  in computer managed instruction, 56
  computer mathematics, 102–103
  drill and practice, 39–40, 42
  geometry, 76, 103. *See also* Logo
  "Log to any Base," 60
  matrices, 249–250
  plotting programs, 75–76
  probability, 249
  problem solving, 58, 60
Mathophobia, 27
Mauchly, John, 31, 32
Memorization software, 81
Memory, computer, 4, 36
Memory, microcomputer
  adding memory, 8
  EPROM, 9
  K (Kilobytes), 8
  PROM, 9
  RAM, 8
  ROM, 8
Memory capacity, importance of, 122–123, 128, 194
Menus, 61, 130–131
Microcomputer as learning center, 268–270
Microcomputer, location of, 265–270
Microcomputers. *See also* Computers
  applications in society, 4, 5, 15
  as a demonstration device, 75–77
  display devices, 11
  memory. *See* Memory, microcomputer
  motherboard, 7
  networking, 184
  operating a, 14

Microcomputers *(Cont'd.)*
  primary components, 4–13
  printing devices, 12, 13
  programming, 14, 16–18
  storage devices, 9, 10, 11
Microprocessors, 9
Microsift, 121
Mindstorms by Seymour Papert, 27, 71
Modeling, 242
Modem, 185
Monitors, 5, 12
Motherboard, 7
Multi-processing, 36
Music
  and CAI, 41
  compositions, 24, 76, 99
  synthesizers, 24, 98–99

National Consortium for Computer Based Music Instruction (NCCBMI), 99
Nested loops, 238
Networking, 77, 184
New command (BASIC), 321–322
Northwest Regional Educational Laboratory, 121
"Nucleic Acid Connection," 76

Objectives, 53, 54, 55, 56, 136
ON-GOTO statement, 235
Operating a microcomputer, 14, 219
Optical card reader devices
  definition of, 11
  uses of, 54, 58, 73, 83
Output, 1, 4
Output devices, 4, 9–13

Papert, Seymour, 27, 71
Pascal, 17, 110, 253, 254, 257
Peer teaching, 62, 64, 269
Periodicals, 16
Peripheral devices, 184–185
PET, 6, 96
Pilot, 113–116, 250, 255–256
Plotters, 13
Portability, 182
Practice. *See* Drill and practice
Pre-packaged software, 3, 14–15
Print statement (BASIC), 225, 230–231, 322, 325–326
Printers
  comparison between, 12, 13
  daisywheel, 13
  definition for, 12
  dot matrix, 13
  hardcopy from, 12, 18
  impact, 12, 13
  need for, 54, 77, 79, 80, 164
  networking, 77